Formal, Transcendental, and Dialectical Thinking

SUNY Series in Philosophy
Robert Cummings Neville, Editor

Formal, Transcendental, And Dialectical Thinking

Logic and Reality

Errol E. Harris

State University of New York Press

Published by
State University of New York Press, Albany

© 1987 State University of New York

For information, address State University of New York
Press, State University Plaza, Albany, N.Y., 12246

Library of Congress Cataloging in Publication Data

Harris, Errol E.
   Formal, transcendental, and dialectical thinking.
   (SUNY series in philosophy)
   Includes index.
   1. Logic. 2. Dialectic. I. Title. II. Series.
BC71.H24   1987   160   86-14463
ISBN 0-88706-429-9
ISBN 0-88706-430-2 (pbk.)

10 9 8 7 6 5 4 3 2 1

Contents

Page

Preface   ix

Introduction: Contemporary Problems   1
    Is Logic Relevant?   1
    The Predicament of Modern Man   3
    Science as Objective Knowledge   6
    Bankruptcy of "the Scientific Outlook"   11
    The Whirligig of Time   13

PART I FORMAL LOGIC

Chapter 1 The Presuppositions of Formal Logic   23
    Logic and Metaphysics   23
    Frege's *Grundlagen der Arithmatik*   25
    The Thesis of this Chapter   31
    Commutation, Association and Distribution   32
    Implication   33

Chapter 2 Formal Logic and Scientific Method   49
    Empiricism and Induction   49
    Physics and "the Interrelatedness of Things"   58
    The Methodology of Science   62
    Perception   65

PART II TRANSCENDENTAL LOGIC

Chapter 3 Kant and Fichte   75
    Synthesis and Transcendental Subjectivity   75
    Coherence   81
    The Emergence of Dialectic   82

Chapter 4 Husserl's Transcendental Logic   89
    Psychologism vs. Formalism   89
    Inadequacies of Formal Logic   92
    The Task of Transcendental Logic   97
    Undeveloped Implications   100

Chapter 5 Dialectical Transcendentalism   105
    A Reformulation of Transcendental Philosophy   105
    Dialectical Parallel   110

Chapter 6 Transcendental Idealism   113
    The Problem of Self-constitution   113
    Merits and Demerits of Transcendentalism   117

Chapter 7 "Independent" and "Nonindependent" Objects   121
    Wholes and Parts   121
    Unresolved Problems   124

PART III DIALECTIC

Chapter 8 The Logic of System   131
    Relations, External and Internal   131
    Overlap of Terms   135
    Organization and System   140
    The Self-differentiation of System   144
    Summary and Exemplification   149

Chapter 9 Negation and the Laws of Thought   157
    Identity and Difference   157
    Dialectic and the Law of Contradiction   163
    Criticisms and Misconceptions   165

Chapter 10 Categories of Perception   171

    The Form of the Facts   171
    Being and Becoming   173
    Quantity, Number, and Formal Logic   182

Chapter 11 Categories of Reflection   189

    Common Sense   189
    Common Sense and Newtonian Science   190
    Contemporary Science   193

Chapter 12 Categories of Systematic Thinking   199

    The Concept, Theoretical and Objective   199
    Conceptual Moments   200
    Scientific Judgement   202
    Scientific Inference   206
      (1) Deduction   209
      (2) Induction   215
    Scientific Advance   221

Chapter 13 Objectivity   227
    Three World Views   227
    Relation of Subjective to Objective   233
    Theory and Practice   236
    Identity of Subjectivity and Objectivity 237

Chapter 14 Value   243
    Dialectical Generation of Value   243
    Desire, Purpose, and
      Objective Standards   244
    Dialectic and World Problems   249
    Man and Nature   250
    Residual Questions   257
      (1) The freedom and individuality of man   258
      (2) The ultimate character of the universal
        whole   261
      (3) Man's relation to universal nature   262

Preface

"The conclusion is that logic, conceived as an adequate analysis of the advance of thought, is a fake. It is a superb instrument, but it requires a background of common sense . . .

"My point is that the final outlook of philosophic thought cannot be based upon the exact statements which form the basis of the special sciences.

"The exactness is a fake."

Alfred North Whitehead

With close approximation, the above statement expresses the main thesis of this book. I argue that formal precision is a specific level of thinking, however sophisticated, which is a useful instrument for many purposes, but which is limited in its applicability, even in science. There is a more concrete form of thought, more universal in its scope, of which insufficient heed has been taken, whose principles need further development and merit closer reflection.

What is revered as "the scientific outlook" has been, and still is, too often confused with the exactitude which Whitehead, in the above quotation, repudiates—Whitehead, who in collaboration with Bertrand Russell, wrote the greatest treatise on formal logic of the present century. By many philosophers it is also confused with philosophical Empiricism. But the scientific outlook of contemporary science has changed in many ways from what it was in the seventeenth century, and the type of logic appropriate to the world-view of the Renaissance requires at least considerable supplementation if it is to be adequate to the science of today and to the problems facing modern civilization.

In the Introduction which follows I have criticized this outdated and now obsolete "scientific outlook"; and in so doing I have spoken of science in what some may consider too harsh a tone. But they may be reassured that it is not science, as such, which is here being castigated, but only a prescribed and limited theoretical attitude, which has run itself into a *cul de sac*, from which it can find no outlet, and from which the escape is indicated in the later chapters of the book, where science once again comes into its own.

My aim has been to reassess the importance of logic and its place in philosophical as well as other forms of thinking, and to consider the question whether the presuppositions of contemporary science may not demand something beyond the current style of mathematical logic to express the principles of structure of scientific thinking. To do this, I have had to present the reader first with an analysis of the presuppositions of formal logic, and a discussion of their adequacy to twentieth century scientific discoveries; then with the alternative possibilities. The first of these is Transcendental Logic, which is neither very familiar nor very much discussed among contemporary philosophers, so I have presumed that many readers would be grateful for a certain amount of introductory explanation, both of its technical terms and of its basic doctrines. This it seemed best to do by direct reference to the major works of the authors who originally expounded it (involving some brief attention to its history). Chapters 4 and 5 may, in consequence, seem to hold up the argument; but if the reader will be patient (for neither chapter is very long), he or she will find that the thread is taken up again in what follows in such a way as to make clear the relevance of what has gone before.

Having set this precedent, it may seem somewhat inconsistent not to have dealt with Dialectical Logic in the same fashion; but, although Part III is unashamedly Hegelian, I have not presented it in the form of a commentary on Hegel's logic. One good reason is that I have done that at length elsewhere. Another is that I wished to set out the fundamental presuppositions of this type of logic, as I had done of the previous two, and so have offered what is in effect a propaedeutic to Hegel, followed by an application of the logico-epistemological principles set out to scientific method and recent scientific theory. The concluding chapters return to the issues raised in the Introduction,

forming in part a completion of the dialectical system, and in part an il-
lustrative development of its consequences.

If, in the notes, I have made what some may consider too many
references to my own writings, it has been only to spare the reader the
tedium of repetition, so that I should not need to say over again what I
had argued at more length elsewhere. Those who have read the earlier
works need only ignore the related notes, while those who have not
may wish to look them up in order to supplement what is argued in the
present text.

One critic, who read the book in typescript, has urged me to draw
attention further to writers like Brand Blanshard and Nicholas Rescher,
whose works (as he put it) lend support to my overall position. I have
acknowledged in former writings (*e.g.*, *Hypothesis and Perception*) my
deep debt to Professor Blanshard and my broad agreement with his
views. But in recent years I have been engaged in debate with him over
at least one crucial matter germane to the argument of the present
work (see *Idealistic Studies*, vols. IX, 2; X, 2; and XII, 3), and I hesitate
to appeal to him as a supporter without reservations when I am unsure
of his unqualified approval. And I can hardly cite Professor Rescher as
one who "lends support to this overall position," because his intriguing
and ingenious version of the coherence theory of truth, no doubt highly
useful heruistically in many fields, is expounded, as he puts it, "in a
manner consonant with modern standards of rigour and precision." He
says it aims at being "exact and *formalized*," and he uses throughout the
techniques of the current symbolic logic.[1] Now, in what follows, I
argue that the tacit but inevitable presuppositions of this logic, and of
its characteristic formalization, are altogether incompatible with the
kind of coherence theory that I espouse, so I can hardly claim support
from Professor Rescher. Also he explicitly allows, as the definition of
truth, correspondence with what "is actually the case" in a sense which
I cannot, and he admits by implication several logical and
epistemological theses that I am compelled by the thrust of my argument to reject. To embark here on an extended critique of Rescher's
theory would be out of place, and to have done so in the body of the
text would have been an unwarranted digression.

My sincere gratitude is due, and freely given, to Dr. Willem

Klever, of the Erasmus University in Rotterdam, who read an earlier draft of this book and made sympathetic and helpful suggestions for improvement; also to the Institute for Advanced Studies in the Humanities, of the University of Edinburgh, for the hospitality and facilities it granted me, as a Research Fellow, at the time when I was doing the work of which this book is the fruit. I have to thank the Editor of the *International Philosophical Quarterly* for permission to reproduce in modified form, as part of the Introduction, and of Chapters 13 and 14, material which has appeared in articles published in Vols. XV and XIX of that journal.

E.E.H.

High Wray
June 30, 1986

[1]Cf. *The Coherence Theory of Truth*, Oxford, at the Clarendon Press, 1973.

Introduction

Is Logic "Relevant"?

Logic is popularly thought of as a very dry and abstract discipline quite devoid of practical relevance. Indeed, contemporary logicians have asserted that all logical truths are analytic and tautological, so that they can never give us new knowledge, even though they may serve to derive hitherto unnoticed consequences from what is already known. But this view of logic is a misconception. After all, it is admitted on all hands that logic is the science that sets out and develops the principles fundamental to the method of every science and identifies the norms that justify the claim of any discipline to be a science at all. And nobody nowadays is likely to deny that science is of practical importance. If so, surely logic, at least indirectly, must have relevance to the interests of practical living.

Moreover, the significance and achievement of any philosophy is closely bound up with the theory of logic that it espouses and upon it will depend what effect, if any, the philosophy will have on practical affairs. Philosophy, prior to the last half-century, was generally credited with great practical influence, especially in the spheres of morals and politics; but more recently such philosophy has been ranked as ideology and has been, for the most part, frowned upon in professional academic circles. That again has been because philosophers have assumed what they regard as a scientific attitude, considering science as properly objective knowledge disinterestedly concerned with facts and eschewing every prejudice or evaluation. Values, once held to be the province of the philosopher, are now assigned to the psychologist, who is himself a scientist and treats them simply as facts, as the determinants of behaviour. He does not and will not claim to pronounce normative maxims. The ideologies rejected by the philosopher thus become grist to the psychologist's mill and form at least part of the subject-matter also of the social sciences.

What then is left for the philosopher? It would be an impertinence for him to encroach upon the fields of the special sciences, whether natural or social; but the principles on which their reasoning is based, those which determine the validity of their arguments, the rules which govern their procedure and the architectonic of their systems are matters which scientists themselves do not usually investigate, taking them simply for granted. These form the province of the logician and are fair game for the philosopher. Consequently, in recent times, philosophy has come to be identified almost, if not quite, wholly with logic.

This retreat of philosophy more or less into the background has left the natural sciences as the most pervasive intellectual influences in our civilization, which is dominated by their theories and permeated by scientific technology in every phase of its activity. Initially this seemed all to the good and the advance of science was hailed as beneficent progress. Latterly, however, scientific technology, though it seemed at one time to promise the solution of all problems and the cure for all ills, has proved to be the source and root cause of the most menacing problems of all; problems, moreover, that, while inseparable from the very progress of our civilization, threaten its continued existence, yet to which that progress seems to offer no prospect of solution.

If logic, as seems clear, has some bearing on the method of science, it should also have some relevance, even if indirect, to these vital issues. But in fact it is not quite so indirect as may appear at first sight, because the practical problems turn out to be not purely scientific and the above conception of science proves, under scutiny, to rest on shaky presuppositions, so that our conceptions of logic and philosophy may well require revision and their importance for practical living may prove to be fundamental.

To convince the reader of this, I propose to begin in this introduction by discussing at some length matters which might not seem germane to the subject announced in the title of this book, but, as will later appear, are the ultimate goal of its argument. For my main thesis is that logic, properly conceived, is inseparable from the structure of the actual world, as well as from our understanding of it. It must therefore, be directly and intimately relevant to the solution of practical problems.

II

The Predicament of Modern Man

European civilization has not always been scientific, although early in its history the spirit of science was born among the Greeks; but in our own day science and its products accompany all our activities and permeate our way of life. Further, what was once known as Western civilization has, in the twentieth century, become pervasive throughout the world. It is the civilization of the scientific outlook, from the effects of which not even the remotest corners of the earth are today wholly immune. Science and technology are no longer the monopoly of the West. They flourish equally in India, China, and Japan, and they affect the lifestyle of all the peoples of the world. In fact, the practice of mankind today is directed by the advance of science, and life is dominated by the machine. Those who still believe in and value spiritual ends will see this as a cause for sorrow and dismay; but those who, borne on the resistless tide of scientific progress, have come to regard the human mind itself as a machine and the belief in the spirit as just one of the machine's aberrations, may (if the word is still appropriate) think it offers an attractive prospect. They might adopt this view were it not, indeed, that technological advance has brought upon mankind a situation in which the very civilization which has nurtured science, and the social structure upon which it rests and from which it derives, is threatened with extinction.

In an overpopulated world, scientific methods of production exhaust the world's resources, be they of energy or of nutriment. Industrial waste pollutes the atmosphere and the hydrosphere, producing acid rain which poisons the earth, its lakes, and its rivers. Other living species, on which the human depends for food, are being decimated, and the whole ecology of the earth is being disrupted. Destruction of the tropical forests with contemporary machines on a scale hitherto impracticable threatens to upset climatic equilibria, as well as to deprive the atmosphere of its chief source of oxygen. Oil spillage, unprecedented in the earth's history, pollutes the seas, destroying marine life, both bird and fish, and settling upon the breeding grounds of the plankton which is its main food supply. The continued advance of science seems only to increase and complicate these troubles, and, apart from creating new problems, has as yet offered little by way of mitigation.

As if this were not enough, science has given us atomic energy, the production of which is accompanied by appalling dangers: the possible overheating and meltdown of atomic cores, threatening explosions of stupendous destructive force; the escape of deadly radioactive gases and the seepage of harmful radioactive liquids; the accumulation of atomic wastes remaining radioactively lethal for hundreds—even thousands—of years, the safe storage of which scientists have not yet devised, and which, when discovered, national economies may well not be able to afford. And these are the by-products of generating atomic energy only for peaceful and domestic purposes. Its main purpose, however, at the present time, is the proliferation of atomic weapons, the use of which in a major conflict would undoubtedly wipe out all civilization, all technology, and all science.

Here again, the very fabric of our civilization, its political form, threatens its survival. Science has flourished and could only do so in a society organized to supply material needs of life and governed so as to maintain social order. Such government is necessarily embodied in a political structure, and that entails legislation and the enforcement of law. This is the function of the state, which can operate only if it wields supreme legal authority and power in the community. Modern civilization is organized in nation-states, each sovereign and independent, and sovereignty is, by its very nature and definition, legally supreme, so that in practice it cannot be subject to any higher law. The mutual dealings of sovereign states, therefore, cannot be effectively regulated. What parades as international law, by its own principles recognizes and purports to maintain the rights of independent national sovereignty. In so doing it disqualifies itself from political enforcement. No authority exists, or could exist without extinguishing national sovereign independence, to enforce international law. The United Nations, committed by its Charter to respect and maintain national sovereignty is similarly disqualified. It follows that international relations are legally unregulable.

In consequence, there is no way of ensuring that treaties will be kept—and it must be noted that international law itself has only treaty status. The only security against external aggression and domination available to any nation, therefore, lies in its own and its allies' power. It is compelled to depend for its own safety on its own means of defence, bolstered when possible by alliances. Yet again it must be remembered that alliances depend upon treaties, which may, in the final issue, not be observed. All international politics, therefore, is inevitably power politics, and its aim is always to maintain a balance of power in the national interest. The unavoidable result is an arms race, which nothing can curb because any advance on either side must always be matched on the other. It cannot be curbed because arms limitation can be secured only by treaty, and there is no means of ensuring the observance of treaties apart from the threat of military retaliation for their breach. Disarmament treaties thus become self-defeating, because they commit the parties to divest themselves of the only means to ensure their observance.

A mounting arms race is thus unavoidable and incurable. This was bad enough in earlier times, but today it has become intolerable and threatens to be finally fatal, because science has put into our hands nuclear weapons, already stock-piled to an extent sufficient to destroy the world's population several times over.

Politicians never tire of assuring us that what prevents and has for forty years prevented the outbreak of nuclear war is the policy of deterrence. The possiblity of "mutually assured destruction" (appropriately acronymized as MAD) restrains either side from using nuclear weapons. But in the strategical thinking of the military, this doctrine has already been abandoned. Strategies of so-called limited nuclear war are now being devised, on the assumptions that such a war can be won and that its victor can survive as an ordered and civilized society. That the assumptions are palpably false, however, must be seen by any intelligent person who carefully considers the scientific evidence.[1] But if these assumptions were true, as they contradict those supporting the doctrine of deterrence, they would remove the alleged safeguard against nuclear annihilation. Moreover, no nuclear war, once started, could be limited, for neither side could rely on the other to observe any presumed limit. Nor is deterrence a valid concept. It depends on the balance of power, and the record of history shows that the balance of power is always unstable. At any time, a change of government, or ideology, or alliance, by any power, may alter the array of opposing forces to give one side the advantage. That would immediately remove the deterrent.

To have maintained the balance for more than thirty-five years is no extraordinary precedent. There were no major wars in Europe between 1815 and 1914, and minor wars have been more numerous and more ominous snce 1946 than were those of the nineteenth century. any one of them could have escalated to become a world-wide conflict. Even now, those in progress might get out of hand and embroil the superpowers. The very nature of power politics generates international crises, and no nation has a reliable means of ensuring that they can be contained. In short, as international politics are conducted today, nothing less than a radical change of thinking and political practice is likely to save mankind from the inevitable nuclear holocaust toward which, like the Gedarene swine, the nations of the world unheedingly plunge forward.[2]

The severity of this political crisis is as much due to scientific advance as any other, for the nature of international power politics has not changed since the eighteenth century, only the destructive power and the sophistication of the weapons at the disposal of sovereign nations. But it is not to science that we can look for any mitigation of the threat or any solution of the problems.

That there are solutions I am convinced, for it is by no means impossible for us to extricate ourselves from our present desperate predicament, although it cannot be by continuing to rely on science. It will require first a deep investigation into the causes of the crisis and the sources of the impasse in which we have become immured. This again will demand examination and rethinking of the fundamental presuppositions of our culture. It is the scientific outlook in particular that needs to be scrutinized afresh, for by that our civilization has become saturated, as it is dominated in its practice by what science has produced. Clearly, this task cannot suitably be undertaken by scientists, unless they can step back from their practice to uncover and examine its presuppositions in a critique which would properly be philosophical. The task is, in fact, that of philosophy, but contemporary philosophy, by adopting what it takes to be a scientific attitude, has largely disqualified itself from undertaking this service. My aim in what follows will be to discover how and why this has come about and to suggest how it might be remedied. One may call this attempt the propaedeutic to the solution of the contemporary predicament.

III

Science as Objective Knowledge

To say that knowledge and truth are necessarily connected is itself a truism. If a belief or opinion is false, it cannot be knowledge. Of whatever we claim to know we must be assured, and if our assurance is not fully justified the claim will be denied. Further, it would be meaningless to say that a belief or opinion was true if it were a mere concoction of the believing subject without any reference to an independently real world. To be known, knowledge must indeed be subjectively entertained, but to be knowledge, it must have some objective reference, it must be true of some independent reality which is the same for all knowers and therefore universal in its validity.

Devotion to the objectivity of true knowledge is, and has been since the sixth century B.C., the characteristic mark of Western civilization. For this reason, our culture is universally acclaimed as "scientific," and the form of its praxis has become distinctively technological; for science is the commonly approved form of objective knowing, scientific research the one recognized form and method of discovering the nature of the independently existing world, and the practical application of what science has found the most effective way of controlling nature and of harnessing its forces in the service of human aims.

This view of science and knowledge would not, until very recently, have been seriously questioned by many, and even today it would be merely perverse to deny, as historical fact, this general characterization of our Western civilization. But the human situation that has resulted from this very prevalence of scientism has, in recent decades, raised doubts in some minds about the validity of the presuppositions of the scientific attitude; and the outcome of scientific thinking itself warrants, and is producing, a modification of outlook, as yet no more than germinal, which should transform our whole approach to objectivity.

To see how this is so, let us first briefly recall the historical origin of objectivism and examine some of its major consequences. The idea of universal objective knowledge goes back at least to Plato, for whom the knowable esentially and exclusively was what was completely translucent to the intellect, absolutely precise, and finally evident to thought: the ultimately intelligible. The one discipline which could, in practice, approach this ideal was mathematics (for it remained problematical just what Plato's dialectic, for him the supreme science, really was). Mathematics, therefore, remained the model for all reliable and self-justifying knowledge until well into the seventeenth century. Accordingly, the seventeenth century architects of the modern scientific revolution segregated all mathematizable elements of our experience and allowed nothing else to rank as scientifically knowable. These elements include the spatiotemporal and the numerable, whatever could be measured and subjected to algebraical calculation. Thus, the real and objective became confined to the so-called primary qualities of things, their spatial and mechanical properties. Everything else was relegated to the merely subjective. All secondary qualities, such as colour, sound, and the like—the purely sensible—were classed as mind-dependent and therefore merely apparent.

The scientifically knowable world was thus conceived as an extended aggregation of material (or mass-) points which moved in the spatial field in accordance with fixed laws. Their movement was determined by forces dependent solely upon their position and mass. The objective world was thus a vast machine with extended, measurable, kinematic, and dynamic properties, altogether foreign to and exclusive of consciousness and feeling, or any other typical property of mind. Values, therefore, which depend upon desire, purpose, and conscious estimation, would be seen as belonging exclusively to the subjective mind and were not to be found in the objective world.

This material, mechanical world, however, was the object *par excellence* of scientific knowledge and so was conceived as presented to the mind independently of its own activity. Yet the mind had somehow to become apprised of its external presence and of its nature. Being thus mutually exclusive, the extended world and the conscious mind were related to each other only externally. The method by which the mind was alleged to become aware of the presence and character of external nature, therefore, was conceived as the transmission, in some way never fully explained, of representative "ideas" from external bodies through the senses. The simplest and most primitive form of these ideas were taken to be sensations, and the senses were regarded as the primary channel of communication between the material world and the knowing mind of the scientist. The objectivity of science, therefore, depended not only on its mathematical reasoning, which as purely formal and algorithmic had no factual significance, but also upon its reference to empirically perceived data in terms of which the algorithm was interpreted.

The twin pillars of objective knowledge, accordingly, came to be recognized as mathematical deductive reasoning and inductive generalization from direct observation. Resting upon these two supports an edifice of value-free scientific knowledge was built, progressively augmented by successive discoveries of a world devoid of any trace of final causation or any vestige of consciousness, not even that of the scientist himself.

Empiricist philosophy, which arose in the seventeenth century co-temporaneously with modern science, was its natural counterpart. All knowledge, on this view, originates from sense-observation which is to count as the basic criterion of truth and the warrant of factual realiability, even mathematical knowledge being an abstraction from what originally comes through sense. In its epistemology a firm distinction is set between matters of fact (discovered by observation) and matters intuitively known through "comparison of ideas," defining strictly the limit between inductive and deductive logic. An equally firm separation is made between these forms of "rational" knowledge and the feelings and sentiments by which men's evaluations and moral judgements are determined.

Empiricism, while typical of the seventeenth and eighteenth centuries, has persisted to our own day and has, in fact, been stronger than ever in the mid-twentieth. Today, it shows signs in many respects of decline, but the one branch which continues to flourish virtually unchallenged is its development of the traditional formal logic into contemporary symbolic logic, as a branch, or rather as the very foundation, of mathematics—the age-old paradigm of rigour and intuitive certainty—an ideal of perfection, however, purchased in our own day at the cost of pure abstraction and analyticity, which disqualifies both mathematics and logic from providing any factual knowledge, and deprives reason of all but a purely instrumental role. Modern logic is commonly described by its exponents as a "powerful tool," but whatever its power, its function does not include the discovery of new facts or the prescription of practical objectives.

So rapid were the achievements of the new science and so compelling in their triumphant success were its methods that the areas originally excluded became progressively drawn into their sphere of operation. First, secondary qualities became correlated with physical motions, and then the processes of life and of the human body, as objects for the growing sciences of biology and physiology. Finally, the activities of the mind itself became subject matter for the empirical science of psychology and in its wake the social sciences came into being, adapting the methods of the physical sciences to the study of social and cultural phenomena.

In order to be drawn into the circle of the scientifically knowable, however, life, mind, and society had to be transformed into the kind of objects which alone such science recognized as real. They had to be publicly observable and reducible to quantifiable properties. To this end, through the mediation of biochemistry, biological processes came to be explained in terms of physics and chemistry; physiology followed suit and, with the help of neurophysiology, psychological phenomena became accessible to the approved methods. Further, the sciences of the mind and of society came to be viewed as behavioural sciences, concerned only with publicly observable and overt movements of human bodies. When cybernetics supplied the means of mechanizing and mathematizing the processes of thinking and the operations of intelligence, the fully objective world picture seemed to have been completed by a thoroughgoing physicalism, reducing everything without exception to material and mechanistic terms in a universal, unified, value-free science.

At this stage, value itself becomes devalued. The science of psychology, in alliance with those of anthropology and sociology, reveals evaluative behaviour as expressive of feelings and moulded by social pressures into cultural traditions. All values and erstwhile philosophical theories of value are shown to be relative, primarily to the chemical mechanism of the individual human organism and secondarily to the cultural unit in which the individual is integrated.

Anthropologists reinforce these results by the discovery of differing and apparently incommensurable codes in different cultures, so that the standards recognized in one society are quite inapplicable in others. The generally accepted scientific doctrine is thus universal relativism, which renders the notion of objective value invalid. Ethics, accordingly, becomes noncognitive, and obligation is reduced to the incidence of social and psychological pressures, which appear as the sole basis for the moral regulation of conduct. But if all values are thus relative, no standard of value has objective validity even within a particular society; for, apart from the fact that all cultures break up into subcultures, to which the same scientific considerations must apply, differences of temperament between persons are unbridgeable. So, even if psychological influences subject every individual to conditioning by social practices, there can be no external yardstick with which to measure conclusively even individual judgements. Much less could any standard be regarded as universally binding upon all mankind.

Pari passu with this thoroughgoing objectivization of scientific knowledge, the advance of technology has overwhelmed every sphere of human practice. Technology is the application of scientific theory to the practical accomplishment of human purposes. Its advance is built into the structure and method of modern empirical science. Science relies for its discoveries on observation, experiment, and measurement, the methods of which are improved and made more precise by the practical application of its own results. Discoveries reveal new means of constructing more efficient instruments for observation which make new discoveries possible. Disclosure of the laws of mechanism which regulate the cosmic machine prompt the invention of machines which, by increasing the power and precision of observation, help to reveal new laws. Laws of nature once discovered can be put to use and inspanned to serve the needs of human life and comfort; and not only is this possible, but the technization of human skills itself ministers to the advance of scientific knowledge. Discovery of the structure of the atom and of the behaviour of elementary particles teaches engineers how to build electron microscopes and cyclotrons, which reveal to physicists new facts about the structure of atoms and the behaviour of elementary particles. Discoveries in electronics prompt the construction of computers which enable scientists in all fields to make yet more discoveries.

The final outcome is a range of technical development that gives man unprecedented powers both of production and destruction. Regulation of human behaviour by means of drugs as well as by implanting electrodes in the brain is already possible. Modification of the genetic code so as to affect future evolution of the species is well within the bounds of possibility. The prospect of prolonging life by counteracting the advance of senility is confidently entertained. As the result of techniques already in use, drastic transformation of the terrestrial environment with far-reaching consequences for the conditions of human and other life is already taking place. This is no longer even a matter of conscious choice, for the techniques already adopted are (as we have seen) exhausting some of the key resources of the planet, polluting its water and its atmosphere, and exterminating useful species of plant and animal life, or injecting into them substances which render them harmful as food for human beings. Destructive capabilities are even more dramatic, for modern technology has produced nuclear weapons that could annihilate all humanity and possibly all life on the planet if used without restraint.

IV

Bankruptcy of "the Scientific Outlook"

All this we contemplate with apprehension and bewilderment. What it means is that the seventeenth century conception of objective

science has generated a method of discovery which has been spec-
tacularly successful within its field, but which has brought man, by its
very success, to a pass where he is faced with problems of survival, the
solutions of which are hardly obvious. To appeal again to science and
technology seems only to produce new and greater problems in the
course of solving old ones. But the real difficulty is that the problems
are not simply technical but are moral. It is not just a question of how
we shall consume the earth's resources, or how we may save them, or
how to conserve the environment or to regulate its change. It is not
simply a matter of how we can vary the genetic code and direct future
evolution; nor how to modify social behaviour by artificial means and
what sort of behaviour to promote. We should not ask simply when to
resort to nuclear warfare or what would be the best strategy. The
essential question is whether we should do any of these things or allow
them to be done at all. The question is not one of what we can do but
of what we *ought* to do: one of right and duty, not simply our own right
and duty and the rights and duties of our immediate associates, but also
of the rest of mankind, however remotely placed, and of future genera-
tions in centuries to come.

These are moral questions unprecedented in any cultural tradition
and unanticipated in any previous theory of ethics. As they are global in
their scope, they are questions, the answers to which demand
reference to universal standards of value; and as they bear upon the
deepest and most far-reaching interests of the human race, the principles to which answers should conform must be ultimate and objective. For it is not only a prediction that we are called on to make as to
what may or will happen, but a judgement of what ought to be done
and one which must be valid for everybody without exception.

Objective and universal standards of value, however, are precisely
what the pursuit of objective scientific truth has eliminated. Such
science is value-free, and, having drawn into its domain every form of
human investigation, it has pronounced value judgements to be subjective and relative to local and temporal conditions.

The issue has been discussed in a brilliant essay by Hans Jonas.[3]
Modern technology, he points out, is "utopian" in its character because
it professes a capacity to remodel and regulate the total structure of
future living. He writes:

> In consequence of the inevitable "utopian" scale of modern
> technology, the salutary gap between everyday and ultimate issues

. . . is steadily closing. Living now constantly in the shadow of unwanted, built-in, automatic utopianism, we are constantly confronted with issues whose positive choice requires supreme wisdom—an impossible situation for man in general and in particular for contemporary man, who denies the very existence of its object: *viz.*, objective value and truth. We need wisdom most when we believe in it least.[4]

But it is the pursuit of objective truth that has destroyed the foundations of objective value. The very authority of science has brought us to the critical impasse. Recent reflections on the nature of science and its methods, however, converging from diverse points of departure, are now calling in question the authority of science itself, in much the same way as science has called in question the authority of value judgements, and, at least by implication, the resulting critique has undermined the very claim of science to ultimate reliability.

V

The Whirligig of Time

Pursuing Husserl's early insight into the beginnings of the crisis we have been outlining,[5] phenomenologists argue that the objective outlook, of which science is the typical expression, is itself derivative from a more fundamental subjective experience. The original involvement of the experiencing subject in his "life-world," from which the scientific view is an abstraction, is forgotten by the scientist, and according to Husserl it is only by tracing scientific thinking back to its original source that we are likely to grasp the nature of the crisis into which it has led us. In so doing he reduces science to a construction effected by the transcendental ego within the subjective awareness of the ultimate subject of consciousness.[6]

Existentialists have emphasized this originating function of the conscious subject, some, like Sartre, stressing its complete freedom to view and construct the world according to its own unrestricted choice. In much the same vein, Heidegger contends in a famous essay[7] that modern science is characterized as research, through the predelineation of an area of investigation which prescribes both its method of procedure and the sort of object which is to count as real and as evidence. In consequence, scientific inquiry becomes the pursuit of an institutionalized professional community, to which its ideas and the canons of its methodology are esoteric. In short, its methods and results are relative to a selected group with a restricted outlook. Meanwhile, R. G. Collingwood has maintained that science, in every period of its history, rests upon a constellation of absolute presuppositions, which are neither empirically derived nor rationally supported and cannot properly be described as true.[8] They are simply presupposed absolutely, and they are peculiar to the historical period under scrutiny. Thus, from three different directions, criticism suggests that objectivist science itself is relative to a more fundamental subjective awareness, or to a closed social group, or to a historical period, or to all three together.

The boat of traditional empiricism had already begun to rock when Karl Popper rejected as psychologistic the criterion of scientific validity in the evidence of sense-perception, when he abandoned inductive reasoning as logically invalid and maintained that scientific hypotheses were mere conjectures, the source of which might possibly be psychologically accountable but was not logically explicable. The hypotheses themselves, he held, were acceptable only so long as they remained unrefuted by empirical evidence. The ultimately "basic" character of such evidence, however, he declared to be a matter of convention, because ultimate data can never be reached, all being subject to interpretation.[9] Empiricists (including Popper himself) did not immediately notice how completely this view subjectivized science (a tendency pushed even further by Popper's follower Imré Lakatos). They tolerated and even welcomed it at first because of the apparently empirical character of what Popper demanded as falsifiying evidence.

But the dovecotes of the accepted philosophy of science were more disturbingly fluttered when Thomas Kuhn declared that science always operates within the limits of a "paradigm" or "exemplar" which prescribes the general outlines of theoretical structure and the methods of procedure. The pradigm also determines the fundamental concepts and defines ultimate entities and the nature of reality. This paradigm has no justification other than that the scientific community accepts it; so once again it is esoteric. And evidence is assimilated to the paradigm—that is, to theory—rather than theory to evidence. As a result, all observation becomes "theory-laden," a thesis maintained originally (in effect) by the British idealists at the turn of the century, and revived (unwittingly) by N. R. Hanson in the middle fifties.[10] Changes of paradigm, when they occur, are said to be revolutionary, so that those prevailing in different epochs are mutually incommensurable, and each is established solely by evidence and arguments recognized and interpreted in the light of its own theoretical terms and concepts. Revolutionary changes occur when the normal process of "puzzle-solving," which articulates the paradigm, breaks down because of an accumulation of "anomalies," each of which taken alone, so long as it does not obstruct the course of research, tends largely to be ignored. But when revolutions *do* occur, the generation of the new paradigm is not rationally accountable and arises from a proliferation of rival hypotheses guided (it would seem) by no systematic principle.[11]

The history of science thus comes to be regarded as a succession of conceptual schemes irrationally generated and selected from among alternatives more or less arbitrarily, each of which is peculiar to its own period and esoteric to a special professional community, each prescribing its own methods, procedures, and canons of acceptability, interpreting its own evidence according to its own principles, recognizing as fact only what conforms to its own concepts, none of which may be legitimately compared with or criticized from the viewpoint of any other.

Finally, in the hands of Paul Feyerabend, science is extolled as a purely and properly subjective pursuit. The proliferation of hypotheses, the more diverse and egregious the better, he regards as advantageous. None of them has, or need have, any logically justifiable origin; the adoption of any of them (a scientific revolution in Kuhn's sense) "cannot be accounted for in any reasonable fashion."[12] What in theory or practice is considered "rational" depends upon rules either accepted at the time or "invented in the course of its development."[13] But no such rules are permanent, for they are all historically relative. Science is a human creation, constructing its own world in its own way according to its own standards. The choice of our basic cosmology is a matter of taste, and science is in this respect, as in all others, on a par with art, aesthetic criteria of satisfaction being paramount in both.[14] The study of its changes is a sociological study and their explanation if any, is a psychological explanation, but the status of psychology and sociology as sciences is (presumably) no different from the rest.

"And thus the whirligig of time brings in his revenges."

The scientific approach to the study of values, a study taken to be wholly objective and value-free, pronounced all standards of value to be subjective and relative. It now transpires that scientific canons and concepts are themselves, in precisely the same way and from precisely the same causes, subjective and relative. But, if this is so we have lost all hold on objectivity and all grasp of truth. For what is subjective and relative, is changeable from individual to individual and from time to time, and no assertion can compel our assent if it is liable to such instability. If what is held to be true at one time is held to be false at another and what is accepted today will be rejected tomorrow, nothing has any justifiable claim and all opinions alike will prove false. If all alleged truths are but temporary illusions that very word will have lost its meaning. For no claim to truth is ever made which does not presume that, however well or ill it may be founded, yet there is some universal criterion by which it may be judged and which gives it significance. Nothing can be rejected as illusory except by reference to some such criterion, and nothing can be accepted as true unless it conforms to some such standard. If there is none, no claims could either sensibly be made or rightly invalidated.

That standards are merely relative, whether of value or of scientific rigour, is an assertion which presumably claims truth. Therefore, by implication it appeals to some presumed standard of truth which is universal and objective. The position is, therefore, self-destructive and untenable. What this standard is has to be uncovered. We must find a way of viewing science which allows for and can relate to this universal and objective standard, even if conceived only in general terms; and one which does not at the same time eliminate a similar relationship in the sphere of values.

We have already seen that science alone cannot solve the problems which we face. In fact, not only does it produce and exacerbate them, but by the contemporary critique its own validity and authority have been undermined. The problems are not, indeed, essentially scientific, but are more porperly philosophical, for they concern values and the standards which ought to be respected—not simply those that are in fact accepted or neglected, as the case may be. The main philosophical question is that of the status and validity of these standards, which have been dissolved away by scientific treatment, while science itself, by a similar argument, has been disqualified from returning a verdict. Contemporary philosophy has so far contributed nothing towards a solution of the practical problems nor offered any answer to the philosophical question. Empiricism, strengthening the seventeenth century outlook, has been an accomplice in the creation of the first, and by its own logic renounces its own right and denies its own competence to answer the second, to define standards of value or to judge of their validity. For empiricists contend that matters of fact belong solely to the province of the special sciences, that all values derive from sentiment and feeling without rational basis, and that logic is purely analytic and instrumental incapable of originating substantive knowledge. Yet it is such logic alone that contemporary analytic philosophy admits as competent.

In a recent lecture on contemporary philosophy, Mr. Anthony Quinton, having explained how the logical positivism of the thirties and its successors in later decades had lost their hold on orthodoxy, remarks, "More generally, there has taken place a very marked re-establishment of the links between philosophy and formal logic." the effect of this reestablishment, he maintains, is the reaffirmation (especially by W.V.O. Quine) of "the view that formal logic in the tradition of Frege and Russell displays the essential structure of thought and language."[15] If this is indeed the case, the ability of current philosophy to contend with the problems set out above will be circumscribed by formal logic; and as philosophy is the discipline upon which the main burden must fall (the nature of the problems being what it is), its capacity to solve them will be proportional to the adequacy of the logic it espouses. If all it recognizes is either induction, as the alleged logic of empirical science, which has engendered the problems, or deduction, the formal procedure limited to purely analytic tautologies, philosophy will be broken-backed and disqualified *ab initio* from rendering assistance in the modern predicament. So we shall be left in our sorry plight without refuge or resource.

Schools, other than the analytic, critical as they are of the more positivist forms of empiricism, have eroded away the claim to objectivity without which judgement is hamstrung and debilitated. We have, in effect, been deprived of any conception of reason which would make its use effectual in our present critical situation. The type of logic which empiricism has bequeathed to us, the only sort currently in vogue, has abandoned every form of rationality that could be productive of remedies to our ills. Our first task, therefore, must be to investigate the nature and foundation of this logic in our search for the root causes of our dilemmas. We may then determine what sort of rationality, if any, can show us the way out of the labyrinth in which we have lost all direction.

Notes

1. Cf. *The Effects of Nuclear Weapons*, Report by the United States Atomic Energy Commission, 1964; The Holifield Committee Hearings on Radiation, United States Congress, 1959; and *Nuclear Disaster* by Tom Stonier, Penguin Books, Harmondsworth, 1963. Neither the facts nor the arguments presented in these documents have yet been superseded; in fact, recent international conferences of scientists have reached still more alarming conclusions of final catastrophe.

2. I have set out the above arguments more at length in *The Survival of Political Man* (University of the Witwatersrand Press, 1950) and *Annihilation and Utopia* (George Allen and Unwin, London, 1966).

3. "Technology and Responsibility, Reflections on the New Tasks of Ethics," *Social Research*, Spring 1973. Reprinted in *Philosophical Essays* (Englewood Cliffs, NJ), 1974.

4. Ibid., p. 50f.

5. Cf. E. Husserl *The Crisis of European Sciences*, trans. D. Carr (Northwestern University Press, Evanston, IL 1970).

6. Cf. E. Husserl, *op. cit.*, esp. *The Crisis of European Humanity and Philosophy*, The Vienna Lecture of 1935, (*Husserliana*, Band VI, p. 343), trans. David Carr, p. 295: "As an accomplishment it [mathematical science] is a triumph of the human spirit. But so far as the rationality of its methods and theories are concerned it is a thoroughly relative one. It presupposes at the outset the fundamental assumption which itself excludes true rationality. Since the perceived surrounding world, as merely subjective experience is forgotten and the scientist is not made a theme [of investigation]." and *The Crisis of European Sciences*, Carr, p. 97, *Husserliana*, Band VI, p. 100: "I myself use the word 'transcendental' in the wider sense, for the . . . original motif . . . which is the most fruitful of meaning in all modern philosophy. . . . It is the motif of inquiring back into the ultimate sources of all knowledge, of self-reflection by the knower into himself and his knowing life, in which all scientific structures which are valid for him have occurred as purposive activity, are preserved as acquisition, and have become and continue to become freely available."

7. "Die Zeit des Weltbilds," in *Holzwege* (Frankfurt-am-Main, 1952).

8. Cf. *An Essay on Metaphysics* (Oxford, 1940).

9. Cf. *The Logic of Scientific Discovery* (London, 1959), pp. 40–47, 94, 104f.

10. Cf. *Patterns of Discovery* (Cambridge, 1958).

11. Cf. T. Kuhn, *The Structure of Scientific Revolutions* (Chicago, 1962–1970).

12. Cf. "Consolations for the Specialist" in *Criticism and the Growth of Knowledge*, eds. I. Lakatos and A. Musgrave (Cambridge, 1970), p. 214.

13. *Op cit.*, p. 216.

14. Cf. *op. cit.*, p. 228.

15. "Current Trends in Philosophy," *The Listener*, 22nd. April 1976, pp. 495–496.

Part I

Formal Logic

Chapter 1

The Presuppositions of
Formal Logic

I

Logic and Metaphysics

The suggestion that logic rests upon metaphysical presuppositions is liable in these days to be rejected with scorn. First, there are some philosophers still who maintain that metaphysics is an impossible and illegitimate inquiry. If this is stated merely dogmatically, it deserves no attention; but the reason which in the past has persuaded thinkers of the impossibility of metaphysics has long been abandoned as unfounded. That reason was originally, that metaphysics claims to reveal the nature of things, but that this can only be done, if at all, by empirical investigation, the only proper method of which is the method of the natural sciences. Any pronouncement about factual matters must be based on observational evidence, and that metaphysics neither can nor attempts to offer. Such arguments, however, have long since been exposed as unwarranted, if only because according to the current conception of scientific method, as held both by practising scientists and by philosophers of science, all science has been shown to presuppose nonempirical presuppositions; but mainly because the very anti-metaphysical argument itself has been recognized by some of its own original proponents (*e.g.*, Ludwig Wittgenstein) as resting upon metaphysical assumptions.[1] The very positivists who originally had declared that metaphysical propositions could have no (factual) sense later came to revise their position. "That metaphysics is nonsense *is* nonsense," declared Friedrich Waismann.

23

Even if this is conceded, however, there are some who will maintain that logic is a purely formal discipline abstracting entirely from the
material content of discourse and concerned solely with the form and
the formal relations of its expressions and that these are wholly independent of metaphysical theories, the subject matter of which is the
fundamental (or elementary) nature of things, and which, therefore, is
concerned directly with the material content of discourse, what it is
about. Further, it is widely held, the logical structure of thought (or of
its expression) neither dictates nor is determined by metaphysical doctrine. That may be whatever it will without in the least affecting the
principles which govern inferential procedures. In fact, the argument
will continue, the principles of valid inference, which it is the business
of logic to investigate, must be prior to any metaphysical speculation,
for in so far as metaphysics derives its conclusions from premises by
reasoning, the principles of that reasoning must be independent of and
prior to both the material premises and the conclusions. The principles according to which the latter are reached from the former cannot
themselves be the consequence of either, and must, therefore, be independent of their content. Moreover, criticism of metaphysical
presuppositions is possible on logical grounds. They may be selfcontradictory, or mutually incompatible, or improperly formulated. If
logical principles were consequences of metaphysical presuppositions,
such criticism would be impossible and self-destructive.

But all these arguments presuppose, first, that form and content
are unrelated and mutually independent, which is itself a metaphysical
assumption. And secondly, validity in reasoning is what guarantees
true conclusions from true premises, and that can be ensured only on
the ground of some real connection in the content. Principles of valid
inference, therefore, can hardly be independent entirely of the nature
of the subject matter, unless they are to be altogether trivial and ineffectual.

Inference, however, is an operation of thought—though most contemporary logicians, anxious to purge their discipline of all taint of
psychologism, prefer to substitute for principles of inference rules of
implication or entailment. Nevertheless, few would wish to deny that
logic is concerned with concepts, with the relations between them, and
between them and the entities of which they are the concepts. Here,
whether we like it or not, there is inevitable involvement with thought,
for a concept is obviously a product of conceiving; and relations between concepts and that to which they apply inescapably implies the

relation of conception to its objects. How we view that relation, moreover, is, or involves, a metaphysical theory. Indeed, logical theory and practice always do presuppose some concept of the structure of fact, which, when made explicit, is a metaphysic. By examining the doctrines and practices of logicians, therefore, we should be able to discover what their presuppositions are, their assumptions about what, if the logical procedures are to be viable, the nature of the concept and its relation to existing things must be.

Logicians, moreover, despite protestations against the dependence of logic on metaphysics, do from time to time admit by implication that the logical character of concepts does depend upon the nature of the objects to which they apply. Frege, for instance, says that strictly the only way we can establish that a concept is free from contradiction is to show that something falls under it.[2] Presumably, then, the nature of the objects falling under the concept determine whether it is self-consistent. Frege also maintains that the rules of calculation are not chosen arbitrarily but depend on the meanings we have assigned to our symbols.[3]

II

Frege and Die Grundlagen der Arithmetik

Despite several precursors, the founder of contemporary logic is undoubtedly Gottlob Frege, whose influence upon Bertrand Russell was profound and, through him and his work in collaboration with A.N. Whitehead, has persisted to the present day. The fundamental principles Frege established have never been seriously questioned or modified by any exponent of mathematical logic. The changes which have been made, though considerable, have been mostly in notation and the methods of its operation, but not of the fundamental ideas which Frege set out in such works as *Die Grundlagen der Arithmetik, Die Begriffsschrift*, and *Grundgezetze der Arithmetik*. It will be sufficient for my immediate purpose to confine attention to the first of these, for such changes in theory and practice as have subsequently been made affect it less than they do the other works.

In his conclusion to *Die Grundlagen*, Frege claims to have shown that it is at least probable, that arithmetic "becomes simply a development of logic" in consequence of the definition of number which he has given. By the use of the expression "one-one correlation" (*beiderseits eindeutige Zuordnung*) and the definition which he gives of that, he claims to have reduced the conception of number to one of purely logical relations. These are relations between concepts and their extensions, for Frege maintains that numbers, although they are "objects" (in his sense of the word), are neither physical nor mental entities. The relations do not pertain to "objects" as such, but only to concepts. The number that belongs to the concept F, he tells us, is the extension of the concept "like-numbered to the concept F," where "like-numbered" (*gleichzahlig*) is defined in terms of one-one correlation. From this claim it follows that logic is concerned only with the nature of concepts and the relations between them, along with the relation of a concept to the objects which fall under it—*i.e.*, its extension.

There should be no objections to this view of logic, for even if one wished to maintain that logic is also concerned with propositions and their mutual relations, it must be conceded that propositions are themselves enunciations of the relations between concepts, between concepts and objects, and between objects so far as they fall under concepts. Or, if one wished to say, with Martha and William Kneale, that "logic is concerned with the principles of valid inference,"[4] it must be admitted that inference depends upon the relations between concepts, for even if it is formulated in purely truth-functional terms, the truth or falsity of a proposition must depend on the relations between the concepts and the objects to which the proposition refers, and inference upon the relation between these and others to which other propositions refer.

Frege insists that "concept" should always be understood, in logic and mathematics, only in its logical sense and not in any psychological sense, nor, as often occurs, in a mixture of the two. What precisely its logical sense should be is not immediately apparent, but we may agree that psychologism and confusion between logic and empirical psychology are to be deplored. Frege, however, does not always give quite the same account of the concept in different writings. In his essay on "Function and Concept" (1891),[5] he identifies the concept with the function in mathematics, saying that it is a function whose value is always a truth-value. Objections have been raised to the consequences of this doctrine which I shall not discuss.[6] Its interest in the present context lies in the fact that a mathematical function gives expression to a principle of systematic relationships between terms, and that its values (or exemplifications) for different arguments may differ widely although they all satisfy the function. What they have in common need be nothing beyond the fact that they do satisfy the function. And this character of functions is much nearer to the account of the concept that I shall seek to advocate later than what Frege says of it elsewhere.

Frege, in fact, consistently ignores the factor of difference in the exemplification of the concept (or function)—except, of course, so far as arguments may differ. He distinguishes sharply between concept and the objects which fall under it, or in alternative mathematical language, between the function and its value range. "Object," he says, is indefinable but is anything that is not a function (or concept), so that no expression for it contains an empty space.[7] The value range of a function—*i.e.*, its values for different arguments—corresponds to (or is the same as) the extension of a concept, which presumably consists of the set or collection of objects that fall under it.

The symbol for an object, therefore, can never significantly be used to fill the place of the predicate in a proposition. That can be done only by the symbol for a concept. And when the name of an object is used in a sentence as if it were the predicate (*e.g.*, in "The morning star is Venus") the word "is" has been used in a different sense from that of the normal copula and stands for identity, or is the same as the equal sign, = . Only terms that represent concepts can be used predicatively.

All this strongly suggests that a concept is a common character, property, or quality, abstracted from a number of objects which are instances of it purely because and in virtue of their having that character, property or quality. The concept is abstract, a class concept, and its instances are concrete objects falling under it because each has the property which is the distinguishing mark of the class. That this is how Frege understands the matter is borne out by his treatment of number.

In developing his famous definition of number, Frege, criticizing earlier views, denies that a number is a property of things,[8] or a set (*Menge*), collection, or group of objects of any kind, or the property of such a group.[9] It is nothing merely subjective, nor it is a concept, for it can be given a proper name ("nought," "one," "two," for instance) which cannot rightly be used in the plural. It is therefore an object;[10] but it is not the property of an object, nor of a group of objects, nor is it a manifold, as several earlier writers alleged. An assertion about number, he holds, is always about a concept, because it is the concept that determines the units to be counted. The concept isolates the instances which fall under it, distinguishing them from other objects as well as from one another, yet it is identical in all of them and so admits of no divisibility within them. Not every concept is of this sort, but those which are, for instance, "moon of Jupiter," are those to which we can assign numbers.[11]

It thus appears that the concept is what is identical in all its instances—their common character—and the units of the number which belongs to it are its instances. Taken together as a group, collection, or set, they constitute its extension.

Now Frege does not define the number which belongs to a concept F as its extension, but as the extension of the concept *gleichzahlig dem Begriff F* ("equi-numbered with the concept F") and to avoid circularity he defines "equi-numbered" as "*beiderseits eindeutig zugeordnet*" ("arranged in one-one relation"). But what are equi-numbered and what are arranged in one-one relation are obviously the objects falling under F.

The extension of a concept is the collection or set of all the objects which fall under the concept. But Frege has told us that a number is not a set. So his definition cannot be taken to mean precisely what it says. Certainly the number that belongs to F is not the number that belongs to "*gleichzahlig dem Begriff F*" although it is said to *be* (is defined as) its extension. Its extension is all those concepts equi-numbered to F; but how can the number belonging to F and to all other equi-numbered concepts *be* the collection of these concepts? Obviously, what Frege means is that the number is what all these concepts have in common, what (as the word *gleichzahlig* indicates) makes them *gleich*. Rather than its extension, it is the intention or common property defining the concept, "*gleichzahlig dem Begriff F*"; that is, the property which the extension of F has in common with the extension of every other concept equi-numerous with it.

These considerations lead us once more to the view of the concept as a common or class property embracing a set of instances—its extension. The instances are what Frege calls "objects" which are obviously particulars, as opposed to the concept which is abstract and general. Moreover, the instances are related to one another simply as instances; that is, in respect of falling under the concept, they are identical. So they can rank as units in a denumerable set.

It would seem then, that not all Frege's earlier denials can be maintained consonantly with his own definition of number. For a number is, after all, a property of what Cantor called *eine menge*—the set or collection of objects constituting the extension of a concept. Certainly, it is not the set itself, but it is the property which it has in common with all other sets whose elements can be put in one-one relation to it. Frege's definition loses nothing in the translation, given by the Kneales,[12] into Cantor's terminology: "The cardinal number of a set is the set of all sets equivalent to it" (where equivalence is the relation between sets of one-one correlation). But to be strictly correct, we ought to say "the common property of all sets equivalent to it," and so to prefer Russell's wording: "the class of all classes similar to a given class," because the word "class" has a convenient ambiguity, meaning common property (or class concept) as well as collection or set. In Russell's definition, therefore, "class" at its first occurrence has the first meaning and at all later occurrences the second.

Further, as the Kneales point out,[13] Frege sometimes allows himself to talk as if number were a second-level concept. "According to the proposed definition," say the Kneales, "a number would be just the common character of all sets of the same size." It would thus be the (second-level) concept of being *gleichzahlig* with a given concept—the common property (or concept) of all concepts which are so *gleichzahlig*—which is surely precisely what that word denotes.

Yet, although Frege insists that numbers belong only to concepts, and that we should not identify a concept with its extension,[14] it is obvious from his treatment of the matter that numbers pertain solely to the extension of concepts, and the extension of a concept is, clearly, envisaged as a set or collection of particulars (*eine Menge*) related one to another only in that they belong to that collection, which they do by falling under the same concept. It is a mere aggregate, the elements of which are wholly external to one another and, apart from their common character of falling under the same concept, are related solely by aggregation. Only on this account can they be arranged in one-to-one correlation with the elements of other aggregates—the extensions of other concepts—and so can be assigned numbers. This purely external relationship between the elements of an aggregate is typical of units which are countable and to which numbers can therefore be applied.

If objects are in this way particulars collected together under concepts, each the distinguishing character of a determinate set,[15] and the extension of each being susceptible to numeration, the relation between concepts will be of the same kind as the relation between numbers; so that logic will in consequence be mathematical throughout.

That this interpretation of Frege is correct, that it involves the assimilation of logical objects to the objects of mathematics, is corroborated by the Kneales as follows:

Furthermore, it is Frege's view that when a satisfactory chain of definitions has been set forth it will be clear that the only undefined notions required for the presentation of arithmetic are notions of formal logic. In particular he wishes to show that talk about natural numbers can be reduced to talk about sets, classes, or manifolds, which in the terminology of logicians are the extensions of concepts, and he says explicitly that the objects of arithmetic are logical objects.[16]

The metaphysical background to this theory is, obviously, the conception of a pluralistic world of particular entities or "objects" classifiable into sets identified by common properties or concepts. The attributive relation between property and object remains undefined, but we may assume that it is a contingent relation. That between objects is wholly external, depending only upon how they are collected together into classes or sets, and so likewise is the relation between sets. The appropriate metaphysical theory is logical atomism, as it was propounded by Bertrand Russell early in this century, and by Wittgenstein in his *Tractatus*. It is the theory which conceives the world as made up of, or as a collection of, facts, each independent of all the rest, so that any one of them may be the case or may not be the case without making any difference to any of the others. The facts are therefore atomic and their mutual relations are external.[17] A fact consists either of the inherence in an object (or a group of objects) of a property (or several properties), or in a relation between objects. But between facts there is no connection such that it would be possible to infer one from any other. This being so, our presumption above is confirmed that the relation between object and property is contingent, for if it were not so, inference from one fact to another would be possible and the alteration of one would entail that of others. An atomic fact can be stated in an atomic proposition, and, as an atomic fact may be combined with others into a complex fact, so atomic propositions may be joined in a complex proposition. These are the metaphysical presuppositions of the logic developed from Frege's philosophy of arithmetic, of the *Begriffschrift* and its successors from *Principia Mathematica* onwards.

Attempts have been made to deny, or to evade, this conclusion by alleging that the metaphysical doctrine is an adjunct unnecessary to the logic, and that its authors were simply misled by the language of mathematics into constructing the metaphysical theory. So indeed they may have been—misled by the language of mathematics into believing that the metaphysical theory was true. But that in no way alters the fact that the logic presupposes and is founded upon the metaphysic. For the language of mathematics is about sets of externally related units, about numbers, as Frege so aptly defines them, a realm of discourse the metaphysical character of which is rightly set out in the theory of logical atomism. What may well be doubted, however, is that the fundamental structure of *the world*, of the concretely real, is the same as that of this essentially abstract sphere of computation and calculation. It is undoubtedly possible to regard all distinguishable objects in the world as if they were externally related particular units which can be variously grouped according to arbitrary principles of classification, and, for some purposes, this assumption may prove very useful. When it is made, objects can be enumerated and mathematical procedures can be applied to them. But the logic appropriate to mathematical calculation may well prove inadequate if the presupposed metaphysic is not true of things as they really are in concrete fact.

III

The Thesis of this Chapter

Before considering the adequacy of the metaphysics, evidence must be inspected which confirms the thesis that contemporary formal logic, in its assimilation to mathematics, is indeed founded upon the metaphysic thus briefly indicated.

The thesis that I shall try to establish in what follows is that logical atomism is an indispensable presupposition and is implicit in the procedures of formal symbolic logic. I am well aware that many logicians today reject the metaphysic, but I shall argue that their logical practice nevertheless requires it as a presupposition. And this may well be the case even if and although they reject the "logicism" of Frege and Russell in regard to mathematics. Nor do I in any way wish to suggest that, because this is the case, mathematicians either subscribe to the metaphysic or presuppose it in their own thinking.

It is, however, only calculation to which procedures of formal logic are assimilated, and mathematical reasoning is by no means restricted to calculation. It should not be surprising, therefore, if it turned out that mathematical reasoning itself in some of its branches exemplified principles outside the scope of formal logic. Nevertheless, so far as the objects of discourse are, can be reduced to, or may be represented as, "sets, classes, or manifolds," we may expect formal logic as elaborated at the present time to be appropriate. Still less do I believe that this metaphysic is presupposed by natural science. In fact, in the next chapter I shall argue that it is not and that, for that reason, contemporary philosophical analysis of alleged scientific method often goes astray.

IV

Commutation, Association, and Distribution

Mathematicians have extended the concept of number to include negative, irrational, and imaginary numbers, and they interpret the symbols for these higher types of numbers so that, in calculation with them, the fundamental algebraical laws are not violated. These are the laws of commutation, association, and distribution. Such laws obviously hold only if the symbols employed stand for entities of the kind defined by Frege; that is, sets of unitary particulars mutually in external relation. Basically, all arithmetical calculation is addition and subtraction, the aggregation and separation of mutually indifferent and externally related units. Multiplication, division, raising a number to higher powers, and extracting roots are all just complications of the basic operations of addition and subtraction. It follows that these operations will conform to commutative, associative, and distributive laws as long as the entities on which they are performed are externally related particular units. Under this condition, the order in which numbers are added will be of no consequence:

$$x + y = y + x$$

and as multiplication is simply the addition of equal sets or numbers

$$xy = yx.$$

For x and y are merely groups of independent units collected together, the mutual juxtaposition of which is entirely indifferent. Such a collection can, of course, be empty, or may contain only one unit, but that will make no difference to its obeying the commutative principle. Associative and distributive laws depend on precisely the same condition. In the case of the associative rule this is obvious:

$$(x + y) + z = x + (y + z) \text{ and } (xy)z = (yz).$$

And the distributive rule holds because the sum of two collections of units multiplied a given number of times is the same as the sum of each of the collections separately multiplied that number of times:

$$x(y + z) = xy + xz.$$

If, however, the units that made up a collection were internally related so that they affected one another in certain ways or constituted one another by their mutual relations, if, in short, we were dealing with wholes and not with mere collections, the order in which the elements were aggregated would not be indifferent and the algebraic laws would no longer hold.

Logicians have been particularly careful to ensure that their manipulation of the symbols which they employ should conform to the three fundamental algebraic laws, and we now see that the condition for this is that these symbols should represent entities that are externally related or are composed of externally related elements. That, we found, was precisely how Frege viewed concepts and the objects which fall under them; these are what logic is about, and the metaphysical presupposition of a pluralistic atomism is again apparent.

Moreover, not only is it the case that formal procedures conforming to the laws of commutation, association, and distribution presuppose an atomic and particulate subject matter, but, indeed, apart from this presupposition formalization (in the sense of symbolization) is impossible. Symbols, if they are to be useful, and if they are to be manipulated algebraically, must represent identical and unchanging terms or entities. Collections of bare particulars are so conceived. The particulars are each identical, constant, and separate from every other. But in a system in which the elements are internally related, so that any change in either part or whole is liable to affect any and every element in the system, symbols representing the elements would be unstable and algorithmic operations with them would break down. The presuppositions of formal logic which we have uncovered are not fortuitous nor are they contingently made. They are essential to it, and without them formalization is not feasible.

V

Implication

The primary rule of inference is generally known as the rule of detachment, the schema for which is

If *P* then *Q*; but *P*, therefore *Q*.

The relation expressed by "If *P* then *Q*" is that of implication and the interpretation of this relation fundamental to contemporary formal logic is what is known as material implication, the doctrine of "the Philonian conditional."[18] The formula for material implication is $p \supset q$, and that it is fundamental in contemporary logic is clear from the fact that it appears (in one form or another) at the head of every set of axioms for general logic which has so far been offered.[19].

The authors of *Principia Mathematica* are quite explicit as to its significance. Among the functions of propositions they list "four special cases which are of fundamental importance, since all the aggregations of subordinate propositions into one complex proposition which occur in the sequel [*i.e.*, the rest of the work] are formed out of them step by step."[20] these are the logical product (or conjunction), the logical sum (or alternation), the contradictory function and the implicative function. The last includes all four because $p \supset q$ is equivalent to $\sim p \lor q$ and to $\sim (p. \sim q)$. My purpose will be served, therefore, by considering the implicative function only. The peculiarities of the relation represented by the function

$$p \supset q$$

have often been noticed before, and it is generally agreed that it differs from the notion of implication in common use outside formal logic, by which we understand that if a proposition (*q*) is implied by another (*p*), the former can be derived from the latter—can be inferred or deduced from it. That this is not always the case when logicians write $p \supset q$ is commonly admitted, but the logical conditional is usually considered to include such cases of possible inference. This, however, is not and cannot be so, because the presupposition of atomic particulars noticed above does not permit of it, as I shall now proceed to explain.

The conditional functor, $\supset$, is so defined that $p \supset q$ is true whenever both propositions are true, or both false, or *p* is false and *q* is true. Attention has been drawn, by H.W.B. Joseph, Brand Blanshard, and others,[21] to the fact that this is not a relation between two propositions so much as a disjunction of relations. No essential connection is required between the truth or falsity of the propositions concerned in order to satisfy the conditions for this kind of implication. There is no essential connection between the falsity of "All dogs are cats" and the truth of "the sun is hot," yet, according to the prescribed rule, the first implies the second because it is false. Now, if all propositions are atomic and state facts which are unconnected, we never can tell in advance of experience and simply from our knowledge of other propositions whether a proposition is true or false. In the usual sense of "imply", no elementary proposition should ever imply any other. But if we can discover that a proposition, p, is true and another, q, is also true, or that p is false and q in some cases true and in others false, we can assert that p materially implies q. Thus, if elementry propositions do state atomic and mutually independent facts, the doctrine of material implication is logically important and useful. But if implication between propositions required interdependence between facts upon which their truth or falsity was consequent, the doctrine of material implication (as a "logical" relation holding between propositions irrespective of their logical interdependence) would have no logical force.

This conclusion cannot be evaded by allowing that material implication includes such cases as involve logical interdependence between the components. If the truth of q is logically dependent upon that of p, it may be said, everything demanded by the doctrine will be fulfilled: when p is true, q will be true; when p is false, q will be false; but if p should happen to be false, q may nevertheless be true. This conformity with the requirements of the doctrine is, however, purely accidental and material implication can never be a criterion of logical interconnection. If it were, cases in which the propositions were logically independent (like the example given above) would not be permissible. More than this, the conditional connective never *denotes* logical interdependence, even where it happens to exist, though symbolic logicians frequently overlook the fact because they tend to confuse the rule for the use of the symbol with a logical relation between propositions.

$$p \cdot p \supset q : \supset q$$

does not entitle us to assert q as true if we know that p is true, for we cannot, with that knowledge alone, assert $p \supset q$. We can do that only if we also know that q is true; and, of course, if we do, the ostensible conclusion is not an inference from p. Consequently, the second implication sign does not signify logical interdependence any more than the first, for it is not the material implicative relation between p and q that entails q when p is true. Likewise, even if the first implication were strict, the second need not be, because the material implication would still hold if either p or $p \supset q$ were false. Accordingly, the sign $\supset$ can never indicate logical interdependence.

This is sometimes held to be disproved by the example:

$$p \supset q \; . \; \supset \; . \; \sim q \supset \sim p$$

Here, the two compound expressions are thought to be related by a strict logical implication, as are the components of the second compound. But this is a mistake. If the first connective is not a strict implication, neither are the other two, and if it is, although they will be also, this, as has been shown, is not what the implication sign denotes. I can conclude from the falsity of the consequent of a conditional to that of the antecedent only if there is a strict logical connection between the antecedent and the consequent in the first place. There is no strict logical connection between

The sun is hot

and

Newton was a man;

therefore, it does not follow strictly that if Newton was a woman the sun must be cold. The validity of the symbolic expression must depend throughout either upon the logical interdependence of all its components or of none. If the former is the case then the sign $\supset$ has *surreptitiously been given a different meaning* from the relations between propositions in terms of which material implication has been defined, and that doctrine will not apply (because it cannot guarantee the logical dependence of q upon p). If the latter is the case, then the relation between none of the components is that of strict logical interdependence.

But $p \supset q$ is *defined* as $\sim p$ v q, it will be maintained, therefore, $\sim q$ leaves no alternative except $\sim p$; thus, the implication is strict. But this is not a strict implication between propositions, but merely a rule determining the use of a symbol. The truth of

Newton was a man

does not depend on that of

The sun is hot,

but must be known independently before we can write $\supset$ between them. And when known independently, it does not entitle us to infer from its opposite to the falsity of the proposition, "The sun is hot," although we are entitled *by the rule* to connect its contradictory with the denial of the consequent by the material implication sign. Where we are entitled to infer, and the truth of the consequent is dependent upon that of the antecedent, the connective does not represent the logical relation between the propositions. It remains true, therefore, that the doctrine of material implication makes sense only if the propositions to which it applies are all atomic and logically independent.

Where a real connection does exist, the doctrine is wholly inappropriate. If Newton was a man, it follows of necessity that his mother was a woman, and if his mother was not a woman he could have been no man; but although "Newton was a man" materially implies "Newton's mother was a woman" (because both happen to be true), "Newton's mother was not a woman" also implies "Newton was a man" (because the first proposition happens to be false and the second true). Thus,

$$p \supset q . \supset \sim q \supset \sim p$$

does not hold strictly, for if q is false it still materially implies p, and if q is true it can equally be implied materially by $\sim p$. We may equally well write

$$p \supset q . \supset . q \supset \sim p$$

(when p and q are either or both false),

or

$$p \supset q . \supset . \sim q \supset p$$

(when p and q are either or both true);
and if p is true and q is false,

$$p \supset q . \supset . \sim q \supset \sim p$$

is still correct even though p does not materially imply q.

Clearly, then, the doctrine of material implication always presupposes the mutual logical independence of elementary propositions, a supposition justified only if they state actually independent facts. In other words, the implicative function, which is fundamental to the whole system of *Principia Mathematica*, presupposes logical atomism. As almost every theorem and demonstration in the logical calculus there elaborated includes this function, it would be fair to say that without it (and so without the presupposition of atomism) the calculus could not operate. The substitution of a different notation makes no difference; for instance $p|q$ or $p|(q|q)$ involves the logical independence of the truth and falsity of the propositions in precisely the same way as $p \supset q$, for the incompatibility sign is defined as meaning no more than that either or both propositions are false.[22]

What is true of material implication is equally true of formal implication, which is the generalized version of material implication and is expressed by the function

$$(x) . \phi x \supset \varphi x$$

In *The Principles of Mathematics* (Ch. III, 40–41), Russell equates this formula with the universal proposition of the traditional logic. "All men are mortal" is said to be equivalent to "For all values of x, x is a man implies x is mortal"[23] The variable cannot, however, be restricted to men, because that would eliminate the implication by eliminating "x is a man." We can determine the truth or falsity of the antecedent (x is a man) only by inspection of each particular case of substitution, which, if x is unrestricted, is an interminable task. We cannot avail ourselves for this purpose of any general rule of recognition, such as "No trees are men," because any such rule is itself a formal implication (in this case, "For all values of x, x is a tree implies x is not a man") and the establishment of its truth would involve a similar infinite process of investigation of particulars. The presumption throughout is that the atomic propositions concerned predicate properties of particular objects *which are not essentially related* to those objects, for any particular may be substituted for x and the truth of the resulting proposition must be checked by some external criterion (for "x is a tree" or "x is a man" cannot be analytic). The issue is not simply that the verification procedure involves an infinite process, but that the truth condition for the conditional implies that its components are logically independent for their truth value. The atomic propositions are not themselves essentially related. The formal implication is not a connection of properties inherent in their natures, it is simply a disjunction of conjoined truth values (as we have seen). Only if the world were composed of bare particulars, externally related to one another and to their properties, and only if the facts of the world composed of such conjunctions of particulars were without any mutual connection, would there be need of an infinite process of inspection to establish an implicative relation between two classes of subjects, so that a propositional function like ϕx can be said formally to imply another φx only if every possible case has been inspected. Once again the principles of the logical calculus presupposes atomicity in the world and we must conclude that the metaphysic is indispensable to it, for if that were abandoned, the whole doctrine of implication upon which the logical system is built would have to be revised.

Sometimes an excuse is offered for the paradoxical (one might say, illogical) character of material implication on the ground that the Philonian interpretation of the conditional is the weakest which will satisfy the requirement that the rule of detachment gives a valid inference.[24] But it is obvious from the foregoing that it does not satisfy this requirement; for unless there is some essential connection between p and q we cannot validly argue "If p then q, and p; therefore q." We ought not even to assert, "If p then q" except on the condition that there is a connection between what the propositions express. The Philonian interpretation licenses the schema "If *P* then *Q*" whether or not there is any connection, so that we might argue

> If pigs cannot fly, Socrates is mortal;
> but pigs cannot fly,
> therefore, Socrates is mortal.

Although this argument is valid according to the current doctrine, the conclusion, as long as it includes the word "therefore" is false, because it alleges in effect that the *reason* for Socrates' mortality is the flightlessness of pigs. Accordingly, we have an implicitly false conclusion from true premisses, and that is precisely what the rule of detachment is supposed to preclude.

We might, of course, change the schema slightly to the form, "If *P*, and if *P* then *Q*, then *Q*":

$$p \cdot p \supset q: \supset :q.$$

But this in effect is the empty tautology

$$p \supset q \cdot \supset p \supset q.$$

which, if the Philonian interpretation is maintained throughout, is subject to all the strictures discussed above, and if it applies only to the first conditional, the last expression becomes false. The material implication,

$$\text{If pigs cannot fly, Socrates is mortal,}$$

does not imply that Socrates is mortal *because* pigs cannot fly.

Quine, in *Methods of Logic*, reserves the term "implication" for a conditional which is, in his terminology, "valid"; that is, true whatever interpretation is given to its literal symbols.[25] For example, if no interpretation of *p* and *q* can make the consequent of the conditional false and the antecedent true, the conditional is valid and amounts to an implication. If, on some interpretations, the conditional is true and on others false, it is "consistent," in Quine's terminology, but not "valid"; and if no interpretation makes it true, it is "inconsistent". Thus,

$$\sim q \supset \sim (p.q)$$

is true however we interpret *p* and *q*.

"If Cassius is not hungry, then Cassius is not both lean and hungry."

i.   If both antecedent and consequent are true, the whole conditional is true.

ii. Suppose "Cassius is not hungry" to be false, then it will materially imply any proposition, so the conditional remains true.

iii.   Suppose "Cassius is lean" to be false, then the consequent of the contitional will be true and will be implied by every proposition. Hence, the conditional cannot be falsified by any interpretation of its literals, and it is a valid implication.[26] Now a logical schema that is true for all interpretations of its component literals is a tautology, so an implication turns out to be a tautological conditional. This is patent from the example given, for

$$\sim(p \,.\, q) \equiv \sim p \text{ v } \sim q$$

and to say that Cassius is not hungry is to say that he is not hungry, whether or not he is also lean.

Note, however, that the logical proof of the validity of a conditional preserves and depends upon the Philonian interpretation, according to which the coincident truth-values of the components (both true, both false, or antecedent false and consequent true) are sufficient. Quine's version of implication, therefore, in no way removes the presupposition that elementary propositions are atomic and have no logical interdependence. Valid inference, on this view, must be restricted to tautologies and its proper symbolization ought to be $p \supset p$. But even so the anomalies consequent upon the Philonian interpretation are not removed, because if p is false it will imply every other proposition, including its own contradictory, and every valid implication will be an instance of *consequentia mirabilis*, in which the conclusion follows from its own denial, and this will be the case, moreover, whatever proposition is substituted for p. Such a conclusion, however, is wholly unacceptable and should lead us to distrust the Philonian doctrine root and branch.

My conclusion is not simply that formalized logic is and must always be truth-functional, and that truth-functional logic implies logical atomism. It is that formalization presupposes the view of the concept as abstract and of its extension as a mere collection or set of "objects," a view common to Frege, Russell, and the Wittgenstein of the *Tractatus*, as well as to the majority of contemporary logicians. Truth-functional varieties of logic merely serve to confirm this thesis, but any formalized system, truth-functional or not, presupposes this theory of the concept, from which logical atomism follows naturally. To reject logical atomism is to hold that propositions can express internal relations between non-synonymous terms and to admit the notion of non-tautological necessity in logic. Such an admission, I contend, must wreck any system of formalization, for the reason given on page 33 above that the commutative, associative, and distributive laws would no longer hold. Further, where relations are internal there can be no bare particulars, and in consequence the rule of substitution for variables cannot be maintained, because their significance would change in differing contexts (*i.e.*, in different formulae).

The replacement of material implication by strict implication in contemporary modal logic has made no difference to the presuppositions I am imputing to mathematical logic in general. In extending general logic to include modal forms, C.I. Lewis introduced strict implication (symbolized by $\rightarrow$) in place of material implication in order to remove the inconveniences to which attention has been drawn. But he did not succeed, because strict implication is defined by the substitution of "impossible" for the negative in the definition of material implication. Where before we wrote

$$p \supset q \equiv \sim(p . \sim q),$$

we now write

$$p \rightarrow q \equiv \sim \lozenge (p . \sim q),$$

and this makes no difference because it is equally true of material implication. There too, it is not possible for the Philonian conditional to hold if the consequent is false while the antecedent is true.

The relations between statements of possibility and necessity set out in modal logic, because its pure formalism must be maintained, leave aside the grounds both of possibility and of necessity, just as general formal logic abstracts from the grounds of the truth or falsity of atomic propositions. It is concerned only with formal transformations of expressions for modal statements; and except for tautology and self-contradiction, what makes a proposition possibly, actually, or necessarily true is not the concern of formal logic. In fact, if I am right, its presupposition is that no proposition is either necessary or impossible except analytically. If it is impossible, then, for q to be false and p true, if p strictly implies q, it is for no other reason than that the implication is tautologous.

Accordingly it transpires, as before, that an impossible proposition implies every proposition and a necessary one is implied by every proposition, which, in the common meaning of "implies," is not the case. The equality of the angles of an equilateral Euclidean triangle is not implied by the mortality of Socrates, nor yet by the innocence of Judas Iscariot; and that the sum of the angles of the triangle exceeds 180 degrees does not imply that the whale is a mammal nor yet that it is a fish. If logical atomism is true, strict implication cannot hold between atomic propositions unless strict and material (or formal) implication amount to the same thing. The difference, if any, can only be purely logical; in other words, to be strict, or necessary, the implication must be a tautology, whereas a material conditional need only be consistent. Yet if strict implication is simply a tautological conditional the consequences of the doctrine, as we have seen, become altogether incoherent for ordinary thought.[27]

So long as the concept is viewed as abstract, as explained above, this does not matter and the logic can proceed unhindered, and it will serve our purpose, nevertheless, as long as no internal connections are assumed between propositions, as long as they are held to be atomic. If the world is made up of mutually independent facts and facts are conglomerations of unconnected particulars with qualities and properties contingently attributable to them, then facts *will* be atomic and so will the propositions expressing them. What I have striven to show is that this is the metaphysical presupposition of mathematical logic, and where internal relations are excluded, mathematical logic does provide a calculus for deducing the relations of such atomic facts and propositions. My thesis is fully supported by Bertrand Russell's explicit statements. In the Introduction to the second edition of *Principia Mathematica* we read that atomic propositions are accepted as a datum[28] and that such terms as can occur in any atomic propositions are "particulars."[29] This is reaffirmed by Russell in his paper on "Logical Atomism" in *Contemporary British Philosophy* (1924), where he maintains that though facts are not simple, all complexes must be composed of simples, which are the limits of analysis. The logical uses, he says, of the old notion of substance can only be applied, if at all, to simples, and such simples are what the simple symbols in symbolic logic represent. In fact it is clear from the way in which Russell writes in this paper, both of symbolic logic and of the world, that he considers the justification of the logical procedures to be their appropriateness to the structure of the real. There can moreover, be no doubt that the account given of atomic propositions on page xv of *Principia Mathematica* is meant to reveal what the authors consider to be the structure of the facts which such propositions state.

Wittgenstein in the *Tractatus*, sets out the metaphysical theory quite plainly, and frankly asserts that logical notation shows forth the form of the facts. Facts, he says, are combinations of objects (*Tractatus*, 2.01), and he uses the word in precisely the same way as Frege does. Clearly, then, the logic rests on the metaphysic and we need not think that Wittgenstein was misled by any error or confusion on the part of

Russell or by any hypostatization of the language of mathematics. Mathematics is itself a part of logic[30]—"a logical method," in Wittgenstein's words (ibid., 6.2).

The reason why the authors of *Principia Mathematica* allege that their notation was "framed with a view to the perfectly precise expression of mathematical propositions," and why they believed that the whole of mathematics could be deduced from certain fundamental logical postulates was that they espoused the metaphysic of logical atomism, and not *vice versa*. The doctrine of extensive abstraction, an essential corollary of logico-metaphysical atomism, the theory of classes and the definition of numbers which go with it, provide the connection between mathematics and the logical notation designed to express the relations between atomic facts. In a world of particulars mutually related in atomic facts, there should be no entities such as classes. The ideal logical notation, therefore, must be one in which classes can be represented by symbols standing for particulars. This is effected by the symbol $x(\phi x)$, meaning "all those values of x for which the propositional function ϕx is true." a number is then defined as a class of classes similar to a given class, and it follows that all propositions about numbers can be represented in the notation designed to express the structure of facts about particulars. It would also seem to follow that all mathematical truths could be deduced from those postulates about the fundamental logical functions which determine the possible relations of atomic propositions. It is not my intention here to criticise this position or to attack the procedures of formal logic consequent to it, but only to demonstrate the indispensability to them of the metaphysical foundation and especially of the view of the concept as abstract.

It will be objected that formal logic has advanced far beyond *Principia Mathematica* and Wittgenstein's *Tractatus* and that many of the later developments belie the conclusion I am seeking to establish. At the same time, it is usually admitted that all later developments rest upon first order logic to which the above arguments apply. It may be alleged that the intuitionist logic of Brouwer and Heyting is not subject to the same presuppositions as other formal logic. But (so far as the differences are relevant) this seems not to be the case. Intuitionist logic seeks to restrict the validity of the law of excluded middle to finite subjects and to demonstrable propositions, but to dispense with it where certain types of infinity are concerned. This indeed introduces new and interesting features into one's methods of mathematical reasoning, and the elimination of the law is common to intuitionists with other multivalued logics, but there is no evidence that it has any effect on the presupposed notion of the concept as abstract with an extension consisting of a denumerable set of particulars. Nor does it dispense with the conditional or interpret it otherwise than as material implication. William Kneale asserts that Heyting's rules of deduction are the same as those of *Principia Mathematica* except that the logical signs (including the conditional) are taken as undefined primitives. But this will not affect the case I have sought to make above if Gödel[31] is right in his proof that Heyting's calculus includes the whole of classical logic. He claims to show that the intuitionists have not even abandoned the principle of excluded middle except in the sense that they refrain from using it in their own mathematical reasoning. Prior asserts that Heyting's calculus restricts implicative theses to those which will justify only such proofs as Brouwer's mathematics will admit. Otherwise implication does not change its character and similar truth conditions prevail for it as in the ordinary propositional calculus.[32] Every false proposition still implies every proposition, a true one is still implied by every proposition, and an indeterminate (or indemonstrable) implies any indeterminate.[33] If, as is suggested by Tarski and McKinsey, Heyting's operators are not to be regarded as truth-functional but as modal, my thesis, as I have argued above, will remain unaffected.[34]

If we do not presume that the world is constructed out of atomic facts, and if we are to take account of internal relations, a very different sort of logical theory is required to make intelligible the connections between facts that justify scientific theorizing. If our logic is not to be wholly extensional, classes, universals, relations, and concepts would have to be quite differently defined and conceived; and if the truths of mathematics could be derived from the principles of this different logic, it would not be by the kind of linear deduction contemplated by Frege, Russell, and their followers.

The foregoing argument must not be understood as an attack on symbolic logic. That is far from its intention. Symbolic logic is a highy developed and technical mathematical science, which has a legitimate and important province and application. But, if my argument in this chapter holds, such logic is necessarily restricted in its application to subject matters conceived as made up of mutually external particulars and sets of such particulars. My object has been no more than to demonstrate from its own doctrine and practice that formalized logic rests on certain metaphysical presuppositions, sometimes openly admitted by its authors, and to reveal what these presuppositions are. I shall show in the sequel that a different approach, which is not bound by the restriction above-mentioned, still recognizes and retains a place for formal logic, the validity and efficacy of which in its own legitimate sphere is neither to be denied nor depreciated.

(Note: The presuppositions underlying the doctrines of the traditional formal logic are not essentially different from those displayed in this chapter as grounding contemporary mathematical logic. Their history is continuous, as the use of the Philonian conditional bears witness. It is largely for this reason that Arisotle, the founder of the traditional logic, is so commonly credited with empiricist views, in contrast with those of Plato. But the doctrines that originated the traditional formal logic appear in the *Prior Analytics*, and elsewhere what Aristotle writes is by no means always compatible with them. His other treatises propound a philosophy much less opposed to Plato than is often believed, one which places Aristotle in quite a different camp from that of the radical empiricists. As Hegel remarks, in his own philosophy Aristotle does not make use of the syllogism the theory of which he sets out in the *Prior analytics*.)

Notes

1. Cf. L. Wittgenstein, *Tractatus: Logico-Philosophicus*, 6.45; J. O. Urmson, *Philosophical Analysis* (Oxford, 1956); and G. J. Warnock, *English Philosophy since 1900* (Oxford University Press, 1958), pp. 41–42.

2. Cf. *Grundlagen der Arithmetik*, § 95.

3. Cf. William and Martha Kneale, *The Development of Logic* (Oxford, 1962), p. 453.

4. Cf. *The Development of Logic*, p. 1.

5. Cf. *Translations from the Writings of Gottlob Frege*, by P. Geach and M. Black (Blackwell, Oxford, 1952), pp. 21–41.

6. Cf. Kneale, *op cit.*, Ch. X, 1.

7. *Op cit.*, Geach and Black, p. 32.

8. *Grundlagen*, §§ 21–15.

9. *Ibid.*, §§ 28.

10. *Ibid.*, § 54.

11. *Ibid.*, § 54.

12. *Op cit.*, p. 466.

13. *Op cit.*, p. 458.

14. Cf. "On Concept and Object," (Geach and Black) p. 44.

15. Frege asserts that the requirement for sharp delimitation of concepts is "that it shall be determinate, for any object, whether it falls under the concept or not." "Function and concept," Geach and Black, p. 33.

16. *The Development of Logic*, p. 452.

17. Cf. D. R. Hofstadter, *Godel, Escher, Bach* (Vintage Books, New York, 1980), pp. 53ff., where the world is compared to a formal system and the "formal" world is said to be one of elementary particles obeying mechanistic laws.

18. After Philo of Megara, who first said that a sound conditional is one that does not begin with a truth and end with a falsehood.

19. Cf. W. and M. Kneale, *op. cit.*, ch. IX, 2.

20. Cf. *Principia Mathematica*, 2nd ed.; A. N. Prior, *Formal Logic* (Oxford, 1962), p. 8: "From a logical point of view, . . . the most important truth-function is . . . the one constructed out of a pair of arguments by means of the operator 'If . . . then . . .'."

21. Cf. H. W. B. Joseph, in lectures delivered at Oxford in 1932 (as yet unpublished) on "Internal and External Relations and the Philosophy of analysis," and in "a Plea for Free-Thinking in Logistic," *Mind*, vols. XLI, XLII and XLIII; Blanshard in *The Nature of Thought* (London, 1939), Ch. XXIX.

22. *Vide Principia Mathematica*, 2nd ed., vol. I, p. xvi.

23. A view originally put forward by F. H. Bradley, but contested by Bernard Bosanquet. Cf. F. H. Bradley, *Principles of Logic* (Oxford, 1922), vol. I, pp. 43ff., and B. Bosanquet, *Knowledge and Reality* (London, 1885, 1892; Reprinted 1968).

24. Cf. Kneale, *op. cit.*, p. 130. The fact that some logicians no longer regard the so-called paradoxes of implication as a problem does not affect the above argument concerning metaphysical presuppositions.

25. Cf. *op cit.*, p. 7.

26. A complete truth table would be

p	q	$\sim q$	$\supset$	$\sim(p.q)$
T	T	F	T	F
T	F	T	T	T
F	F	T	T	T
F	T	F	T	T

27. Efforts to develop a formalism appropriate to quantum physics (called quantum logic) seem to be an adaptation of the more normal formal logic so as to take account of peculiarities in the physical theory of testing. These affect the truth of $p.q \supset p$ when the determination of q affects the experimental conditions so as to alter the value of p. Logicians have therefore had difficulty in defining the implicative functor. This is an embarrassment, for as J. J. Zeman remarks "To be a logic . . . a formalism must possess an implication relation." ("Quantum Logic with Implication," *Notre Dame Journal of Formal Logic*, 29, 1979). The general result of their efforts seems to have been to convert the implicative sign into a modal operator, which, if what is said above is correct, would have no bearing on my main thesis.

28. Cf. *Principia Mathematica*, 2nd ed., vol. I, p. xv.

29. *Ibid.*, p. xix.

30. The truth is rather the reverse. Hilbert observed long ago that symbolic logic could be treated as a branch of elementary number theory (*Verhandlunge des dritten internationalen Mathematiker-Kongresses*, 1904), and the detailed correspondence has been worked out by Gödel (*Über formalunentscheidbare Sätze der Principia Mathematica und verwandter Systeme'*, *Monatshefte für Mathematik und Physik*, XXXVIII, 1931).

31. "*Zur intuitionistischen Arithmetik und Zahlentheorie,*" *Ergebnisse eines mathematischen Kolloquiums*, Heft IV (1932), pp. 34–38.

32. Cf. A. N. Prior, *Formal Logic* (Oxford, 1962), pp. 250, and 252.

33. That the rule of detachment is ultimately the same for the intuitionist implicative function as in the ordinary propositional calculus has been shown by Lucasiewicz; cf. "On the Intuitionistic Theory of Deduction," *Nederlands Akadamie voor Wetenschap Proc.*, Ser. A, 55 (1952) pp. 202–12.

34. The belief held by some that intuitionist logic rests on Kantian presuppositions is a grave misunderstanding. Kant did indeed maintain that mathematics depends for its cogency on what he calls "the pure forms of intuition." But Kant's thesis is that these forms (space and time) are inherent in the mind which can therefore deduce synthetic results from them *a priori*. In contemporary intuitionist logic no such metaphysical doctrine is reflected.

Chapter 2

Formal Logic and
Scientific Method

I

Empiricism and Induction

The presuppositions of formal logic uncovered in the last chapter may be summarized as follows:

1. The ultimate constituents of the world are purely particular atomic entities (bare particulars).

2. Relations between particulars are wholly external.

3. Particular entities are variously associated with a multiplicity of attributes or characters.

3.1 The relation between a particular entity and its characters is wholly fortuitous (or, if it is not, we cannot know the intrinsic connection).

4. Particulars may be grouped together according to the similarity of their characters to form classes, collections, or sets.

4.1 The identifying mark of a class is the common character or concept of which the particular instances together form the extension.

4.2 Concepts are abstract and general.

5. The inherence of a character in a particular thing, or the relation obtaining between particulars, or both, constitute an atomic fact.

5.1 Any atomic fact can be the case or not be the case and all the rest remain the same.

6. A statement of an atomic fact is an atomic proposition.

There follow as corollaries: (a) that atomic propositions are not deducible one from another; (b) that deductive inference is purely analytic; (c) that facts can be known only by direct observation and inductive inference from direct observation.

Historically these theses have developed from the last. It has been assumed or asserted that facts can be discovered only through sense-perception, which primarily reveals only sensible qualities, and never reveals any connections between them. We do however, by its means, experience conjunctions between sensibles, which, when they occur constantly together, we take to inhere in particular things (or "substances"). Constantly experienced conjunctions of sensibles leads us to expect repetition of such associations and so gives pretext for inductive inference, but becuse no connections are ever revealed, deduction of one fact from the occurrence of another is never possible (facts and propositions are thus atomic), and formal reasoning does no more than develop the consequences of the definition of terms. This doctrine is known as empiricism and it is the presupposition of contemporary formal logic. In fact, these metaphysical presuppositions may be called the "deep structure" of formal logic, and they have epistemological consequences. To repeat, where facts constituted solely of contingently associated particulars are atomic, and atomic propositions are unconnected by any essential logical link, the knowledge that any proposition q is true is never derivable from the knowledge that any other proposition p is true. If we know that p q and that p is true we can assert q, but we cannot know that p q unless we know the truth or falsity of q independently, for the conditional is valid only if either both propositions are true, or both false, or else if q is true irrespective of p. The knowledge that q must have been otherwise ascertained and cannot be derived from the knowledge that p. The truth or falsity of any atomic proposition, therefore, can be discovered in either one of only two ways: (i) by direct inspection of the fact, or (ii) by induction from past experience. Intellectual intuition is necessarily confined to tautologies, for *a priori* intuition of facts—synthetic propositions—would involve a connection between particulars (whether substantive or adjectival) that was not purely fortuitous, a relation between them that was not wholly external, and so a violation of the metaphysical principles presupposed.

Deduction, therefore, of one proposition from another is inevitably restricted to tautologies and is strictly analytic. The discovery of facts must always be and can only be empirical, either by direct observation or inductive generalization. A further metaphysical presupposition is here involved having epistemological force: that direct perceptual intuition of particular immediately presented fact is possible. If it were not, no factual knowledge would be attainable, since induction is dependent upon past perceptual experience and no atomic fact is intellectually intuitable.

Adherence to these metaphysical principles commits one to the treatment of facts as if they were governed by pure chance. This follows naturally from the externality of their mutual relations, for if no connections between particulars are binding and necessary, they may be conjoined—or may not be conjoined—in any way or in any order, and how they will occur will be entirely fortuitous. Causal connection has then to be treated simply as a generalization from past experience of constant conjunction between events otherwise altogether unconnected. It is a conjunction the constancy of which has no ground and is on a par with an unbroken series of heads in the repeated tossing of a coin. Accordingly, any attempt to predict the occurrence of conjunctions can proceed only by the calculation of probabilities based on the proportion of similar occurrences already experienced among the totality of possible cases. Logical theories of induction, therefore, are always closely associated with mathematical theories of probability, and the formalization of inductive procedures, like that of deductive, is founded on the same presupposition of a world of externally related particulars.

If these metaphysical and epistemological presumptions are made and are strictly maintained, an insoluble problem arises with respect to induction; for the lack of connection between atomic facts makes the prediction of future conjunctions always unjustifiable on the grounds of past experience, no matter how many instances have been observed or how frequently. Only two empiricist philosophers seem to have understood this problem thoroughly: David Hume, who was led, by recognizing its insolubility, to scepticism, and Bertrand Russell, who saw that it could only be solved, and scientific knowledge could only be salvaged, if wholehearted empiricism were abandoned.

The principle of induction is, in general terms, that constant (or frequent) experience of the occurrence of the conjunction of particulars in the past warrants prediction of their conjunction in the future, either invariably (universally), or probably, that is, with a more or less definitely assignable frequency. But if there is no connection which binds them necessarily together, no instance of their conjunction at any time gives ground for predicting their conjunction at any other time, however often such conjunction may have been experienced in the past. But, in the absence of inductive generalization, knowledge disintegrates; for even the recognition of individual objects depends on the assumption that qualities which have in the past been experienced (in Locke's words) to "go constantly together" will continue to do so in the future. Some logical justification must therefore be found for induction if empirical knowledge is to be possible at all, and, if none can be found, the metaphysical presuppositions of formal logic cannot be retained as the foundation of natural science.

It is commonly agreed that deductive justification for inductive inference neither can be given nor ought to be sought; for deductive reasoning follows precise rules relevant only to analytic procedures, whereas induction is empirical generalization involving synthetic statements and requiring entirely different rules of its own. But whatever such rules may be, they cannot rightly include the principle of induction itself, for to state dogmatically that prediction is justified by past experience is to contradict the metaphysical presupposition of atomic disconnection between facts which makes inductive reasoning epistemologically indispensable. The metaphysical assumption of the atomicity of facts makes deductive inference from the known to the unknown impossible and so compels us to introduce an alternative procedure for empirical science. But the same assumption, by implication, forbids the inductive process from past experience to future prediction, rendering the commonly recognized procedure of empirical science invalid. If facts are atomic no inference from their past to their future occurrence is warranted, yet no other form of reasoning is left open to the natural scientist.

It is not, therefore, surprising that philosophers who have openly or tacitly subscribed to the metaphysical presuppositions of formal logic have been tireless in their efforts to find a justification for inductive generalization, or somehow to extricate it from Hume's criticism, which first unerringly set out the difficulty indicated above. Nor is it surprising that they have invariably failed. The so-called pragmatic justification of induction, which claims that the procedure is vindicated by its ubiquitous success, fails, because, first, no attempt is ever made to demonstrate the prevalence of the alleged success. It is simply assumed that the triumph of empirical science is that of inductive reasoning because it is assumed that no other method is available. No investigation is made by those claiming this kind of justification for induction into the actual procedures adopted by practising scientists, and it has never been established that induction as traditionally described—inference from observed conjunction of particulars to the recurrence of similar conjunctions—has ever been the source of major scientific discoveries. Secondly, however, even if it had, the argument from past success of the method as a justification of its future use is a *petitio principii*, because it invokes the very principle it is meant to justify.

Another argument frequently put forward is equally futile, that the demand for justification of induction misconceives the nature of empirical truth by requiring certainty where only probability is possible. For probability (high or low) of future conjunctions is as little deducible from past occurrences as certainty. Hume made this clear at the very inception of the discussion, as well as the circularity of the pragmatic justification.[1] No appeal to the mathematical calculus of probability is even relevant to this problem. This was fully recognized and clearly demonstrated by Bertrand Russell.[2] The mathematical calculus of probability is a purely deductive algorithm and it can be applied to empirical cases only on the assumption that the principle of induction holds good. It cannot justify that assumption. It is based upon the ratio of two numbers, one representing the totality of possible cases under consideration, the other representing the favourable cases hitherto observed (or in certain circumstances, the number of possible favourable instances). What may or may not occur in the future is in no way determined by this ratio, which has no causal efficacy, and expectation of a certain frequency of occurrence can only be based upon belief in the validity of the inductive principle.

As I have shown at length in *Hypothesis and Perception*, arguments based on probability theory all collapse as soon as this veiled *petitio principii* is uncovered. Donald Williams' elegant proof of induction[3] rests on the assumption that samples are being taken of a given "population" of facts in which a fixed proportion (unknown but calculable from the samples) is favourable to the hypothesis being tested. But this assumption does not allow for the possibility of future change in the population and the proportion of favourable cases. Any attempt to cover that possibility leads to an infinite regress. The belief that the proportion is invariable invokes the principle of induction which the argument seeks to justify—*i.e.*, it is the belief that the future will resemble the past and the present. It is the condition of the proof and not its result.[4]

Similarly Reichenbach's frequency theory and its related justification of induction is unsuccessful because it confuses a mathematical series, which is convergent, with an empirical series, which can be presumed convergent only if the principle of induction is assumed valid.[5] Reichenbach admits that there may not be any limit in the empirical series and that the probability estimate is only a posit, but he claims that the best way to discover whether there is a limit and what it is (in fact, the only rational way) is by the method of induction. This, however, is what has to be proved, and it can be true only if the principle of induction is first assumed, namely, that what has hitherto been found (a seemingly convergent series) will continue in the future as it has been found in the past, that the empirical series of events will coincide with the mathematical series calculated from past conjunctions.

The same sort of fallacy infects the argument of G.H. von Wright,[6] who admits that no valid justification of induction has been or ever could be given, but argues, following Reichenbach and Braithwaite, that induction is the best policy to adopt because it is "self-correcting." Once again, however, what has to be proved is being assumed. The self-correcting tendency depends upon the assumption that if two classes, A and B, have in the past been found to overlap there will be a precise proportion of As that are Bs and that this proportion will remain constant in the future. In that case, as we collect more instances, we continually approximate to the actual proportion of B to A and so correct earlier discrepancies. This is, in fact, the same thesis as that maintained by Williams, and it suffers from the same fault. The initial assumption entails the principle of induction; if that is assumed to be valid, it is natural to believe that our use of it will be self-corrective; but if it is not valid, our use of it will not be self-corrective. The fallacy is further illustrated by von Wright's discussion of what he calls "counter-inductive policies." He maintains that a " reason" for believing that the relative frequency of B among A regularly declines may be that, among the first 500 As we have observed, the proportion of Bs has decreased with each hundred, thus: in the first hundred 50%; in the second, 49%; in the third, 48%; and so on. We might then conclude that in the sixth hundred the proportion will be 45%.[7] If we do so conclude, however, we presume the validity of the inductive principle. Neither can our series validate that principle, nor is our conclusion "counter-inductive." The assumption is that the empirical series will continue in future as the mathematical series does in theory, and that assumption alone, can ground the belief that our "policy" will be successful, or self-correcting, or have whatever advantage we attribute to it.

von Wright is not the only thinker to argue along these lines. It is often said that even if no justification can be given for induction, it is still the most rational procedure because it is the best, or the only one available. This however is simply the presupposition underlying formal logic and is a grossly dogmatic assertion, for the reason already given. No effort has been made to show that there is no alternative procedure, or that other methods have not in fact been used by scientists who have made the most significant discoveries, or that any reputable scientist ever really argues inductively in the manner alleged. I have shown in detail that the actual method prevalent among scientists is a different one and, in agreement with Sir Karl Popper, have maintained that the traditional form of inductive reasoning is not used in, and is not typical of, empirical science.[8]

To claim that induction is the best or most reasonable policy for scientific investigation, or even, as some writers have done, that it is precisely what we mean by "reasonable," is highly dubious. First, we may note that what we usually mean by "reasonable" is "deductively valid," which inductive inference is not. Secondly, as facts are assumed to be unconnected and to occur on the same principle as the outcome of spinning a roulette wheel—as they are (tacitly) assumed to be governed by pure chance—it is hardly reasonable to believe that the longer run of luck makes its own continuation more probable than the shorter. In fact, mathematically (*i.e.*, deductively) considered, a frequent recurrence of chance conjunctions either reduces the probability of their repetition (if, for example, the length of the unbroken sequence is considered), or leaves it unchanged (if simply the probability of the next occurrence is calculated).

Finally, in company with others (like Max Black), von Wright argues the failure to justify induction rests on linguistic confusion—a demand for the guarantee of the truth of a proposition which is logically constructed so that no such guarantee can be given. This is, of course, strictly correct on the presuppositions underlying formal logic which were disclosed in the foregoing chapter. If facts are atomic, and likewise propositions, as the result of allegedly purely external relations between existent particulars, to ask for a justification of inference from observed facts to the unobserved is to demand the impossible. But in a world of such externally related particulars, empirical science as we know it would be impossible. This is what Kant understood long ago, and the fault must surely lie in the metaphysical presumptions from which this result would follow rather than in any linguistic confusion.

Before investigating this possibility, we must notice the conception of science that emerges when these metaphysical presuppositions are adopted. It is that set out clearly, accurately, and elegantly by R. B. Braithwaite in his book, *Scientific Explanation*.[9] The fundamental postulate is that all empirical laws of nature are statements of the constant conjunction of characters. They are derived from direct observation by way of inductive generalization, which produces hypotheses to be tested by further observation. The procedure for such testing is to deduce from the hypothesis consequences which are observable, the deductive process being formal and largely mathematical. Resort may be made to the introduction of postulates and theoretical concepts, defined arbitrarily and adopted for convenience, to assist in this process. The deductive procedure is purely analytic and is conducted with the help of calculi into which empirical terms are introduced by substitution for variables. The inductive procedures are more or less complicated forms of empirical generalization using statistical methods in which the mathematical calculus of probability plays an integral role.

The key concept in this view of science is direct observation, which must be the source of all factual knowledge and on which all inductive inference ultimately rests; and direct observation is overtly or tacitly taken to be an immediate registration by the mind, without distortion or modification, of the fact which it records. Interpretation, where it enters at all, is something superadded; it is fallible and subject to correction in the light of new observations or revised calculations, and it accounts for the purely theoretical elements in science, which must, however, ultimately be rooted in direct observations (Bertrand Russell's "hard data") that are not subject to doubt. Philosophers who deny the possibility or need for certainty in their protestations in defence of induction overlook this presumption of the infallibility of direct observation on which they all rely in their pursuit of probable knowledge.

In recent years, the above conception of science has come under attack, notably from Sir Karl Popper, who rejects induction and denies the possibility of verification of empirical hypothesis in direct perception. For him, science is the invention *ab initio* of hypotheses, for which there are no logical rules and which depends solely on psychological causes. The approved deductive process is then used to elicit from the hypotheses consequences testable by observation. "Corroboration" (understood as the repeated appearance of favourable instances), however frequent, is never complete, for future falsification always remains possible, and the only conclusive proof, when it occurs, is of falsity. The logical principle here invoked is the syllogistic rule that affirmative general conclusions can never be validly derived from particular premisses, but the negation of universal propositions can validly follow from any one particular negative instance. Falsification of this kind, however, still rests in principle on the assumption of infallible direct observation of particular instances, although Popper actually rejects the assumption and adumbrates a quite different theory of scientific discovery (in *obiter dicta*) which he never develops explicitly.[10]

A further consequence of the empiricist conception of science has direct bearing upon the practical dilemma in which mankind finds itself: the dilemma occasioned by the fact that the continued advance of technology creates global problems for the solution of which appeal is made to the very techniques which, as they develop, exacerbate the problems. The metaphysical presuppositions we have been discussing are closely associated with the notion of an 'objective' world independent of all knowledge processes. Immediate registration of facts in direct observation then becomes a necessity if knowledge is to be acquired by a mind to which such facts are external. To be true, this immediate apprehension must be free from all subjective interference. No imaginative embellishment is allowable, and any emotional qualification arising from wish or desire would inevitably distort the faithful registration of the objectively real. As that reality is assumed to be particulate and pluralistic, an aggregation of externally related elements, objective knowledge must consist solely in observed facts, inductive generalizations, and mathematical analyses. Evaluation in any other than a mathematical quantitative sense must be excluded and science must be unrelentingly value-free, in the first place because value is presumed to be absent from what is wholly objective, and, secondly, because valuation involves desire and purpose, subjective elements in experience which must be rigidly eliminated from all record of the nature of the external world.

The world which such science investigates is conceived as a mechanical system of externally related parts. As science discovers the laws of its working, it can apply them so as to enable scientists increasingly to control the mechanism for their own purposes—and such applied science is technology. But the purposes for which it is used, though (in one or more of its branches) science may inquire what they are, it cannot criticize in the light of any criterion of what they ought to be. To do that would be to introduce value judgements into science and value judgements are held to be subjective. If science and technology give rise to problems involving value judgements, they are problems a value-free science is not competent to solve. This is the root of our contemporary dilemma and the soil in which it grows is a metaphysic, for the most part unrecognized and disowned by those who persistently presuppose it. It is, moreover, a metaphysic which is internally incoherent and demonstrably false.

A great body of contemporary philosophy, even if its proponents disown metaphysical commitments, persists in its faith in the omnicompetence of formal logic, deductive and inductive, and concomitantly in the infallibility of direct observation. This persistence carries with it, despite disclaimers, evasions, and qualifications, tacit acceptance of the metaphysic of empiricism. That formal logic has its uses and is not to be despised I have no wish to deny; but there are spheres of investigation and discourse in which another kind of logic is requisite and operative. My object in the sequel will be to show that this is so, as well as to show that formal logic has its legitimate use in its appropriate place.

II

The Wide Interrelatedness of Things

As I have shown elsewhere,[11] empiricism is the metaphysic approprite to and required by the science of the seventeenth and eighteenth centuries. But since the middle of the nineteenth, the presuppositions of science have changed dramatically. Consequently there is sharp conflict between empiricism and the findings of contemporary physics, biology, and psychology, and a demonstrable discrepancy between the alleged inductive method and that actually practised by scientists. For, although the seventeenth- and eighteenth-century scientific world-view gave some pretext for the belief in atomic facts, close attention even to *its* implications would show that it belied that doctrine. Nor was the form of reasoning employed by scientists even in these earlier centuries by any means that alleged by empiricist philosophers. This I have shown in detail in Chapters 5 and 6 of *Hypothesis and Perception*.

For Newtonian science the world consisted of bodies—in the last resort, mass-points—moving about in absolute space under the impulse of forces dependent upon their masses and mutual distance. From these data, the movement and position at any given time of any or all bodies at any prior or subsequent time could be calculated. Mass-points were regarded as independent, for their position and motion, of absolute space, which was indifferent to them and was related to them as a containing receptacle. Mass was held to be independent of velocity and mutual positioning was taken to be (at least initially) purely for-tuitous. Thus, maintaining that such a world consisted of facts each of which might be the case or not or be the case and all the rest remain the same seemed plausible. Yet, clearly, it could not be so, for the mo-tion of every particle must be influenced by the position and mass of every other, hence even in Newtonian mechanics every fact is depen-dent upon every other and whatever is the case in one part of the universe at any one time would affect whatever was the case elsewhere (however slightly) at any other. For this reason, Laplace could claim that an infinite intelligence knowing the mass, position, and velocity of every particle in the universe at any given instant could calculate the position and velocity of every particle at any other instant.

When we turn to contemporary physics and cosmology, we are left in no doubt of the intrinsic and inextricable interdependence of facts, on which the most eminent scientists of our era have insisted repeated-ly and with emphasis. Max Planck, commenting on the quantum theory, declared that "the nature of any system cannot be discovered by dividing it into its component parts and studying each part by itself, since such a method often implies the loss of important properties of the system."[12] And again: ". . . it is impossible to obtain an adequate version of the laws for which we are looking unless the physical system is regarded *as a whole*."[13] Sir Arthur Eddington demonstrated in-separable connections between the fundamental constants of physics, and between the fundamental properties and quantitative relations of space-time, on the one hand, and those of elementary particles, on the other. He showed that the structure of the universe *in toto* and the radius of space curvature determined all the fundamental physical quantities and interrelations among its constituents. His demonstra-tions, he said, "make vivid the wide interrelatedness of things."[14] Eins-tein established the interdependence of space and time, matter and energy, velocity and distance, in fact virtually all elementary physical measurement. The unified field theory, which integrates all physical facts into a single interrelated system, was first advanced by Weyl and Schroedinger and was a persistent goal of Einstein's thinking, is also ad-vocated by Heisenberg. The attainment of a "unified understanding of the world" and the discovery of "a fundamental law of matter" are, he says, the final aims of physical investigation.[15] The theory suffered a temporary eclipse, but has since been revived by elementary particle physicists, who seek, and think they have found (in the so-called quark), a fundamental particle (with which, like all other particles, a field is associated), one from which all others are built up. Such a fundamental particle should, then, correspond to an energy field which is universal and ubiquitous, in which other particles and their combinations are enfoldments, or wave-superpositions.

Even though the view that the quark is the fundamental subatomic particle is not final (and so far physicists have found it necessary to postulate six different kinds of quark, each in three different forms or "colours"), the tendency of current physical theorizing is still steadily in the direction of unification. The recent quantum-field theory, combining relativity and quantum ideas, and the S-matrix theory, uniting space-time, energy, and matter afresh, reinforce the holistic trend. The striking speculations of Professor David Bohm, emphasize still further this contemporary insistence on holism. He envisages an "implicate order" enfolded into what he calls the "holomovement," using the hologram as an analogy, in such a way that a universal principle of order is immanent throughout the physical world, and manifests itself in diverse ways in particular phenomena, the whole being implicated in every part and in every event.[16]

Professor Paul Davies writes:

> there is a feeling among the scientific community that the subjects of cosmology on the one hand and the fundamental forces within matter on the other are coming together to provide a unified description of the cosmos. It is a description in which the ultra-microscopic structure of matter is intimately connected to the global structure of the universe, each influencing the development of the other in a delicate and complex fashion.[17]

It is not just interdependence of objects and events which is revealed by these theories so much as unity and wholeness of the entire universe. D. W. Sciama has displayed this integrity and unification in a detailed study, in which the inseparability of distinct facts, whether they be the swing of a pendulum on earth or the position and movement of the fixed stars, is incontestably made evident.[18]

For contemporary physics, the atomicity of facts and propositions is sheer nonsense and the systematic wholeness of both the macrocosm and the microcosms it contains (atoms, molecules, crystals, and the rest) is unquestionable. Such unity of differences is still more undeniable for organic wholes of the biological sphere, and even more emphatically for psychology. In biology, not only are organisms unmistakably integrated wholes the structure and functioning of whose parts are inextricably interwoven, but the relations between organism and environment, which include those between (relatively) separable organisms, are themselves organic, so that they form biocoenoses or ecosystems, within which the life of every member is intimately connected with and deeply dependent upon that of every other, and all are adapted to and integrated with the physicochemical conditions of the common environment. Lewis Thomas, in his fascinating book, *The Lives of a Cell*,[19] describes the whole earth as a single organism, and that is the current conception of it, common to modern biologists. Taken together with what physicists tell us of the interdependence of physico-chemical facts, this conception links up with their insistence on the unity of the universe and establishes the unity of the biosphere as one with it.

And there is yet another way in which the oneness of the world makes itself evident. All the various levels of living species are mutually continuous, and living forms emerge continuously from non-living. There is an unbroken series of interdependent natural forms from matter and energy to intelligent beings. Space-time curvature is equivalent to energy field, energy to mass, material forms interact chemically and form compound molecules and crystals, macromolecules and what Shroedinger called aperiodic crystals constitute living matter which is a perpetual interchange of chemical cycles. Finally, metabolism and the physiological functioning of organic beings integrate and find expression as the sentience and preception of conscious animals, culminating in intelligence and in self-knowing minds. The whole gamut is one unbroken continuous series in which no phase is separable from any other without modification or dissipation, yet all are distinguishable and relate to one another in precise ways.

All this has been set out in detail in my earlier book, *The Foundations of Metaphysics in Science*. Its relevance here is that such unity as is displayed by the world, both as a whole and in its subordinate parts, implies internality of relationships between the elements of the whole, and we have seen that the presupposition of formal logic is of a world of externally related particulars. Such logic cannot, therefore, be appropriate to contemporary empirical science, for where internal relations obtain its definitions and rules no longer hold.[20] The presuppositions of science in the present era imply and require logic of an entirely different kind.

III

The Methodology of Science

A similar conclusion emerges from an examination of scientific method. Recent attacks on the hitherto accepted empiricist theory have led to much hedging and qualification by its proponents, but no clear alternative has been offered by any of the major critics. Professor Popper was the earliest to reject induction, but the theory of hypothetico-deductive method which he and his followers substituted for it, is unsatisfactory so far as it still gives allegiance to formal logic. The theory maintains that from hypotheses (which are conjectures by inspired scientists) consequences are deduced and are then tested by experiment and observation. But, if the deduction is purely formal, according to the current doctrine this should be impossible. Deduction, we have noted, as understood by contemporary formal logicians, is and can only be analytic and tautological. The hypotheses of natural science, however, are empirical, and experimentally testable results must be factual. If different facts cannot be deduced from one another, observable phenomena cannot be deduced from empirical hypotheses. At best, only synonymous formulae could be so derived. No legitimate escape from this difficulty is to be found by alleging that empirical statements can be added as axioms to a deductive system, or may be introduced by substituting empirical terms for variables, because these devices in no way alter the analytic character of formal deduction, which, however empirical its premises, cannot produce conclusions with new empirical content. Any "deduction" that could do that would have to be of a new kind, capable of producing synthetic statements *a priori*. If, as is likely, scientists do proceed from hypotheses to testable predictions, the deduction must be of a different sort from that countenanced by formal logicians. A different type of logic altogether must be employed. So Popper, who comes a long way in the right direction towards an acceptable theory of scientific method, is really committed to an entirely different logic from that which he uses and advocates. It cannot be (as a result of his own repudiation) inductive, nor can it be deductive in the currently accepted sense.

Popper was also among the first to recognize (albeit more or less in passing) that direct observation is not a matter of passive acceptance of data.[21] He clearly stated that every scientific statement goes beyond "immediate experience" and that all observation is interpretative.[22] N. R. Hanson followed[23] by arguing that observation is always theory-laden, and Thomas Kuhn's doctrine of "paradigms" involved the same consequence.[24] This is a direct attack on the fundamental principle of empiricism that immediate perception of fact is not only possible but basic and original to all empirical knowledge. Its demolition undermines the whole empiricist epistemology and leaves the theory of induction unsupported by any foundation, for induction depends at base on belief in the possibility of direct observation of factual conjunctions. If observation is theory-laden the test of acceptability for hypotheses must be altogether different from that commonly presumed, and even the hypothetico-deductive method must rely on some other touchstone of falsification, or corroboration, than immediate observation.[25]

What we find when we investigate the actual form of reasoning and argument used by practising scientists who have made significant discoveries is that they certainly do not argue "inductively," if by that is meant from the occurrence of *AB* constantly, or frequently, to the probable occurrence of *AB* universally. Nor do they deduce by formal process observable consequences from conjectured hypotheses. Another procedure is discernible in every case analysed, whether that of Kepler searching for the orbit of Mars, Galileo working out the mechanics of falling bodies, Newton investigating the nature of light, or Harvey discovering the circulation of the blood; the same is true of Lavoisier's research into the nature of combustion, of Darwin as he marshalls his evidence for the theory of evolution, and of C. D. Anderson revealing the existence of positive electrons.[26]

This other procedure is at one and the same time both deductive and inductive in character, but in neither case in the commonly accepted meaning of those terms. A new word would be necessary to name it more appropriately. I have suggested "construction" in place of both the traditional names, and Newton himself spoke of "deduction from phenomena,"[27] a procedure altogether excluded by contemporary logical theory. The obvious implication of the phrase is that from phenomena—observed facts—other facts, or better, empirical laws, can be deduced. The modern empiricist would say that they might be inferred inductively, but can never be deduced. Yet, in his own work and reasoning, Newton appears to do precisely what contemporary theory pronounces to be impossible.[28]

All these scientists, we find, are engaged in organizing a body of fact by means of an hypothesis, derived or modified from one previously accepted. The observed phenomena are always interpretations in terms of previously acquired knowledge itself already theoretically systematized. Hence the observations are always theory-laden. But the prior hypothesis, in each case, has proved unsatisfactory because it has led to conflicts and contradictions within the system. The aim of the research is to remove these contradictions, and its process is the collection of evidence as varied as possible, which nevertheless fits together in mutually supporting testimony to form a system. The principle of order in this system emerges as the new theory.

In Galileo's case, the conflicts were those of the Aristotelian doctrine of motion exacerbated by the introduction of a heliocentric cosmology that removed the earth from the centre of the universe. Galileo tended to argue deductively from *Gedankenexperimente*, scorning as deceptive the evidence of the senses (to which his opponents appealed).[29] Kepler, using the Copernican and Aristotelian hypothesis of circular planetary orbits, modified it by successive steps, until he could organize without conflict the empirical evidence collected by Tycho Brahe, to produce an elliptical orbit for Mars. None of the evidence had recognizable significance unless and until it was interpreted in terms of one or other of the current hypotheses.[30]

William Harvey, spurred on by the contradictions he found in the Galenic teachings, experimented on animals and with tourniquets on human limbs, gathering a body of diverse pieces of evidence, which, together with that brought to light by his predecessors, meshed into a system such that, in Harvey's words, "it cannot be otherwise" than that the blood, driven into the arteries by the pumping action of the heart in systole, circulates continually, seeping back through the capillaries and the veins.[31] In like manner, the contradictions arising from the theory of Phlogiston moved Laviosier to seek a new system into which he could fit the results of experiments by the English pneumatic chemists, and by his French contemporary Guyton de Morveau, and of his own experiments on combustion and calcination with sulphur, phosphorus, mercury, and lead. The organizing principle of the system was the hypothesis that a gas existed in the air which eminently supported combusion and respiration and which combined with the burning or calcined substance.[32]

Darwin did likewise, collecting his material from a whole range of sciences and from investigations covering the entire surface of the globe. But what is most important about the evidence that he mustered is not its mere extent so much as the use he makes of it, fitting it together to form a system of interdependent facts such that, despite lack of direct observation in many respects, the conclusion to the theory of natural selection is overwhelmingly cogent.[33]

In every instance, the scientist constructs a whole, a system of evidence, of facts so interlocked that they mutually support one another and make the conclusion inescapable—facts which are the opposite of atomic. Such interdependence of evidential material is what should properly be meant by corroboration, not the mere repetition of like instances and similar conjunctions. Truly corroborative evidence should be as varied and different as possible, and the more diverse the sources from which it is drawn, the more compelling is the inference to the conclusion it supports. This is the real strength of the arguments (especially Darwin's) of the scientists mentioned. Their method of reasoning is never merely that of inductive generalization, and when it takes deductive form it is always concerned with empirical facts from which new factual conclusions are derived. The presuppositions and rules of formal logic as currently formulated seem here to be quite irrelevant and some other form of logic must be operative to provide the principles which the arguments and methods exemplify.

IV

Perception

A third source of testimony to the need for a different kind of logic, other than the merely formal, is the nature of perception. The possibility and occurrence of direct perceptual apprehension of given objective fact is, as we have seen, one of the essential presuppositions of formal logic. But the implications of this idea are incoherent and it is hardly surprising that every epistemological theory associated with it breaks down when pressed, and that physiological and psychological evidence runs counter to it. If self-existent facts are presumed independent of cognition, and if perceptual apprehension of them is to be immediate and infallible, some process of transmission of factual information from the external world into the seat of cognition in the organism must operate. The physiological evidence at our disposal contradicts any belief that what is registered in the brain through the sense organs and nerves has the least resemblance in any respect either to the correlative phenomenal experience or to what its object is taken to be. Reaction in the visual area, the occipital lobe of the brain, for instance, to stimulation of the retina by the image of a solid body, is confined to a complex pattern of electrical discharges having quite different spatiotemporal relations from the parts of the perceived object and none of the qualities that are experienced.[34] Psychologists are generally agreed that sensory stimuli are always perceptually ambiguous, and that they require elaborate organization and interpretation in reference to a context both spatial and temporal and to a body of already acquired objective knowledge in order to become perceptual objects.[35] There is thus no scientific evidence of any process of copying by the percipient organism of objects in its environment nor any transmission of precise replicae of external things.

The very notion of a transmission process whereby factual information is conveyed to the brain or to the mind is nonsensical as an explanation of perception. For perception is a form of knowledge, and is knowledge of objects as external to the perceiver in a spatiotemporal objective world. Therefore, it involves knowledge of the relation of the object to the perceiver as well as of the character of the object itself. But the most that a transmission process could achieve would be the production of some sort of image confined to the end result of the process in the percipient's brain. That could include neither its relation to the object nor the causal chain by which it was introduced. Even if we did perceive in this way, we could never know or discover that we did, or how the factual information was conveyed to us, and could never frame the hypothesis that it was so conveyed. In fact, we could never form any conception of an external world or of our own relation to it. For, if by some such process, a replica of external objects could somehow be constructed in the brain, it would not amount to perception. It would be a mere image which would still have to be perceived within the brain as a replica of something without. And if there were an agency (like the soul which Descartes presumed) capable of perceiving it so, it would of necessity require independent access to the external object if it were to cognize its relation to the internal model or picture and the process by which it had been introduced. Thus the model or picture would still fail to amount to perception, and, for the actual percipient (the soul), would be supererogatory.

The doctrine that the perceiver constructs his knowledge out of simple sense-data conveyed into the mind by sensation from external things is vulnerable to the same objections. If the existence of external things is not postulated and the assumption is that we begin from sensations as the subjective building blocks out of which we construct our objects, the criterion of veridical perception—the exact correspondence of the sense-data to real architypes—has to be forfeited. Moreover, the sense-data are, in such a doctrine, taken to be immediately perceived, and nothing of the sort is ever isolable in experience, nothing free of interpretation, whether in terms of context or prior knowledge, nothing which can rank as pure data. Nor is there any basis for assuming their occurrence in physiological evidence (which is the original pretext for the assumption), nor in psychological discovery. As may well be expected, therefore, the sensedatum theory has come under attack from all sides. Many of these attacks (*e.g.*, that of John Austin in *Sense and Sensibilia*) are ill-argued, psychologically naive, and easily repulsed;[36] but that cannot save the theory. The sounder criticisms, when they are based on any internally consistent alternative doctrine, all imply, even when they do not explicitly propound, a view of preception as the cognitive interpretation of sensuous material, a judgemental act involving, as Kant maintained, conception and thought as well as intuition, the latter without the former being blind.[37]

But if direct perceptual apprehension of independently existing fact is neither actual nor even possible, the epistemological presupposition indispensable to formal logic is removed and its metaphysical underpinning is destroyed. For, if all perception essentially involves interpretation in the light of context, perceived facts cannot be mutually independent. There must be logical connections between them and not all relations can be external. A logic of internal relations is required, such as formal logic neither provides nor countenances, a logic demanded likewise by both the contemporary scientific account of the world, and by the methods of reasoning and discovery employed by practising scientists.

This conclusion must throw serious doubt upon the claim made by Anthony Quinton[38] for Quine's book *Word and Object*, which was said to have demonstrated that formal logic in the tradition of Frege and Russell, displays the essential structure of thought and language. It is an odd claim, for the book is bracketed with Wittgenstein's *Tractatus* and Carnap's *Aufbau*, both of which had already been discredited even by analysts before Quinton wrote. In fact, Quine's views, before his

book was published, had been rendered obsolete by the works of
Merleau-Ponty, Popper, and Hanson, followed immediately by that of
Kuhn, to say nothing of Noam Chomsky.[39] Quine's account of
language is based upon the behaviorism of B. F. Skinner and assumes
that speech is a stimulus-response reaction complicated by conditioning, a view that much weighty psychological evidence belies and the
best established psychological and physiological theories reject.[40] The
doctrine of "stimulus meaning" which Quine exploits is rendered
altogether untenable by the recognition that perception is impregnated
with conceptual content, as has now become incontestable. So far from
demonstrating that formal logic displays the structure of thought and
language, Quine assumes this from the start and proceeds *ab initio* from
the presuppositions that we have unveiled in Chapter 1. Assuming the
structure of formal logic to be fundamental, he adapts his theory of
language to its requirements. In short, what we have here is just one
more prominent example of the inadequacy and unsuitability of formal
logic to the contemporary situation.

Notes

1. Cf. *Treatise of Human Nature*, bk. I, pt. III, sec. vi.

2. Cf. *Human Knowledge, Its Scope and Limits* (London, 1948), pp. 374–379.

3. Cf. *The Ground of Induction* (Harvard, Cambridge, Ma, 1947).

4. Cf. *Hypothesis and Perception* (London, 1970), pp. 36–37.

5. Cf. H. Reichenbach, *Experience and Prediction* (Chicago, 1938); "On the Justification of Induction," *Journal of Philosophy*, 37, 1940; and my critique in *Hypothesis and Perception*, pp. 37–42.

6. Cf. *The Logical Problem of Induction* (Blackwell, Oxford, 1957), ch. VIII.

7. *Op. cit.*, p. 172.

8. Cf. *Hypothesis and Perception*, chs. V–VI; K. Popper, *the Logic of Scientific Discovery*, ch. I.

9. Cambridge, 1953.

10. Cf. Popper, *op cit.*, pp. 94f, and 107, n 2. Both Popper's theory and that which he criticizes have come under attack from other quarters. It will

not serve my immediate purpose to discuss here the issues involved. See, however, my *Hypothesis and Perception*, pp. 72–79, "Epicyclic Popperism," *British Journal for Philosophy of Science*, vol. 23, 1972; also Imré Lakatos, in *Criticism and the Growth of Knowledge*, eds. I. Lakatos and A. Musgrave (Cambridge, 1970).

11. *Nature, Mind and Modern Science* (London, 1954), chs. VI, X, and *passim; The Foundations of Metaphysics in Science* (London, 1965), chs. II, III, and *passim.*

12. *The Philosophy of Physics* (London, 1936), p. 33.

13. *The Universe in the Light of Modern Physics* (London, 1937), pp. 25–26.

14. *The Expanding Universe* (Cambridge, 1933), pp. 104–105, 120.

15. Cf. p. 176 below, and *Philosophical Problems of Nuclear Science* (London, 1952), ch. 7, p. 95; *Physics and Philosophy* (New York, 1962), p. 72.

16. See David Bohm, *Wholeness and the Implicate Order* (London, 1980, 1983). Also Fritjof Capra, *The Tao of Physics* (London, 1975, 1983).

17. *God and the New Physics* (London, 1983; Harmondsworth, 1984–1986), p. 160.

18. *The Unity of the Universe* (New York, 1961).

19. New York, 1974, Cf. also Marston Bates, *The Forest and the Sea* (New York, 1960).

20. Cf. p. 32f. above.

21. Of course, this had been recognized by many long before Popper (by Kant, Hegel, and all the British Idealists from T. H. Green to Bernard Bosanquet, H. H. Joachim, and Brand Blanshard), but Popper was among the first modern critics of the empiricist theory of scientific method to acknowledge it.

22. Cf. *The Logic of Scientific Discovery*, pp. 94f., and 107, n 2.

23. Cf. *Patterns of Discovery*, ch. I and *passim.*

24. Cf. *The Structure of Scientific Revolutions* (Chicago, 1962), esp. ch. V and p. 112.

25. It is here especially that Popper has wavered; for he insists on "basic statements" as ultimate falsifiers of hypotheses, giving at least the impression that these are "immediate" observations, while he denies that any observation can be immediate and asserts that what scientists accept as basic is a matter of convention. (Cf. *op cit.*, pp. 104–105, 111.) For a fuller discussion, see *Hypothesis and Perception*, ch. IV.

26. Cf. *Hypothesis and Perception*, chs. V–VI, and "Empiricism in Science

and Philosophy," *Impressions of Empiricism*, ed. Godfrey Vesey, (London, 1976).

27. *Principia*, General Scholium.

28. Cf. *Hypothesis and Perception*, ch. VI, p. iii., where I have set this out in full.

29. Cf. *Dialogue Concerning the Two Chief World Systems*, trans. Stillman Drake (Berkeley, Ca, 1962), pp. 12–14, 28–29, 141–149, 172, 180f, etc. *Hypothesis and Perception*, pp. 93–102.

30. Cf. *Hypothesis and Perception*, pp. 124–139.

31. Cf. *De Motu Cordis*, ch. VII, and *Hypothesis and Perception*, pp. 139–154.

32. Cf. *Hypothesis and Perception*, pp. 167–178.

33. Cf. *op. cit.*, pp. 178–189.

34. Cf. Sir W. Russell Brain, *Mind, Perception and Science* (Blackwell, Oxford; Springfield, Il, 1951).

35. Cf. J. J. Gibson, *Perception and the Visual World* (Boston, 1950); M. D. Vernon, *The Psychology of Perception* (Harmondsworth, 1969), pp. 66, 68; H. W. Ittleson, "Size as a Cue to Distance: Static Localization," *American Journal of Psychology*, vol. 64, 1951, pp. 52–67; Sir Frederick Bartlett, *Remembering* (Cambridge, 1961), ch. II.

36. This is not the place to present detailed criticism of Austin, but in this book his case is ill-argued because it misrepresents the views of the philosophers it attacks (G. E. Moore, C. D. Broad, H. H. Price, and A. J. Ayer). This is well-demonstrated in two admirable papers, one by H. H. Price, "Appearing and Appearances," *American Philosophical Quarterly*, vol. I, 1964; the other by A. J. Ayer, "Has Austin Refuted the Sense-Datum Theory," *Metaphysics and Common Sense* (San Francisco, 1970), ch. 9. These papers give support to the judgement that Austin's attack is easily repulsed. It is psychologically naïve because it ignores, and by implication contradicts, a great body of experimental work (to which reference has been made above) by eminent psychologists. One small example of Austin's naïveté is his denial on p. 12 of *Sense and Sensibilia* that mirror images involve illusion and that we are commonly deceived by seeing our own faces in a mirror. Was he unaware of the well-established fact that what appears to the viewer in the mirror to be of normal size (the reflected face the same size as the actual face) is in fact only half the size of the original? In this way, mirror images always involve illusion and we are always in some measure deceived when we see our faces in the mirror.

37. For further discussion, see *Hypothesis and Perception*, ch. VIII, and *Perceptual Assurance and the Reality of the World* (Clark University Press, New York, 1974).

38. Cf. p. 17 above.

39. Cf. M. Merleau-Ponty, *The Structure of Behaviour*, trans. A. L. Fisher (Boston, 1963); *The Phenomenology of Perception*, trans. Colin Smith (London, 1962); K. Popper, *op. cit.*; N. R. Hanson, *op cit.*; T. Kuhn, *op. cit.*

40. Cf. K. S. Lashley, *Brain Mechanisms and Intelligence* (Chicago, 1929), and *J. Gen. Psychol.*, 26 (1942) pp. 241–68; K. Lewin, *Psychologische Forschung.*, 7, pp. 294–329; R. Leeper, *J. Genet. Psychol.*, 46, pp. 3–40; W. H. Thorpe, *Lerning and Instinct in Annuals* (London, 1963), p. 81; N. Tinbergen, *A Study of Instinct* (Oxford , 1952), p. 2; Le Gros Clark, "The Anatomical Perspective," *Perspectives in Neurophsychiatry*, ed. D. Richter (London, 1950) p. 23; E. L. Hutton, *ibid.*, p. 161.

Part II

Transcendental Logic

Chapter 3

Kant and Fichte

I

Synthesis and Transcendental Subjectivity

The consistent development of empiricism by Hume led him to a sceptical conclusion. His principles forced him to deny the possibility of universal and necessary connections between facts, without which there can be no scientific laws. Kant, therefore, called in question the primary presuppositions that knowledge of facts can be directly acquired only through sense-perception and that "concepts must conform to objects." These are presuppositions that lie at the root of formal logic, but Kant failed to notice this connection and regarded formal logic as a fully developed and perfected science to which nothing further could be added. The recognition, however, that the main empirical principle was in need of examination and revision—Kant proposed to replace it by its opposite, that "objects must conform to concepts"—is in effect a demand for a critique and a remodelling of the presuppositions of formal logic.

Kant proceeds to fulfil this demand by raising the question, How is science possible?, subdivided more particularly into: How is mathematics possible?, How is pure physics possible?, and How is metaphysics possible?, all of which he sums up in the question, How are synthetic judgments *a priori* possible? The possibility of *a priori* synthetic judgments would be established by the demonstration of the existence of wholes with internal relations between their parts, for once the principle of organization is known, universal and necessary judgments about the structure and its parts would be possible *a priori*. Principles of organization Kant identifies as concepts or categories, *a*

priori determination by which, he proceeds to demonstrate, is the indispensable condition of any experience of objects whatsoever.

The new science in which this conclusion is deduced Kant called
transcendental logic, the investigation into the ultimate conditions of
the possibility of the experience of objects, and so of there being any
experience at all in the empiricist sense of that word.

Transcendental logic is a form of speculation the development of
which is usually omitted from contemporary histories of logic, for only
formal logic is recognized by their authors as rightly belonging to the
subject. However, as introduced by Kant, transcendental logic is clearly the attempt in the first instance to provide a logic of internal relations
consequent upon the organization of experience by synthetic principles, shown to be the ultimate and indispensable conditions of the
cognition of objects, and so of the possibility of scientific knowledge.

Whereas the presuppositions of formal logic are such as enable the
logician to abstract entirely from the substantive content of knowledge,
it is impossible for the transcendental logician to do so; for the conditions under which objects can be experienced may, on the one hand,
depend upon the general nature of the objects, and, on the other, may
well affect that general nature. Contemporary logicians would dismiss
any such investigation into the conditions of cognition as
epistemological and outside the sphere of logic, involving
psychological considerations foreign to their discipline. But, unless
logic is to be altogether irrelevant to science and truth, it can hardly
separate itself rigidly from epistemology, to which some psychological
aspects of experience may well be material. Of course, if truth is held
to be wholly dependent upon correspondence between the result of a
mental operation and sensuously intuited existent fact, formal logic
would have at most a marginal relation to it, if any at all, and conditions
governing its attainment would be very largely psychological. Formal
deduction, so far as it is incapable of leading to any factual information,
would fall outside the scope of epistemology, and induction, in spite of
Hume's contention that it depends upon a psychological propensity,
would be rendered ineffectual by the logical invalidity of its process.
But this separation of logic and epistemology derives from the presupposition that the knowledge of facts comes only through direct perceptual observation, whereas the interdependence of observation and conceptual interpretation, now generally admitted, links logic inseparably
with epistemology; for if all knowledge involves the use of concepts,
the theory of the concept and its particularization, which is fundamental

to logic, will also be integral to the theory of knowledge. Indeed, what led Kant to embark upon transcendental logic was his insight that perception (*Anschauung*) without concepts is blind, and his transcendental deduction of the categories in the first *Critique* established its foundations once and for all.

In the transcendental deduction, Kant argues first that the cognition of any object necessarily involves a synthesis of elements which must be held together as a whole in order to be apprehended as an object. If each successive presentation were separate and isolated, and if it dropped out of consciousness completely as it passed, not even a succession of changes could be perceived. Kant illustrates this truth from the drawing of a line in space and the computing of successively presented units into a sum. He is unquestionably right, for isolated sensations are not apprehensible as objects (if apprehensible at all). Only structures, the simplest of which is a figure-and-ground *Gestalt*, are ever cognized. Even though a number of differentiable elements are presented simultaneously, they must be, as Kant puts it, run through and held together as one object,[1] and any series of such groupings could be apprehended as such only if combined into one and grasped as a single series. Every object must be held together as a whole of contrasted elements, as a unity of differences combined as one configuration. Accordingly, the cognition of any object whatsoever requires a synthesis of a maniford—a grasping of a plurality in unity.

Following this insight, transcendental logic becomes a logic of wholeness and synthetic unity, developing a coherence theory of truth and objectivity. This is evident from its beginnings in Kant's work[2] and is still more explicit in its later development.

A condition prior even to the foregoing, Kant recognizes next, is that the synthesis be effected by an identical and unitary subject of consciousness. For if each element were cognized by a different subject, or even by one and the same in separate and incommunicable moments, the manifold could never be synthesized, the elements could never be apprehended together as forming a single whole, and no configuration would emerge. Further, as a succession of presentations, in order to be seen as a succession, must be held together and unified, the subject aware of it as such must be distinct from it, cannot be itself an item of the succession involved in the flux of presentations.

It should, therefore, be obvious that this identity of the subject is no mere psychological condition of the experience of objects, for it is prior to all psychological phenomena in the field of consciousness. It is prior likewise to the apprehension of all psychological events as empirical objects, the subject matter of an empirical science, whether they are regarded as states of consciousness or as patterns of behaviour. The knowledge of all psychological processes and the causal laws governing their occurrence presupposes this transcendental condition, which is, therefore, with everything that logically follows from it, independent of psychological conditioning.[3] Whatever might be the psychological conditions of consciousness, unless its diverse presentations were synthesized by a unitary subject (and they could not otherwise be synthesized at all), no cognizable object could be constituted.

The next step is to observe that experience, to be coherent, must be one experience. It must all be mine, the experience of my world; that is, a comprehensive unity of differences, which is possible only for me as a unitary subject of experience. No knowledge is possible and no theory intelligible unless it relates systematically to one another the elements it takes to be objective, and no systematic relating can take place unless the related terms are held together in one objectified whole for a single identical subject. This indispensable and inescapable self-identity of the subject of consciousness is the fundamental prior condition of all experience of objects and of all theorizing. Kant's statement is incontestable that knowledge is a whole of related and connected presentations,[4] which it could be only as apprehended by a single subject of awareness.

The ground and origin of synthesis in the self-identical subject Kant called the original transcendental unity of apperception. But this unity could be imposed upon the variety of its objects only through its self-differentiation into categories, or principles of organization which thus become the primary principles of objective knowledge. Clearly, if knowledge is to be a whole of related and connected elements, it must be ordered by structural principles determining the connections, and these will necessarily be particularizations of the one original presiding unity of transcendental apperception. To discover these principles, Kant adapted the classification of the judgement in traditional formal logic, transforming it somewhat dubiously into his table of categories; but his successors became aware of the tenuousness of the connection and saw that the categories must be more intimately related to their transcendental source, the cognizing ego. That, moreover, was not merely a simple blank and analytic unity, as Kant in some of his pronouncements alleged. As he points out, the representations (*Vorstellungen*) which it synthesises are all in principle prefaceable by the rubric, "I think . . ." Thus it is the *cogito* of Descartes, necessrily implicating existence, the very meaning of which, both for itself and for its objects, is posited in its own synthetic activity. It is essentially the self-conscious and self-reflective ego, at once subject and object in its own self-awareness, and therefore *ab initio* a differentiated unity. Moreover, because its being and its self-consciousness are one and the same and because its activity is nothing other than the constitutive synthesis of objects (the content of its experience), apart from that content there would be neither activity nor ego. The experienced world and the identical subject whose world it is are thus inseparably correlated, and the former lies implicit in the self-differentiating (self-conscious) activity of the latter.

The self-identity of the subject is, then, the fundamental principle and starting point of transcendental logic, and once it had been established by Kant, his successors exerted themselves to deduce from it more rigourously than he had done, not only categories, or organizing principles, necessary to unite a given manifold of sense into an objective world, but the very manifold itself and the stream of its production in consciousness. They were constrained to do so by the inexorable consequences of Kant's own demonstrations in the Transcendental Analytic. For his argument makes it apparent that even the *a priori* forms of intuition, space and time, are incomprehensible apart from the principles of the understanding; and the postulated source and cause of the manifold of sensations, things in themselves, becomes an idea of reason, a noumenon, itself resulting from the conceptualization imposed by the categories upon the content of experience. Hence there can be no source from which that content could originate except the activity of the transcendental ego, the original synthetic operation of the identical self-conscious subject. All forms of knowledge, therefore, should be derivable from this primordial activity of the ego, and such derivation was the task set for themselves by Fichte and Schelling.

That they were, in this enterprise, immediately concerned with epistemology is obvious, and this is indicated clearly by the very title under which Fichte forthwith presented what he regarded as essential philsoophy, *Wissenschaftslehre*, theory of knowledge (or science), which turns out to include, in fact ultimately to depend upon, what is equally the foundation of ethics. Thus logic, ethics, and epistemology are inseparably welded together in a doctrine which is at the same time a metaphysic. It is a metaphysic because it is an investigation into the presuppositions of science, the conditions under which there can be any science at all and on which it can have objects. As natural science claims to be the objective knowledge of the actual world, research into its presuppositions will clearly have implications for the nature of its objects. And, in fact, as we have already to some extent seen, concern with metaphysical presuppositions was the initial pretext for introducing transcendental logic. Kant was perhaps the first modern philosopher openly to declare that no presuppositions in philosophy, or any other form of knowledge, are exempt from criticism.[5] But his final decision that metaphysics as hitherto presented could never be made scientific persuaded his successors to avoid the term. Following him, Fichte identified metaphysics with dogmatism (attributed primarily to Spinoza, whose system Fichte considered the only form of dogmatic philosophy legitimately alternative to critical idealism), and this practice persisted in the work of both Schelling and Hegel. The effect of transcendental logic, however, is to unify logic and metaphysics insofar as the latter seeks (as Collingwood held it essentially must) to uncover the ultimate presuppositions of science.[6]

The tendency in Kant and his successors to trace the fundamental principles of theoretical knowledge back to those of practical philosophy, the principles of value, is for us today of profound significance, because our major problems are concerned with values, which, through the influence of empiricist prejudices, have been extruded from scientific treatment except insofar as they can be treated descriptively as facts of social behaviour. Such empirical study, we have found, commonly leads to a relativism which denies the existence of objective standards, and finally comes to infect the objectivity of science itself, implying a radical scepticism attended by the most devastating and deleterious consequences.

If, however, in Kant and his successors, epistemology, metaphysics, and ethics are all rolled into one, does it follow that what they give us is in any sense logic? The answer to this question must depend on how logic is defined and on what definitive description of it we accept. Hitherto we have regarded logic primarily as the study of the concept and its instantiation, but we have also noted the description of it as "concerned with the principles of valid inference," and have incidentally referred to it as directed to "the structure of thought and its expression." We maintained however, that the principles of validity in inference must derive from the nature of the concept, the structure of which in relation to its extension must also determine the logical structure of thought and its faithful expression. If that is so and if the precondition of the experience of objects is that they be brought under concepts (as Kant maintained), then transcendental philosophy is certainly concerned with logic. Moreover, if the concepts are principles of organization or synthesis, they will determine the structure at once of thought and of its objects, and so necessarily of its proper modes of expression. That the theory of the concept must be central to transcendental philosophy is unquestionable, and in its subsequent efflorescence into dialectic, under the husbandry of Hegel, this centrality of the concept is put beyond dispute. That being so, we have every right to speak of transcendental logic, and an even better right to accept the dialectical logic of Hegel as appropriately named. But here logic, epistemology, and metaphysics cannot be divorced from one another, and presuppositions are under scrutiny all along the line of philosophical discussion.

II

Coherence

The endeavour of transcendental logic is to give an account of the experience of an objective world in terms of the necessary synthesis effected transcendentally by the subject of awareness; effected, that is, *a priori* in the act of cognition, as the condition of apprehending any object whatsoever. The major contributions of Kant to this development were to establish (i) the inseparability of perception from conception (of observation from theory); (ii) the indispensability of synthesis to all cognition, of unity in multiplicity—the integration of a manifold; (iii) the impossibility of this synthesis unless it be effected by a single apprehending subject to whom the synthetic unity is objectified; (iv) the consequent enjoyment by the subject of a unified whole of experience; and (v) the necessity, for such an experience, of organizing principles coordinating and structuring the manifold presented to the subject in the flux of experience. These Kant shows to be the conditions of science—the knowledge of an objective world. But Kant restricts our experience of such a world to one solely of phenomena, the relation of which to reality (to things in themselves) is (or in accordance with his theory should be) unknowable. All knowledge, therefore, however "objective" in relation to illusion and mere fantasy, still ranks for him as no more than appearance, subjective to our minds; and that of which it is the appearance remains beyond our ken. Nevertheless, for Kant, the mind's persistent endeavour to reach the reality, its incurable tendency to apply the categories beyond the range of experience, even to things in themselves, gives rise to transcendent ideas, which regulate both action and the pursuit of knowledge, and upon which (among other things) the very criterion of empirical truth is finally made to depend.[7]

That this criterion is coherence within the systematic totality of the experienced world stands to reason, as a consequence of the original synthesis which is the condition of any such experience. Not only does this make the ideal of all knowledge a complete unification of all the sciences into one system—in Kant's view the essential regulative principle of all research—but it is also the common criterion by which alone decision can be reached whether a perceived object is real or imaginary.[8] Inseparable from transcendental logic, therefore, is the conception of truth as coherence, the one criterion that can be made effective, the persistent drive of the intellect towards which is the prime incentive to the advance of knowledge.

A logic of coherence, however, is essentially a logic of wholes (or of *the* whole) and must accept and give a systematic account of internal relations; for what is coherent is a whole, and what is a whole is composed of parts adapted one to another so that their mutual relations determine what each in itself actually is—its intrinsic nature. In other words, the relations between the parts are internal to them. Transcendental logic, accordingly, is or ought to be, essentially a logic of internal relations. This is, moreover the consequence of the new theory of the concept which emerges. In Kant's doctrine the transcendental concept is a principle of organization, a principle of structure governing a synthetic whole. Such principles, Kant repeatedly tells us, make *a priori*, synthetic knowledge possible, and this claim will clearly be justified, for if the organizing principle of a system is grasped it will be possible to infer *a priori*, by its means, to the general character of the interrelations of the elements, and so from one element to another within the system. Such inference will legitimize *a priori* synthetic judgements.

III

The Emergence of Dialectic

Fichte, a devoted follower of Kant, committed to the critical method in philosophy, realized that the postulation of things in themselves (the existence of which Kant had said it had never occurred to him to doubt), as well as the supposition that they were somehow the cause of our sensory experience, were as much products of the spontaneous activity of the transcendental ego as were the categories and the ideas of reason. He saw that one could not legitimately appeal to any source beyond consciousness for the genesis of experience, and that to be consistent the transcendental philosopher must trace back all knowledge, at every level and in every aspect, to the self-consciousness of the original subject. The form of self-consciousness, and in particular the self-identity of the ego, became for him the indispensable conditions of any experience whatsoever and the foundation of all being and of every form of knowing.

The very concept of self, of I, involves self-objectification. To say "I" immediately signifies an awareness of self in which I am both subject and object; and it is this opposition to itself (*Gegenstandlichkeit*) that Fichte strives to develop into the whole system of knowledge, theoretical and practical. The primary characteristic of self-consciousness is self-opposition, and that is the form of all awareness—the oppositedness of subject to object. But opposition involves mutual limitation of each other by the opposites, and self-awareness thus requires the self-limitation of the ego by its own activity—a self-contradiction that has to be removed at the outset if any progress is to be made.

Outside of the ego and independently of it nothing can be posited; for any and every positing can be done only by the ego itself. It is, therefore, all-inclusive, unlimited, and infinite. How then can it, by its own activity, limit itself so as to become its own object? The answer to emerge is: by sensing, in which a sensory object is set as unconscious opposite against a conscious subject. Only in becoming aware of the opposition to itself of an object can the ego become aware of itself as subject. Its limitation by the object is thus the condition of its self-consciousness; but, because nothing can be imposed upon it from without, the sensory object must be its own product, and the effect of its own activity somehow turned back upon itself, by an inexplicable *Anstoss*—a self-opposing which we have already found to be self-contradictory. Fichte's solution to this apparent impasse is to demand and to discover a synthesis of opposites, on the principle that every antithesis implies synthesis (a sound Kantian principle) and conversely that every synthesis involves antithesis.

This is the next great step in transcendental logic, lying implicit in Kant's reasoning, and brought to light and developed further in Fichte's *Wissenschaftslehre*. It is the discovery of a new principle of logical deriva-

tion through contradiction and the reconciliation of the antithetical opposites. At the stage so far reached, the basis of synthesis can be no
other than the self-identity of the transcendental ego, and it is from this
original unity that Fichte derives its possibility, as does Schelling in his
wake.[9] Synthesis from now on becomes the key term in philosophical
logic, and Fichte insists on its necessary supplement, antithesis, implying that contradiction is not just the mark of absurdity and logical
failure, but is the result of a concrete opposition which is a stepping-
stone to logical advance. To remain stuck with opposition and immersed in contradiction is, of course, logical failure; and the presence of
such logomachy is therefore the spur to further progress towards its
resolution in new and more satisfactory concepts.

As we have observed, the primary principle and foundation of
transcendental logic, insisted upon by Fichte and reasserted by Schelling, is the necessary and inescapable identity and self-awareness of the
knowing subject. This is the ineradicable condition of any experience
whatsoever, of any sort of object and any form of presentation. And the
identity of anything with itself ($A = A$), whatever it may be and whether
or not it exists, is posited in the self-identical ego, apart from which
positing it is absolutely unknown and unknowable. Further, the unity
of the ego imposes a corresponding unity on the object of its experience, and the identification of A with A is correlative to the non-
identity with A of not-A. Thus, A and not-A in their antithesis form a
synthetic whole of mutually determining opposites. As $A = A$, so $I = I$;
but whereas A is identical with A whether or not A exists, $I = I$
necessarily involves existence, and it is only in and through this
necessarily existent self-consciousness that the identity of A with itself
and its non-identity with not-A can be posited. Thus the positing of the
identity and the opposing of the negation have the same source—the
self-identical ego. But just as A implies a correlative not-A so I involves
a correlative not-I. Yet this opposition is and can only be posited by
and within the identity of the ego itself. Thus the ego is opposed to
itself and is in contradiction with itself. But the contradiction cannot
annul its activity and (what is identical with it) its being, for its self-
existent activity is involved even in the contradiction. Consequently,
the contradiction must be resoluble. The ego is the source of, for it
posits, both identity and opposition and the resulting contradiction is
resolved only by seeing that I and not-I constitute a single whole or
unity which is divisible, or differentiated. In consequence, both the
subject and its object, each annulling the other in part, prove to be a

differentiable unity and together constitute a whole of correlative opposites.

So Fichte recognizes that all antithesis or opposition is made in terms of some hallmark of distinction determing the opposed factors within a wider identity, and that identity subsists only between distinguishable terms,[10] in short, that both identity and difference rest upon a common ground. Accordingly, opposites imply a higher uniting synthesis, and every synthesis short of the absolute whole (or 'thesis') involves an antithesis, both within it, which it implies, and beyond it, with which it must in turn be unified. The whole is system, one and absolutely final—but, in Fichte's view, attainable only through the endless (and in itself impossible) convergence of finite and infinite.[11]

The identity and integrity of the self-conscious subject ensures for transcendental logic a corresponding integrity of the object and of experience as a single system; and from this wholeness emerges the dialectical process by which the system develops. As with Kant, so with Fichte, and even more emphatically with Schelling,[12] the whole and its principle of unity, the transcendental subject, determine the nature and interrelation of its constituent elements, which are as much phases in its own self-development as components of its structural pattern, forms of its self-expression as well as opposing or antithetical complementaries. This feature of transcendental logic is its most important, because it establishes it as a logic of internal relations as opposed to formal logic, the logic of external relations. The elements of the whole are dependent for their intrinsic characters on one another, as mutually determining opposites (as indicated by Fichte's term *Wechselbestimmung*), as stages of development of an identical and continuous complex, and as specific forms of a universal concept. We shall find later that these features are fundamental to dialectic, which has its roots and origin in the transcendental philosophies of Kant and Fichte.

The process of self-development of the whole is the dialectical process, which, for Fichte, throughout, is the result of the drive of the self-conscious ego to realize to the full its thoroughgoing and all-inclusive self-identity and self-adequacy. The process is the activity of the ego developing the implications of its own self-objectification, indispensable to its own identical self-completeness. In the course of the development, all the categories of empirical knowledge are generated along with all the forms of human experience; sensation, imagination (representation), intuition, understanding, and reason, practical as well as theoretical. Judgement and inference are simply phases in this process, and the logical theory of them is just the detailed transcendental doctrine of the unfolding of conscious experience.

My purpose is not to give a detailed commentary on the doctrines of Fichte and Schelling. If it were, notice would have to be taken of numerous far-reaching insights, especially Fichte's recognition of the mutual determination of opposites in systematic relation, and Schelling's of the generation of successively more complex forms of experience by the persistent effort of the ego to objectify its own activity. Leaving aside the detailed elaboration of these insights, however, what must again be stressed is that transcendental logic stems as a whole from the identity and self-consciousness of the subject, on which the unity of the object and its coherence is made to depend. The object is a whole because of the necessary synthetic activity of the subject, an activity indispensable to cognition through and by means of a flux of representations. This emphasis on the activity of the subject, important as it is, as well as the reflection (frequently reiterated by transcendentalists) that all knowledge comes and can come only through consciousness, of which the identity and self-awareness of the subject is the unavoidable condition, commits transcendental logic to an idealism which brings with it insuperable problems, despite the disavowals by its authors of subjectivism and their common protestations against the accusations of their critics. To the difficulties it encounters we shall return in due time, but first let us take notice of a more recent author and a form of transcendentalism that is still current in our own day.

Notes

1. Cf. *Kritik der reinen Vernunft (Critique of Pure Reason)*, A99.

2. Cf. *ibid.*, A155, B194: "There is only one whole (*Inbegriff*) in which all our representations (*Vorstellungen*) are contained, namely the inner sense, and its *a priori* form, time. The synthesis of representations rests on the imagination, the synthetic unity of which, however, (required for judgement) rests upon the unity of apperception. In this, accordingly, the possibility of synthetic judgements is to be sought, and as all three [of the above faculties] contain the sources of synthetic *a priori* representations, they must also account for the possibility of pure synthetic judgements." See also A156–157, B195–196, A651, B679; and cf. my *Nature Mind and Modern Science*, ch. VIII.

3. It is something very much to this effect that Husserl labours persistently to demonstrate in his *Logical Investigations* (to which later we shall have occasion to refer), endeavouring to establish the need for a transcendental logic supplementary to a purely formal, or apophantic, logic.

4. Cf. *Critique of Pure Reason*, A97.

5. Cf. *op. cit.*, Preface, A vi n.

6. Cf. R. G. Collingwood, *An Essay on Metaphysics* (Oxford, 1940).

7. Cf. *Critique of Pure Reason*, A237, B296; A651, B679.

8. Cf. *op cit.*, B279; "*Ob dies oder jene vermeinte Erfahrung nicht blosse Einbildung sei, muss nach den besonderen Bestimmungen derselben und durch Zusammenhang mit den Kriterien aller wirklichen Erfahrung ausgemittelt werden.*" "Whether this or that supposed experience be not mere imagination must be ascertained according to its particular determinations and through its conformity with the criteria of all actual experience."

9. Cf. *System des transcendentalen Idealismus* (1800). English translation: *System of Transcendental Idealism*, by Peter Heath (University of Virginia Press, Charlottesville, VA, 1978).

10. Cf. *Grundlage der Gesamten Wissenschaftslehre*, Erste Teil, 3 D 4.

11. *Ibid.*, D 7.

12. Cf. *op. cit.*

Chapter 4

Husserl's Transcendental Logic

I

Psychologism vs Formalism

A century later than Fichte, Husserl has revived a great many of his ideas, though in some respects he is closer to Kant, and (making scant acknowledgment to either of those philosophers—in fact, ignoring almost entirely his debts to the former) he has become the outstanding advocate of transcendental logic in the twentieth century. He professes to abjure subjectivism and to have escaped all taint of solipsism—with what justification we shall have to consider anon. The dialectical consequences which emerge from the thought of Fichte and his successors have no place in Husserl's theories, for he makes no move in that direction and he rejects with deprecation the views and the method of Hegel.

Husserl's attitude to formal logic is not unlike that of Kant, to which he makes reference in his *Formal and Transcendental Logic*[1] as too sweeping, although he himself maintains that its central structure and content have persisted unchallenged since Aristotle. Formal logic, in Husserl's view, is the science of science, the doctrine of the principles of systematic and rigorous ordering of thought and knowledge, which are the criteria of scientific adequacy. He distinguishes "objective" logic from "subjective" (which proves to be phenomenological or transcendental) logic, and divides the former into "formal apophantics" and "formal ontology." Formal apophantics has three phases: judge-

89

ment logic, consequence logic, and truth logic, the third apparently coinciding or overlapping with formal ontology.

In his *Logical Investigations*, Husserl argues justly and at length against psychologism in logic. His protest is against confusion between the mental processes accompanying thinking and principles of validity and essentially logical concepts. The latter, he (rightly) contends, depend on the content of thought and are objective; they are quite independent of the subjective processes by which judgements are formed in the mind or inferences made. The confusion, Husserl asserts, is between the real, or factual, and the ideal, and is characteristic of the theories of several of his eminent contemporaries, like Sigwart and Erdmann, as well as of earlier thinkers like Mill and Spencer. There is, he maintains, a pure logic, free and independent of psychology and logically prior to it, as it is prior to all special sciences.

While Husserl's attack is explicitly against psychologism, much of his argument is directed against empiricism; in particular, the empirical approach to logic adopted by John Stuart Mill. But the implication of empiricist presuppositions in contemporary formal logic and in the work of his contemporary Frege, seems to have escaped Husserl altogether. For, as we shall presently see, he takes over intact the whole of formal logic with its contemporary developments, and (like Kant) simply proposes to supplement it with a new discipline which he calls transcendental logic. The need for this supplement is not that the presuppositions of formal logic limit it to the abstract and to subject matter abstractly conceived as aggregates of particulars, but, in Husserl's view, that formal logic is a special science which takes no account of the transcendental conditions of its own fundamental ideas and operations. These are yet other hidden presuppositions which require investigation, giving rise to what he calls transcendental logic, or eidetic science.

There may be grounds for cavilling in detail at some of the statements and arguments in the case made against psychologism in *Logical Investigations*, but Husserl's main thesis is undoubtedly sound, for logical connections are in no way determined by psychological processes and are not dependent upon or derivative from mere mental associations. Psychological laws are, in the main, causal, whereas logical laws are, as Husserl contends, eidetic. The former govern the relations between events, the latter the relations between concepts. Consequently, the first are empirical laws and are in the last resort only probable, while the second are *a priori* and hold apodictically. The difference between them, Husserl declares is unbridgeable (*unüber-brückbar*).

It does not, however, follow from all this that psychological considerations are always entirely irrelevant to logical investigations, and at a later stage Husserl himself appeals to phenomenological characteristics of experience which are in some sense psychological. Moreover, if mental processes do not determine logical relations, the converse is not always true, for psychological processes of reasoning are in large measure determined by logical relations. Be that as it may, Husserl's main concern is with the presuppositions of valid thinking and the logical conditions of its possibility, which, as will presently transpire, are the fundamental bases and the starting point of transcendental logic. To these, all positive sciences including psychology, are posterior and all scientific thinking subject.

And this is true equally of formal logic as the science of science,[2] which Husserl classifies as itself a special science. It proceeds from what he calls the naïve or natural attitude, in which we accept what comes to us in experience in terms of traditional prejudices and unquestioned beliefs, taking it more or less at its face value. This is true of the empirical scientist as well as of the layman, although the scientist is more reflective and critical in refining, ordering, and systematizing his knowledge and checking his result. The formal logician accepts in the same naive spirit what he finds in scientific procedure. He analyses its structure and the forms of its reasoning, classifies the types of judgements which it makes and determines the principles of connection which render its inferences sound.

Husserl sees the identity between principles and presuppositions of formal apophantics and those of formal mathematics. He enunciates, in his account of formal logic, a position having much in common with that of Frege. He acknowledges the consequence of radical formalization, the consequent extensional character of the resulting logical calculi, their affinity to mathematics and the correlations between forms and relations of judgements and those of sets.[3] The resulting science is what he calls formal ontology, and this Husserl holds to be a perfectly legitimate discipline, in fact one that has hitherto not been properly recognized. At its final and most general level it is a general theory of manifolds, which unites logic with mathematics and is the ultimate theory of calculi and deductive systems. This contention is in great measure consonant with what has been argued above, and by implication supports our view that the presupposition of formal logic is a world of bare particulars gatherable into sets belonging to or coming under abstract concepts.

Husserl never questions or criticizes these presuppositions in their metaphysical bearing. He does, however, complain that formal logic cannot exhaust the scope of philosophical logical inquiry because its attitude and approach to its subject matter is purely naïve and unphilosophical. It ignores the implicit phenomenological character of the thought acts and the logical processes involved in thinking and knowing. Accordingly, like Kant, he proposes to introduce a further study—transcendental logic—the character and method of which as he expounds it next demands our attention.

II

Inadequacies of Formal Logic

Formal logic is naïve or, as Husserl sometimes puts it, "positive," in the same way as the (other) special sciences. In the first place, the existence of the material world is taken for granted as it is in the natural attitude, and the natural sciences direct themselves to it empirically as a world of material objects existing independently and presenting themselves for our inspection. Logic assumes all this similarly and accepts the sciences in their naïveté, reflecting critically upon the forms of judgement and inference which they use and prescribing norms for validity and truth. But in all this unnoticed and uncriticized presuppositions are made of which the formal logician is unaware but which the philosophical logician cannot overlook.

Critical though the approach both of natural science and of formal logic in some sense may be, there are, Husserl tells us, two grades of criticism.[4] There is the critical reflection upon common judgement and reasoning typical of the sciences, and of formal logic as directed to its special topic, the principles of scientific thinking. But besides this there is a higher critique which seeks the *a priori* conditions of the former sort and of the types of experience involved in it. It is this second grade of criticism which notices and investigates the naïve presuppositions, not only of the natural attitude in general, but also of the more critical disciplines which arise out of it and are based upon common experience. In the case of logic, Husserl gives the following examples as illustrations of the tacit and unexamined presuppositions that it makes:

i. He points out that logical acts (such as judgement and inference) and logical concepts and relations, independent though they are in essence of the psychical processes in which they occur, do in fact appear in those processes, not just once and for all, but repeatedly and in varying forms and contexts. The formal logician assumes that at each occurrence he is dealing with the same concept, judgement, inference, or whatever, without questioning the basis of this assumption or considering how, or on what grounds, the identity of the logical object is constituted.[5] In short, an inquiry is needed into the conditions of the possibility of judging, inferring, concept-formation and the like, and of the identity in different psychical occurrences of their products.

ii. Similarly, the ordinary logician takes it for granted that a judgement made on primary evidence is the same as when it enters into a train of reasoning, overlooking the fact that its meaning-structure and significance are modified by such a transition, as well as by a movement from mere inference to positive assertion as truth.[6] The mere form of statement expressing a significant judgement will not in itself serve as the premiss of an argument, for in order that it may do so the grounds of connected fact on which its meaning rests must be invoked. What Husserl seems to be hinting at there is something like the doctrine expounded independently by F. H. Bradley and Bernard Bosanquet (and derived originally from Hegel) that in inference the judgement is being expanded and developed, as it is itself an expansion and development of the concept.

iii. Thirdly, logic and in particular mathematics, make frequent use of the notion of continuous series, which, they assume, continue uniformly in conformity with some stated rule of procedure, *e.g.*, $n + 1$. This characteristic is expressed in the phrase "and so on." What is the ground and justification of the assumption? How is the "idealization" (as Husserl calls it) of "reiterational infinity" (*iterativen Unendlichkeit*) constituted?[7]

iv. Further, there is the notion of contradiction and the mutual exclusion of opposites. What makes this compulsive?

In all these cases the "objective" aspect, which is accepted in logic, has a "subjective" correlate requiring investigation, analysis, and criticism. In each case, we have to determine the subjective evidence and the manner of constitution.

Further questions arise concerning the presuppositions involved in the attribution of truth, underpinning the laws of noncontradiction and excluded middle, and the rules of *modus ponens* and *modus tollens*, but just what these are it is difficult to extract from Husserl's averrations. They are mainly connected with his very obscure and puzzling conception of "evidence,"[8] about which we shall have more to say in a moment. Problems, also, concerning the "objectivity" of truth, of experience, and of the world of fact, and the "absoluteness" of truth and of being are mooted.[9] These are bound up with intersubjectivity, a matter very troublesome to Husserl, discussion of which is deferred to a later chapter. One point of great interest, which he explains all too sketchily in *Formal and Transcendental Logic*, but of which he gives a fuller account in *Experience and Judgment*, is the tacit acceptance in common thought and discourse of a general "situation horizon" permeating and shaping the meaning of everyday judgements, the intentionality of which, he tells us, requires examination.

In order to grasp the evidence for these concepts and to discover the manner of their constitution, it is necessary, Husserl maintains, to suspend all beliefs and assumptions about the reality of the presented world, all prejudices and common assumptions, and to return to the point of departure established by Descartes in the *cogito ergo sum*. But Descartes did not go far enough. Husserl accuses him of confusing the transcendental ego with the empirical psyche[10] and of failing to note (or at least to develop the consequences of) the fact that the content of *cogitatio* is as indubitable in its phenomenological presentation as the existence of the ego itself. From this absolute consciousness everything in experience is processed, and how its objective significance is developed can, and must be, determined by description and analysis of the "intentional performance" of the experiencer, which constitutes its "sense," whether as transcendently existent reality, categorial necessity, or logical consequence.

In *Formal and Transcendental Logic*, Husserl's treatment of the subject is programmatic rather than substantive. He tells us what needs to be done and the kind of method by which it should be done, but the projected logic itself is hardly set out in any systematic detail. His pupils and successors have embarked upon widespread phenomenological investigations, but nothing remarkable has been accomplished by them in the field of logic.[11] What Husserl does offer, not only in the *Formal and Transcendental Logic* but also in *Ideas* and at more length and in more detail in *Experience and Judgment*, is the outline of an epistemology which contains tantalizing suggestions of highly fruitful theories, he does so in such ambiguous and vague, even obscure, language, full of special technical and mostly unexplained usages, that one is often doubtful how he should be interpreted. Certain points emerge, however, about which we may risk committing ourselves.

The first step to be taken is to effect the transcendental reduction of consciousness indicated above—the *epochē*—the suspension of all beliefs concerning the external reality of the content of consciousness. That content must be regarded simply as it is presented primordially with its own direct and immediate evidence. Precisely what Husserl means by "evidence," however, is not easy to determine. Sometimes he speaks of it as primordially given—"primordial dator consciousness"[12]—and sometimes as that consciousness in which the object (in the widest sense of that word) is "itself given." Although these appear to be two ways of describing the same thing, there are grounds, both general and implicit in Husserl's writing, for concluding otherwise (see below). In the case of material objects, he often seems to suggest that this is direct sensuous perception although there are massive reasons, many of which Husserl himself provides, for denying that direct sensuous perception ever presents us with a material object as "itself given."

Frequently he speaks like a naïve realist, telling us that at a certain level (the prepredicative), or in a certain stratum, of experience objects are pregiven (or self-given) and are primordially evident—the implication being that this primordial evidence is unmediated self-evidence. Sometimes we are told that such primordial "objects" (which constitute the substrates of all predicative judgements) are sensuously perceived static spatial bodies, as if we could immediately apprehend such bodies by sensuous intuition. But elsewhere, or even in the very same context,[13] we are told that the presence and existence of such a body "confirms itself in the harmony of experience." In that case it cannot be primordially self-evident *qua* body, for what is so self-evident requires no confirmation.

The recurrent suggestions of naïve realism are not in keeping with Husserl's analysis of preceptual experience, with his description of it as presenting us with incomplete and one-sided *Abschattungen*, partial views of objects which have to be synthesized, together and with imaginal supplementation, in order to constitute the actual objects we perceive. In fact, we are explicitly told in the following section (§ 13, pp. 59ff) that the apprehension of the substrate objects consists of cognitive acts of rudimentry judgement. Husserl also maintains that the awareness of objects, even at the most primitive level, is always in the context of a wider horizon (*die Lebenswelt*) which gives sense or meaning to the object at the center of attention. Clearly, then, the cognitive act must always be discursive (he insists that even the sensuous level of consciousness is itself a phase or level of constitutive activity[14]), involving implicit and inchoate reference from elements in focus ("prominences," *Abgehobenheiten*) to others in the horizonal background as well as relations between these elements.

This description of the perceptual process, with its direction of attention and interest to prominent features in the perceptual field, and the exploration or explication of them along lines prescribed by prior experience and implications in the horizonal background, a process involving continuous activity of synthesis on the part of the ego, is not only highly suggestive and epistemologically pregnant but is in standing conflict with any view of "primordial evidence" as the direct sensuous appearance of spatial objects.[15]

Moreover, not all objects are material objects. There are ideal objects (sometimes called "irreal") such as concepts and judgements, and they are just as little presented intact in the psychic stream of consciousness, but are also in need of synthetic constitution and identification. In reference to such objects, when Husserl speaks of "evidence," he claims that it is a sort of conviction of logical necessity, an intuition of apodicticity. Again he speaks at times of this as dependent upon systematic relations between different presentations, both of the object concerned and of others with which it is associated or connected,[16] strongly suggesting a coherence theory of truth.

At other times he refers to the intuition of essences as *Wesenserschauung*, describing it as the apprehension of an invariant in the free, arbitrary, and unrestrained imaginative variation of the object.[17] This, he says, requires three steps in the process of ideation: (i) the productive activity involved in running through the variations, (ii) the grasp of the whole succession of variations as one series revealing continuous correspondences (*Deckung*), and (iii) the active identification and selective apprehension of the congruence in contrast to the differences. Clearly, this threefold activity is a discursive process at every step and no *Wesenserschauung* could occur without any one of these three phases. Yet the grasp of the essence is still regarded as an immediate intuition analogous to direct sensuous apprehension.

Husserl warns us that such "seeing" is in no way sensuous (even in imagination), yet it is difficult to understand what other kind of "seeing" is intended, unless one adopts Spinoza's dictum that "the eyes of the mind by which it sees and observes things are solely demonstrations,"[18] in which case the evidence of *Wesenserschauung* would indeed by discursive and not sheerly immediate. Husserl's doctrine becomes most fruitful and productive through suggestions and implications of this kind, revealing the close connection between the transcendental approach and the requirements of system, coherence and mutually determining relations.

III

The Task of Transcendental Logic

The task before us is to examine and inquire into the constitution of the sense, or meaning, of what is primordially given in absolute consciousness and we begin (not unlike Kant) by observing that it is all *mine*. "There is no conceivable plane," Husserl writes, "where the life of consciousness is broken through, or could be broken through."[19] Any transcendency discovered can only be what is intended by and constituted within the subjectivity of transcendental consciousness. And *I myself* am that subjectivity; it is my consciousness and mine alone that is available to me. As there is no consciousness without an object, everything of which I am aware is *intended* and constituted by my intentional performance as experiencer.[20] Nothing comes into experience from an alien source. Consciousness is not, as Locke pictured it, a light shining into a dark room simply revealing objects, for everything—my own psyche and physical organism, the external world, other subjectivities, being, illusion truth, and falsehood—whatever I experience—is transcendentally constituted by the activity of my transcendental ego. " 'I am' is for me, the subject who says it, and says it in the right sense, the *primitive basis for my world* . . ."[21] "the right sense" is the transcendental sense.

Once we have grasped the fundamental priorities, we can appreciate the importance of discovering how sense and meaning are constituted for the transcendental ego and bestowed upon all its intentional objects, and we can proceed to uncover the principles by which this is done. Anything that can exist and have specific character for a conscious subject is "something of which he is conscious by virtue of an appertinent 'sense-bestowing' (*Sinngebung*)", that is, by virtue of intentionality as a constitutive performance.[22] What has to be uncovered is the precise nature of this performance in specific cases and in experience as a whole.

How this is to be done and what exactly the investigation reveals is, in *Formal and Transcendental Logic*, very vaguely and obscurely described by Husserl. He demands that the "style" of intentionality of any (and every) object be traced through the multiplicity of possible and actual forms of experience (perception, memory, imagination, etc.) in which it can occur, and which relate together 'harmoniously' (*einstimmig*); that this be done for all forms of objectivity, and that "the entire life of consciousness" be viewed as an all-embracing unity, governed by a universal constitutional *a priori* including all intentionalities. We must inspect the modes of appearance in which objects take shape as "synthetic unities" seeking for "the systematic universe of possible experiences," or "for the *idea* of a complete synthesis of possible harmonious experiences," the synthetic product of which the object in question would be.[23] Just what he intends by "harmonious" experience is never explained, but it surely must be experience without internal conflicts—that is, coherent experience—and the suggestion is very strong that what is being advocated is a logic of coherence and system.

The primary question of transcendental logic, we are told, is not so much "How is science possible?" as "How is Logic possible?" and this is answered by a phenomenology of reason. The account Husserl gives of this discipline is confused, repetitive, and diverse, nor is it entirely self-consistent; but we may try to piece together as best we can the kind of investigation he contemplates. In *Ideas*,[24] he seems to be indicating some sort of epochal evolution of consciousness similar to that expounded by Schelling (following Fichte) in his *System of Transcendental Idealism*, but Husserl's adumbration of this structure is much too dim and indistinct for us to attribute it to him with any assurance. At all events, he does speak of a hierarchical sequence of problems, apparently corresponding to a hierarchy of levels of evidence.

Only the transcendental reduction, Husserl declares, with its universal *epochē*, can open the way to the required investigation. This furnishes us with a sphere of transcendental subjectivity which is, in the first instance, purely solipsistic, and investigation of this level of consciousness (the "egological") requires its own solipsistic logic. But

Husserl gives us no guidance as to what this would be or how it would operate. One is tempted to assume that what is revealed in the sphere of transcendental subjectivity is primordially evident—it is surely "primordially given". Yet Husserl speaks of two levels even here, one naïve and the other "sense-bestowing"[25] (presumably constitutive).

The nature and types of evidence and self-evidence seem to be the main concern of the phenomenology of reason, which, Husserl appears to hold, is primarily directed to the intuitively self-evident.[26] Yet he gives different explanations in different contexts of just what such self-evidence is. In fact, there seem to be three different kinds, sense-perceptual (as in viewing a landscape), apodictic (as in mathematics, or the grasp of a logical nexus), and "hyletic"—whatever that may be, for we are never clearly told, though the strong suggestion is of a primitive sentience of which no further account can be given. At the same time, if we are to understand evidence as "self-evidence," it is somewhat surprising and not a little bewildering to discover that evidence may be more or less adequate, perfect or imperfect, genuine or spurious.[27] The common understanding of the word "evidence," more especially "self-evidence," is the immediately apparent givenness of knowledge. No question then arises as to its adequacy or degree for it is always superlative. But this is not Husserl's consistent usage.

Such distinctions might lead one to conclude that the sort of evidence to which Husserl is referring is the sort that could support a hypothesis, and this interpretation is further strengthened when we are told that, at least in the case of perception, and indeed also in the case of ideation, adequate evidence only supervenes upon a complex process of construction and identification in differences, of diverse instances, in the synthesis of differing forms of harmonius experience.[28] As maintained above, this can hardly be intuitive self-evidence. Yet, again, we learn that to grasp an object *primordially* is to grasp it in its full adequate meaning to which there corresponds a form of consciousness apprehending it in a primordial and adequate way; and such full and adequate meaning is, surely only what has been built up through the complex process of identifications and distinctions in continuous and varied, actual and possible, harmonious experiences that was earlier described, in which case it would be no more primordial than immediately given.

In several places Husserl maintains that there will emerge from the phenomenological investigation rules of construction and categories of formative synthesis, recalling Kant's principles of the understanding.

But he never gives a comparable list of categories, although, in *Ideas*, §§ 10–11, he gives numerous examples.

IV

Undeveloped Implications

The promise of a systematic development of transcendental logic is not fulfilled even in *Experience and Judgment*. There Husserl gives a detailed phenomenological description of the psychological basis and background of apophantic logic, full of insight and perspicacious analysis of the constructive activity of attention, and containing further suggestions of holism, the logical implications of which are unfortunately never fully worked out. Husserl maintains that he is tracing the genealogy of logic through a series of levels or strata, from the passive, prepredicative apprehension of substrate objects to the active and explicit predicative judging in which knowledge becomes a permanent possession at our conscious and voluntary command. The prepredicative level divides into simple apprehension and explication of substrate objects, and the apprehension of relations of connection and comparison between them. At the predicative level, similarly, simple categorical judgements are constructed as objectivities of understanding, assume modal forms, and give rise to the higher levels of constitution of generalities or universals.

The movement and active discrimination by attention of the moments, aspects and qualities of objects and how they overlap, coincide, and are mutually distinguished is traced in detail. But, as we saw the primitive substrate object is taken to be a spatial body sensuously apprehended as "self-given," while the process of apprehension is seen to depend on explication, and correlation of spatiotemporal relations to elements in both the internal and external horizon, without which no such apprehension is conceivable. The strong implication is that a still deeper level of sentient awareness must occur, or one possibly preconscious, from which these elements are elicited and made evident by the active attention and so converted into what Husserl calls "prominences" (*Abgehobenheiten*). Within the horizon of the *Lebenswelt* these explicated objects are related by comparison against a background, in various groupings or as connected by mutual foundation in concatenations.[29] From the descriptions given, these relations ought to be internal to their terms and determined by the wholes within which they are distinguished. But they are not delineated as such and the logical consequences of their interdependence is not worked out. On the contrary, substrate objects, as well as certain types of parts and wholes are alleged to be separate and independent, so that relations between them remain merely external. But, external or not, no proper logic of relations develops.

On the foundation of prepredicative consciousness the forms of judgement are erected. But they turn out to be no other than the traditional forms of formal apophantic logic, the psychological presuppositions of which have been examined, but the metaphysical presuppositions of which are not discerned.

When he comes to the constitution of generalities or the universal (*der Allgemein*), Husserl says that empirically, it is based on common properties, and *a priori* or essentially, on an invariant form discernible amid arbitrary variations. The strong suggestion in all this of a unity in and of differences is left undeveloped, and the final result is an acquiescence in the view of the universal as abstract—the common property of a contingent or arbitrary collection—the traditional universal of formal logic. This is the case whether the universal is merely an empirical concept, based on contingent objects and contingent similarities, or the essential *a priori* concept inseparable from the apprehension or imagination of the object.

Nevertheless, a subtle implication of something more is discernable. The account we are given of *Wesenserschauung* describes its constitution as the grasping together, as a whole, of a succession of free and arbitrary imaginary variations of an object. For example, sound may be considered as variable in pitch, tone, melodiousness, harmony, etc. All these variations considered together reveal an invariant essence without which they would not be identifiable as sound. Husserl treats other examples similarly; a house, the colour, shape, or materials of which may be varied *ad lib*; a colour, which may be bright, dim, or whatever you will. But what remains obscure is how the distinction is made between the invariant and the variable unless the essence is presupposed *a priori*. If, like Locke, I think of the sound of a trumpet as scarlet, is it still sound that I envisage? If not, it must be because I have prescribed in advance what is to count as essential to it. If I imagine a house with no roof, horizontal walls, and windows in the floor, is it still a house? If not, is it because I have determined beforehand what "houseness" requires? The constraints imposed by the eidos are indeed *a priori* and they subject its possible exemplification, as Husserl affirms, to *a priori* necessary laws.

The source of this *a priori* and its necessitation remains unexplained, though we may suspect that the integrating apprehension of a diversity of variations might have something to do with it. But the origin, the generation, and the logical efficacy of this *a priori* is what the true business of transcendental logic should be; and while Husserl brings us to its threshold the "Open Sesame" to its interior structure is never divulged.

In sum, the phenomenology of reason, or transcendental logic, seems to be, for Husserl, the tracing out of various forms and levels of evidence, involving a study of the operations of the transcendental subject in constituting the ranges of intentional objects comprised in its experience, with special attention to logical concepts and relations and to the discovery of the categories which govern this constitutive performance. The upshot of this investigation apparently should be, or should include, an account of truth as the coherence, or harmonious concurrence of diverse forms of actual and possible experience, which builds up complexly into a unitary system, structured both hierarchically and temporally, through "sedimented" retentions which form a "sleeping" background, or horizon, of knowledge.[30]

Much in what Husserl writes is suggestive and valuable, especially the indications he gives of a system of principles and operations determining the construction of a unitary and coherent experience of an ordered and law-governed world. The theory of perception he seems inclined to advocate is one in which the apprehension of objects is a constitutive activity of interpretation operating upon a stratum of unformed hyletic data. We are, in fact, strongly reminded of Kant's manifold of intuition, to which the schematized categories must be applied in order to produce knowledge of objects in space and time. The constitutive activity which Husserl seeks to describe is apparently one of interpretation and judgement, informed and supported by a background of knowledge, a context (or "horizon") systematically constructed in the course of experience according to principles of order which are *a priori*—that is, inherent in the intentional performance of the transcendental subject. This is all very Kantian and, so far as it goes, is none the worse for being so. But the system, whether of categories, constitutive activity, or experience as a finished product emerges from Husserl's exposition with any degree of clarity only in some few cases (for example in the Fifth Cartesian Meditation and in

The Phenomenology of Internal Time Consciousness). For the most part, the principles are not defintively revealed nor the logical structure of the intentional operations described in sufficient detail or with the requisite degree of precision.

Notes

1. *Op. cit.*, Introduction.

2. Like Fichte, Husserl calls logic *Wissenschaftslehre*. It is, he says, "the science of the logos in the form of science, or as the science of the essential parts that constitute genuine science as such." Cf. *Formal and Transcendental Logic* (Trans., Dorian Cairn), Preparatory Considerations § 5 (*Husserliana*, band XVII, pp. 31–32).

3. Cf. *Formal and Transcendental Logic*, § 25.

4. *Op. cit.*, § 68.

5. *Op cit.*, § 73.

6. *Ibid.*, cf. also § 88.

7. *Ibid.*, § 74.

8. *Op. cit.*, §§ 76–80.

9. *Cf. ibid.*, § 81.

10. *Op. cit.*, § 93, b. Husserl, as we shall see, is not himself entirely innocent of this confusion.

11. Alexander Pfander contributed a treatise on Logic to Husserl's *Jahrbuch* containing several interesting submissions, but for the most part it follows the traditional programme and reveals no special insight due to the phenomenological approach. (*Jahrbuch fur Phänomenologische Forschung*, vol. IV, 1921.) Andre de Muralt has made some attempt to present Husserl's doctrine dialectically, although he claims for him more affinity with Plato than with Hegel, and to his exposition we shall presently turn. Cf. *L'Ideé de la Phénoménologie: L'Exemplarisme Husserlien*, (Presses Universitaires de France, 1958), trans. Garry L. Breckon as *The Idea of Phenomenology, Husserlian Exemplarism*, (Northwestern University, Evanston, IL, 1974).

12. *Ideen zu einer Phänomenologie und Phänomonologischen Philosophie* I, trans. W. R. Boyce Gibson as *Ideas* (George Allen, Unwin, London, 1931, 1952), §§ 136, 144.

13. Cf. *Erfahrung und Urteil* (Felix Meiner Verlag, Hamburg, 1972), p. 54, trans. J. S. Churchill and Karl Ameriks as *Experience and Judgment* (Northwestern University Press, Evanston, IL, 1973), § 12, p. 54.

14. Cf. *Ibid.*, § 16, p. 73.

15. Cf. also *Ideas*, § 138.

16. Cf. *Formal and Transcendental Logic*, §§ 105–106.

17. Cf. *Experience and Judgment*, part III, ch. 2.

18. *Ethica*, V, Proposition XXIII, Scholuim.

19. *Formal and Transcendental Logic*, § 94.

20. Cf. *ibid.*, §§ 94 and 97.

21. *Ibid.*, § 95.

22. *Formal and Transcendental Loic*, § 97.

23. *Op. cit.*, § 98.

24. Cf. *Ideas*, § 4, ch. II.

25. Cf. *Formal and Transcendental Logic*, § 102.

26. Cf. *Ideas*, §§ 142, 145.

27. Cf. *Formal and Transcendental Logic*, § 106.

28. Cf. *Ideas*, § 138; *Formal and Transcendental Logic*, § 107.

29. Cf. ch. VII below.

30. Cf. *Formal and Transcendental Logic*, § 107 d.

Chapter 5

Dialectical
Transcendentalism

I

A Reformulation of Transcendental Philosophy

All this may be seen in a new and somewhat different light as interpreted and presented by André de Muralt,[1] but his version of Husserl's doctrine is as much a reconstruction as an exposition, giving grounds for maintaining that de Muralt is going somewhat beyond Husserl's explicit doctrine in the direction of a dialectic such as Hegel developed more fully. This would allign Husserl even more noticeably with earlier transcendental idealists revealing in his doctrine the kind of dialectical progression initiated by Fichte and Schelling which Husserl himself might well have repudiated. I shall therefore, treat de Muralt's account of the idea of Phenomenology separately (if rather more briefly than, perhaps, it deserves).

de Muralt presents Husserl's theory as a continuous dialectical idealization moving from "factical" object (or 'reality') to irreal eidos. He contends that intentional analysis always moves in two (opposite) directions at once, from real (factical) object to idea, and from idea to object. The former (factical object) "motivates" the movement to the latter, while the latter (the eidos) equally motivates the intention (or, presumably, the constitution) as well as the development of the former. The first direction he calls the descriptive-phenomenological, the second, the transcendental-phenomenological.

The aim of knowledge is complete and perfect cognition of its object, but this is never fully achieved, in spite of persistent efforts, which range themselves in graded series from lesser to greater clarity. The series constitutes a development or teleological process tending towards ideal knowledge, and in its course, the later, more successful form of cognition ranks as provisional end (or "telos") in relation to its predecessors. While this can be said of any object, it is equally true of science as such—in fact, what is true of the object is *ipso facto* true of the science (which is the endeavour to know the object). Science strives for ever more perfect, more complete and more lucid, knowledge, and does so by progressively reconstituting itself as a theoretical structure, each successive development representing more adequate knowledge than the preceding versions.

From this teleological series critical reflection can elicit the ideal at which the series aims and which ranks as its ideal telos. This would be the eidos of the object or of science as such. So, de Muralt says, the factical example is an examplar for the discovery of the eidos, but the eidos is essentially what the factical example is trying to be (or become) and is alone what gives it its essential character and meaning. The eidos is, therefore, equally (or more eminently) the exemplar for the constitution of the thing. These two poles are dialectical opposites which unite in the recognition of eidos as the norm of the factical process of realization.[2]

As in Plato's doctrine, the relation between the two is "participation", but this is not a merely static relation, for the "fact" is continually tending (or striving) toward realization of the eidos, just as an artist strives to embody an idea in a work of art. The complete realization of the eidos is, however, never possible in actuality and the approach toward it at best asymptotic.

Accordingly, a method is needed to grasp the eidē of things (and sciences), their essences in their purity, a science which is in no way concerned with facts, but which is purely ideal. Its objects will not be real in any sense, but will be purely "irreal", and between them and the facts (which nevertheless "participate" in them) is an impassable gulf forbidding factical realization.

While this is the case from one point of view (the merely static), it is not Husserl's final position which, it is claimed, is teleological. The dynamic relation is that of progressive approach to the telos or eidos, which, in the end and after all, proves to be nothing but the totality (or integral sum) of the infinite asymptotic process. It is in this sense infinite, yet *in itself* it is a definite, finite, self-giving idea. It is only "irreal" and never real, although it is attained by suspending the reality and conceiving it *as if* the process of development were completed. It is this completed whole which is the true reality from the transcendental point of view, and it is always the whole which explains the part, and the end (telos) which explains the process.[3]

The special interest of this conception of science is its implication of a scale of forms in which the higher serve as exemplar to the lower and reveal more adequately the truth or essential being of the prior forms—a scale which is teleological and the ideal end of which is at once the whole series and the explanatory principle which makes every incomplete premonitory phase intelligible. To a conception such as this we shall return in the next Part, where it is shown to have fundamental significance as the structure of thought and knowledge answering to an identical structure in the nature of things. But in de Muralt's version there are distinct echoes of Kantianism and of Fichte, the ultimate aim of knowledge being an ideal (or idea) of reason not empirically attainable but toward which approach is made asymptotically in an infinite progression.

Now if the special sciences are taken as factical examples, the science of the theoretical norm (or norms) which, in their endeavour to perfect themselves, they seek to observe, will be the science of logic—*Wissenschaftslehre*. This, in fact, is traditional logic, but as each of the diverse objects of the special sciences requires its own appropriate method of study, traditional logic abstracts from all objects and restricts itself to apophantics. It then takes itself to be independent of the substantive sciences on which it is actually based. This, however, is a mistake, for it is in principle related to them teleologically and its theoretical forms are "motivated" by those of science. It therefore, requires criticism in the light of the "ordinary" experience by which it is "preconstituted," and the demand arises for a transcendental logic.

Prior to this, however, is the recognition that although the empirical objects of science are not amenable to *a priori* treatment, we can formalize them as "objects in general" and elaborate a *Gegenstandslehre*, which is formal ontology. Formal apophantics and formal ontology are then combined into a single science with two dimensions; and because it is as much ontology as logic, it lays claim to being "a philosophy", or science of pure being, like what Plato envisaged as Dialectic.[4]

But formal logic, as the science of science, is still a factical science and it too, throughout its history, has shown progress towards an ideal of logic, in the light of which it must be assessed and criticized. What is now sought is a science of the idea of logic, or a logic of logic, which is at the same time a logic of being. This is transcendental logic, the condition of which is the epochē or transcendental reduction, suspending the truth-claims of all particular sciences, while it seeks the essential form of objects as such and of science as such. It criticizes traditional logic to elicit its telos, as traditional logic elicits that of science but to do so it must also concern itself with the object, that is, with intentionality. So it becomes at once the phenomenology of both being and reason, and coincides with philosophy as such. It situates us in the intentional life of transcendental subjectivity, which is absolute being and which is its own norm. It takes us back to the transcendental ego, which is the presupposition of all presuppositions and the ultimate foundation of all phenomenology and all knowledge.

The critique of formal logic outlined by de Muralt (following Husserl closely) is based on quite other grounds than its formalism, which is accepted as appropriate to its relation (as critique) to the special sciences. The defect of formal logic alleged is its naïveté with respect to the constitutive *a prioris* of logical forms which it recognizes and their roots in the originary experience, from which both the special sciences and logic as their norm derive.

The phases of transcendental logic set out by de Muralt are three:

(1) The transcendental reduction presents us with the lived experience of the *Lebenswelt* as pure phenomenon ("merely presented"), which is the originary source (or evidence) of all objective knowledge. Our first task is to describe this *cogitatum* phenomenologically as noema. As such, however, it presents a problem, namely that of its intentional constitution. The object is presented in different ways and with different forms, it is perceived, remembered, or imagined; as fact, supposition, or subject to doubt, etc., but in all these secondary characters it is the same object, with the same "sense" or meaning. The problem is how this sense is constituted, for it is never actually presented, as it were, in its naked essence. Moreover, this essence or sense is a telos having ideal relation to the object, to which its diverse noematic forms tend or which they adumbrate. Thus, the problem arises of how such a sense is constituted and a second phase—that of reflection—is needed to seek its solution.

(2) This reflection discovers the dependence of the constituted *cogitatum*, or noema, upon the constituting *cogito*, or noesis. The question is how a given world is constituted in the intentional life of consciousness. Here de Muralt summarizes the complex Husserlan doctrines first of time constitution, through the media of retentions and

protentions, and the immersion of objects in its flow, so that their "sense" is constituted in terms of, and in relation to, "horizons" of experience both past and future, which prescribe recollections and expectations. It is in relation to the temporal whole that the objects are constituted and only in this whole is their sense made concrete. Next, comes the doctrine of the structure of experience as doxic, in varying doxic modes. Third, there is the doctrine that objects are apperceived in, or from, a stratum of sensuous hylē (the hyletic stratum). The hylē in itself is "blind" and acquires cognizable form only through the constitutive functioning, the intentional performance (*Leistung*) of consciousness. It is nevertheless indispensable, for without it the *cogito* would have nothing to inform: "the matter (hylē) without intentional form is blind, and the noesis without the hyletic datum is empty."[5] The constitutive function of the noesis is that of unifying, or ordering intentionally in a synthetic unity, the multiplicity or manifold of the data of sensation.[6]

The intention, however, is teleological. The empirical object thus synthesized prescribes a sense which seeks validation. It is an implicit sense which has to be explicated. This, we are told, involves the adequation of the meaning to the originary givenness of the object meant. It is a process of fulfilment depending on concordant or discordant sequences of experience. This theory would be more easily comprehensible as a coherence theory of truth, if it did not include the insistence that perception gives the maximum degree of objective fulfilment, meriting the title "rational consciousness" in that it gives "the bodily presence of the object."[7] For if perception is the mode of originary givenness, no further "adequation" is necessary; and if "validation" of the sense of the object is sought, it must surely be found in some other and superior form of "evidence".

Evidence is divided into three types or states—perceptual, categorial, and eidetic—and we are told that the last two are founded in the first, yet the third gives the telos or exemplary idea and is said to be the originary mode of rationality. It is, however, only "ideatable" *a priori*; it is never actually attained, but only thematizes an infinite process—"and so forth". The truth, it seems is a perpetual *Jenseits*; it can be approached only asymptotically.

(3) The third phase of phenomenological analysis is a further stage of reflection. Without the ego there can be no *cogito*. Kant's formula from the transcendental deduction is explicitly adopted: "The 'I think' must be able to accompany every representation." So from the *cogito*

we are inevitably led back to the transcendental ego and seek to thematize it as *fons et origo* of intentionality.

But strictly the ego cannot be thematized. It lives only in its *cogitationes*, in its noeses. These are intentional, so the concrete experience, in which the ego is activated, is always bipolar, always noesis and noema in concrete unity, and the concrete subject is intentionality itself. It is its "habitualities," its constitutive dispositions of apperception and thinking. It is the absolute beginning of intentionality and is immanently transcendent to the manifold of its concrete life, in and through which it constitutes itself as the transcendental-subjective pole from which the transcendent object is constituted. The ego is the transcendental absolute which is intuitively justified in "the infinite totality of the lived flow" of its experience.[8]

Here, then, the ultimate truth of all objects and all science is presumably to be found in a total coherent experience which is subject and object in one. The transcendental *ego* as a concrete whole of infinite experience proves to be the final truth of constituting *cogito* and constituted *cogitatio*.

II

Dialectical Parallel

The parallelism of this tripartite exposition of Husserl's transcendental phenomenology to the three major divisions of Hegel's logic is of arresting interest. The descriptive phenomenology of the *cogitatum* corresponds to Hegel's Doctrine of Being. They both relate to the level of perception and immediate presentation, Husserl's to the reduced presentation of the *Lebenswelt*, Hegel's to the immediate (unreflective) in general. The intentional analysis of the *cogitatum* by the *cogito*, which de Muralt says is the first phase of reflection, corresponds to Hegel's doctrine of Essence, which is precisely the logic of reflective thinking; and the thematization of the transcendental ego, *qua* transcendental subjectivity, corresponds to Hegel's Doctrine of the Concept, which he explicitly identifies with the Kantian unity of apperception.[9]

For Hegel, the Concept is the unity of Being and Essence as for de Muralt's Husserl the transcendental *ego* is the concrete unity of *cogitatum* and *cogito* (noema and noesis). This is the truth and is the whole of lived experience. And for Hegel, too, the truth is the whole, and the whole is the Concept self-realized as absolute Idea, which is the telos of both Being and Essence, as the ego for de Muralt is the telos, of all *cogitans* and all *cogitata*.

There are, however, at least two significant differences. First, de Muralt's telos, even the ego, which like all other eidē is infinite, is in the last resort an unattainable goal thematizing "and so forth," whereas Hegel's Idea is an eternally realized Absolute.

Secondly, the whole of Husserl's *Lebenswelt* is constituted and circumscribed by the transcendental ego, save perhaps for the hyletic stratum; while Hegel's Idea is both subject and object in one. It is not merely transcendental, but is at once universally immanent and transcendent, both substance and subject, Nature and Spirit. For Hegel, the hyletic stratum of experience (if such a phrase is permissible) is sentience, which is the dialectical outcome of Nature, through which it has been generated, and which in it is inwardized (*erinnert*) and transmuted as the matrix of consciousness.

Husserl's phenomenology remains, even as expounded by de Muralt, strictly within the circle of transcendental subjectivity and is, in consequence, and in the last resort, nearer to Fichte's *Wissenschaftslehre* (with the hylē corresponding to the *Anstoss*) than to Hegel's logic. For this reason it is subject to the same kind of criticism as Hegel levelled against Fichte and Kant. It falls victim to its own transcendental reduction by which it is inexorably subjectivized and from which the objective world can never genuinely re-emerge.

Notes

1. Cf. *L'idee de Phenomenologie, l'exemplarisme Husserlien*, translated by G. L. Breckon as *The Idea of Phenomenology, Husserlian Exemplarism* (Northwestern University Press, Evanston, IL, 1974).

2. Cf. *op. cit.*, p. 35.

3. Cf. *op. cit.*, p. 61.

4. Cf. de Muralt, *op. cit.*, p. 92.

5. de Muralt, *op. cit.*, p. 303; Husserl, *Ideas*, p. 247.

6. *Op. cit.*, p. 301.

7. de Muralt, *op. cit.*, p. 310, following Husserl, *Ideas*, p. 334f.

8. Cf. de Muralt, *op. cit.*, p. 333.

9. Cf. de Muralt, *op. cit.*, p. 329 ff.

Chapter 6

Transcendental Idealism

I

The Problem of Self-Constitution

In spite of his own disclaimers and those of many of his folowers, Husserl's transcendentalism is ineradicably subjective. In his, as in all transcendental philosophy, the I, who am, is prior to all objective awareness, even to "I, this man", to I as person or psychophysical individual in the world.[1] From and within my transcendental consciousness the world is constituted, with my pschophysical being as a member of that world, as well as other persons with psyches of their own. In fact, the world is experienced by each of us as intersubjectively common, and this very intersubjectivity is constituted by my transcendental ego. Accordingly, my transcendental ego is not the same as my psychophysical self, although I say "I" in both cases, for the content of each differs from that of the other. The transcendental "I" is prior to all possible objects, whereas my psychophysical self is an object experienced in part introspectively and in part through outer sense.

Husserl acknowledges the problem of self-constitution and the even more acute problem of constituting other selves with primordial experience of their own. He concedes that the objectivity of the world, even (or rather precisely) as constituted by myself, depends on its intersubjectivity; yet the other egos, to whom my world is common, are all constituted by me within my transcendental awareness, even despite the fact that the immediate consciousness of others is necessarily unavailable to me. In *Formal and Transcendental Logic*,[2] these problems are mentioned and a very sketchy resolution of them is outlined; in the fifth of the *Cartesian Meditations*, however, Husserl makes a determined effort to give a coherent account of the possibility of such constitution of an empirical self and of other subjects. I have criticized his argument elsewhere[3] and have shown that it fails. In any case, as he states the position in *Formal and Transcendental Logic*, the *hysteron proteron* is apparent. Without the objective world there can be no psychophysical self, for that is delineated in terms of, and as a constituent in, the world which it inhabits, in relation to other beings, both animate and inanimate, which make up the world. Further, prior to the constitution of the psychophysical self, no other selves can be conceived, for, as Husserl argues more explicitly in *Cartesian Meditations*, V, other subjectivities are "appresented" by empathetic projection from the psychophysical self. Yet there can be no fully objective world which is not intersubjectively common and intersubjectively constituted. The impossible situation is thus generated in which the world, the psychophysical self and other selves are each necessarily prior to the others.

In the *Cartesian Meditations* he proceeds more carefully and systematically, but his persistent and insistent declarations that all experience of whatever level or kind is confined to consciousness and that nothing comes into consciousness from outside, while it seems obviously unexceptionable and undeniable, has drastic consequence for the position which develops. No mere statement that intentional objects may be transcendent to consciousness (that is, independently real) will serve to extricate him from this subjectivism. For transcendence itself, and whatever sense can be given to "reality" and "independence" is professedly, and can only be in this theory, constituted by the intentional performance of the transcendental subject. It is not, of course, a psychological, or worse, a psychophysical, subjectivism. That, as Husserl clearly shows in his *Cartesian Meditations*, would be blatantly self-refuting. It is a transcendental subjectivism, committed willy-nilly to transcendental solipsism. True it may be that the *epoché* only suspends, and does not deny, the independent reality of the world; but as all that that can mean is constituted solely by the transcendental ego, even possible independent reality remains transcendentally subjective. Husserl was acutely aware of the problem, and he wrestles with it manfully in the fifth meditation, but the way in which he professes to solve it is hardly satisfactory and is effected only by a sort of sleight-of hand.

He first announces the necessity for a second reduction, by which consciousness is restricted to exclusively mine—"my primordially own"—abstracting from everything that requires the recognition of the existence of other selves. This is supposed to give me a subjective world of my own in which other persons figure only as objects in the same way as inanimate things. I then set my own ego in this world by "mundanizing" it, with all its cognized content, to constitute my empirical self. This step is, however, illegitimate. I cannot mundanize the transcendental ego without paralogism, for everything mundane derives from it and is contained within its transcendental awareness. Nobody could be more emphatic on this point than Husserl himself. If so, it cannot consistently be inserted into one item (my physical organism) in the world constituted by its own intentional activity. The psychophysical self is constructed from materials contained within transcendental consciousness, as are other objects. It is, of course, complicated by the attribution to it of the contents of sentience (the hyletic stratum), the peculiar substratal relation of which to the rest of experience generates immediately an insuperable difficulty. But Husserl glosses this over simply by attaching the sense-fields to the mundanized psychophysical subject, although the psychophysical self must itself, along with other objects in contradistinction to it, be constituted from material derived from the hylectic stratum now being attributed to it as its psychical field. Previously Husserl has emphatically assured his readers that the transcendental ego is not and cannot be "I, this man", and that the contents of the former and of the latter subjectivities are radically different. The mundanization of the ego, therefore, is nothing less than a confusion and conflation of these two different subjectivities, the distinction between which should be (to use a favourite term of Husserl's in another, not unrelated connection) unbridgeable (*unüberbrückbar*).

The constitution of other minds is dependent upon and derivative from this false move. To constitute them as parallel psychophysical entities presents no great difficulty, but to attribute to each of them its own transcendental ego, constituting its own world from its own primordial awareness, is quite another matter. Husserl contents himself with a form of argument from analogy: by "pairing" of like objects and correlating their characteristics, we attribute to other persons, from the similarity of their bodily movements and behaviour to our own, experiences similar to those of which we are concomitantly conscious, and we project empathetically into them the whole constitutive intentional performance of our own transcendental ego. But this argument can serve only if the original mundanization of my ego is accepted, and that involves the logomachy of attributing to the intentional object the constitutive activity of the intending subject.

This defect is endemic to all transcendental idealism. As noted above, it dogs the heels of Fichte throughout the *Wissenschaftslehre*, and it surfaces again in Schelling's *System of Transcendental Idealism*, where the major ambiguities (some of them shared with Fichte) are in the fundamental concept of the ego, which is somehow both absolute and universal, and yet limited, finite, and individual. It generates all knowledge and consciousness, as well as the whole of nature, out of itself, yet admits of other intelligences outside of itself, which restrict its individuality, and an objective world common to them all, which is objective in the full sense only because of them. Of course, Fichte and Schelling are aware of these contradictions, and in a sense, the whole of their philosophy is a persistent effort to overcome them or explain them away; but Fichte never finally succeeds, and Schelling had yet to go further. The persistent problem is that of limiting the illimitable transcendental ego, so that it may be conscious of an object opposited to itself, or alternatively of how it can determine itself so as to become its own object, since its essential being is self-consciousness; or again, it is the problem of relating the ego of *cogito ergo sum* with the finite self which knows its own finitude as a member of the world in which it lives and of which it is conscious.

The ego, for Fichte and Schelling, is pure activity; but to act the agent needs some passive substance on which to work. Activity implies passivity, and correspondingly consciousness, the essential being of the ego, requires an object. Both Fichte and Schelling stress this obvious point in the same way as Husserl. But if nothing exists except the ego, and nothing comes into consciousness from outside, what can be the source of the object? It must stand over against the subject (it must be *Gegenstand*). It is the term and limit, the aim of end of the subject's activity (as Husserl has it, its intention), but the subject is held to be infinitely active. By what can it be limited or caused to reverse the direction of its activity? Fichte struggles with this quesiton unavailingly. The ego, he maintains, posits itself as limited by the non-ego. But how and why should an all-inclusive, infinite, pure activity do this? It cannot cancel its own activity, yet to limit itself it must do so and must transfer some portion of its activity to the non-ego, which by definition is non-active. This self-positing as limited by a non-self involves self-contradiction, and Fichte's effort to remove this contradiction by successive syntheses of antitheses, leading by successive steps through the categories and the diverse forms of experience, does not finally resolve the problem. Fichte is, to the end, stuck with a mysterious and inexplicable *Anstoss*, which he postulates as the source of objectivity and which takes the place in his philosophy that the thing in itself takes in the philosophy of Kant, though Fichte repudiated that. The demand that the object should be encompassed by and should conform to the unifying principles of the subject's activity (reason) proves to be a practical demand, one which cannot be met theoretically; and the moral urge to satisfy it issues in an endless endeavour constantly opposed by a resistance for which no explanation can in principle be given.

For Schelling, the whole problem is one of self-consciousness. To be object to itself the ego must determine or limit itself; and how it does so by self-opposition leads it into endless, ultimately unavailing, avatars of experiential forms. Schelling resolves the problem ultimately on the virtually mystical union of the conscious with the un-conscious—an unconscious which, for transcendental idealism, is itself a product of self-consciousness. Later he elevated the identity of subject and object to the Absolute, and significantly modifies his whole position.

Fichte and Schelling came finally to confess the identity, in the last resort, of the transcendental ego with the Absolute, or God, revealing thereby a great gulf fixed between it and the empirical self, a gulf which Fichte, like Kant, bridges by means of an urge to infinite never-ending approximation of the "is" to the "ought to be". Schelling resorts to a preestablished harmony between nature and spirit converging in an in-difference point in the Absolute where all distinction is absorbed and abolished. But Husserl makes no appeal to anything beyond finite con-sciousness, which, however, in its transcendental subjectivity is ab-solute and in principle unconfined. But the persistent problem of mun-danization cannot be legitimately solved, and with it ineradicable dif-ficulties remain for intersubjectivity.

II

Merits and Demerits of Transcendentalism

While transcendental logic moves in the right direction, it fails because of its subjectivism. It reestablishes the mutual dependence between the objects of knowledge and logical concepts, maintaining no divorce between logic, epistemology, and metaphysics (ontology). Further, it establishes the unity and coherence of experience centered in the activity of the knowing subject, and reveals its importance for inference and truth. But in subjecting everything to the transcendental ego, it ultimately undermines the concept of truth, so far as it is truth about the world, for that is a relation between an independent world and our knowing, a relation of which transcendental philosophy can give no satisfactory account. In it the empirical self is restricted to the status of object (as it is legitimately in psychology), but *qua* object its self-knowledge and its consciousness of other objects is inexplicable. Physiological transmission theories of perception inevitably fail,[4] as Kant and Fichte, as well as Husserl, clearly understood, but the transcendental idealism offered by these thinkers goes to the other extreme and banishes the knowing subject altogether from the world which it claims to inhabit by making the world its own internal construct. The two types of theory are really mutually obverse, for the denouement of every attempted realism, as with Berkeley and Hume, is radical subjectivism. It was this consequence in Hume's epistemology which provoked Kant to reverse the assumption of Locke, that ideas are conveyed into the mind from external objects through the senses. The ideas (or concepts) had to be projected on to the sensuous material of consciousness derived, as Hume had decided, from unknown causes (things in themselves). It soon became clear that this postulation of unknown causes was itself a subjective act, and so the objective world, carrying with it the empirical self, became internal to the activity of the knowing subject, and the subjectivity of empiricism and of transcendental idealism coalesced.

Yet another feature of transcendental philosophy (to which brief reference has already been made) ought not to be passed over without further comment, for it has weighty and constructive implications for practice. This is the tendency already evident in Kant's system, to give primacy to the practical, a primacy on which both Fichte and Schelling insist. It is less apparent in Husserl's thought, yet if his principles are to be strictly followed, it should emerge in the phenomenological study of value—phenomenological axiology. Husserl does affirm the interconnection of practice, value, and theory,[5] but makes theory predominant. There is good reason also for this, which does not destroy the significance and justice of the saying that all theory is for the sake of action—did not Plato argue similarly in the *Theatetus* that the ultimate criterion of success in practice must be theoretical knowledge, which in the *Republic* disclosed itself as knowledge of the Good? But my present purpose is not served by reviewing the arguments pro and con. It is simply to observe the transcendental ground for linking truth to value which these philosophers reveal.

The unremitting urge of the ego to realize its full transparent self-knowledge and, in the course of so doing, the complete knowledge of all else, sets before it an ideal of reason, which it unceasingly endeavours to actualize. Theoretical knowledge of the ideal as existent is declared to be unattainable, but the idea of it exercises an indispensable regulative influence upon the quest for knowledge and an imperative demand for its realization in practice. This demand, as it were, spills over from practice into theory, so that the postulation of an absolute system as the standard of all truth is the product of the practical *conatus*. In consequence, the ultimate standard of value coincides with the ultimate standard of truth and the separation of fact from value, of theory from practice, is overcome.

With a doctrine of this kind there cannot be one logic for factual truth and another (or none at all) for values. Factual knowledge cannot be divorced from evaluation, as it is in all forms of empiricism; nor can value statements be reduced to non-cognitive expressions of feeling and sentiment. For transcendental philosophy, feeling, sentiment, impulse, and desire are all equally products and expressions of the activity of the transcendental ego striving to become fully self-identical in self-conscious clarity. Husserl would say that their sense and meaning are constituted by its intentional performance, while Fichte and Schelling see them as the direct expression of the drive of the ego to full self-awareness. Its active self-identification and self-consciousness is the essence of reason, so that feeling, sentiment, impulse and desire are all subject to rational regulation and become the media of practical reason and the material on which it works. The activity of the transcendental ego is also equally the ground of all theoretical knowledge and truth. Hence theory and practice cannot be divorced, but are inextricably interwoven. In the next phase of the development of idealistic philosophy—Hegel's—their relationship is worked out more systematically and proves to be dialectical, in a manner more explicit than, though already foreshadowed in, the doctrines of Fichte and Schelling.

While the transcendentalism of Fichte and Schelling produced the beginnings of a dialectic, Husserl's phenomenology of reason stops short of that issue. Even in de Muralt's reconstruction the dialectic is of a very general kind and is not systematically worked out. Husserl's phenomenological analysis leads back simply to apophantic logic in its traditional forms. It adumbrates but does not develop, even to the extent to be found in Kant, a systematic doctrine of the transcendental concept, which, if it were adequately worked out, should revolutionize the formal doctrine and completely transform our notions of logical procedure. In so doing, however, it would go beyond the limits of transcendentalism and free itself from subjectivism, as in Hegel's development of the dialectic of Fichte and Schelling, so as to relate the knowing subject to the objective world dialectically. In consequence Hegel was able to show how finite subjectivity with genuine apperceptive spontaneity could generate itself from Nature, a world in which the Idea (what in Hegel's theory the transcendental ego becomes) is already immanent. Thus the metaphysical problem is resolved and a logical procedure is offered which promises to be more fruitful than those examined hitherto.

Yet in Husserl's thought, seeds of a dialectic can be discerned demanding further and more consistent development, besides what we have already noticed and what de Muralt makes apparent. A logic of internal relations is further anticipated in *Logical Investigations* (III), where Husserl expounds a doctrine of wholes, although it never fully or satisfactorily develops as its implications require. Before turning to the discussion of dialectic proper, it may be helpful to examine this feature of his doctrine, which is considered in the following chapter.

Notes

1. Cf. *Cartesian Meditations*, I, § 11.

2. § 96.

3. "The problem of Self-Constitution in Idealism and Phenomenology," *Idealistic Studies*, vol. VII, no. 1, 1977.

4. Cf. my *Foundations of Metaphysics in Science*, ch. XIX.

5. Cf. *Ideas*, § 139.

Chapter 7

"Independent" and "Non-Independent" Objects

I

Wholes and Parts

The dominant principle in Fichte's dialectic is what he calls *Wechselbestimmung*, mutual determination, of opposites. This is a relation internal to its terms, for each is what it is in virtue of and as determined by its opposition to the other. The dialectic is thus a logic of internal relations, and it is this that we must now investigate. But first let us consider an attempt by Husserl to examine the nature of wholes, treated nondialectically, to see how far it goes toward the type of logic required. Internal relations are the peculiar features of the constituents of a whole, for what justifies our calling anything a whole is the interdependence of its parts; that is, the internality of their mutual relations. Where relations are (if conceivable) wholly external, there is no coherence among the terms and they do not form a whole of any sort, not even a collection (as we shall shortly argue), for a collection, regarded as one, is at least a rudimentary whole and its elements cannot be entirely external one to another. In the third of his *Logical Investigations*, Husserl discusses the relation of whole and part and, in some measure, without using the terms, he is addressing himself to the nature of external and internal relations.[1]

He begins with the assertion that objects relate to one another as wholes and parts, but not every object need have parts, because some are simple. Although it is not explicitly stated, the general way in which Husserl uses the word "object," and the examples he gives (when he does), strongly suggest that what he means is "intentional object" of consciousness. He does say that "part" is taken to mean anything really (*reell*) distinguishable in an object; and, as later he speaks of certain types of part as "abstract," this cannot mean that what is "really" distinguishable is actually or physically separable (though the converse must be true), and he denies that existence is a part of anything. The intention seems then to be that distinguishable parts must differ either qualitatively or quantitatively, or in spatial or temporal position. He seems therefore, to imply the parts of a whole are the differences distinguishable within it. At the end of the Third Investigation, however, he draws a distinction between examples in the field of pure intuition and empirical examples, which is puzzling. For surely any empirical example must be experienced in the field of pure intuition even if, in the natural attitude, we assume that the general run of empirical objects exist independently of our experiencing them; and if we impute actual relations to external objects that we do not find in pure intuition (*e.g.*, causal relations), it is only (on Husserl's own showing, though admittedly at a later stage in his philosophical development) because we constitute the externality of objects *a priori* in terms of relations such as substance and accident, cause and effect, and similar quasi-Kantian categories.

This distinction of Husserl's between pure intuition and the empirically discoverable has interesting consequences for the ontology assumed in his essay, but, because it does not enter into his main discussion of the relation between parts and their wholes, it may be ignored for the time being.

A simple object, then, is one which has no parts. The natural meaning of complexity, however, (he tells us) "points to a plurality of disjoined parts." By "disjoined," Husserl again seems to mean distinguishable rather than separable for he says that, while colour and redness are not disjoined, redness and the extension it covers are, because they have no community of content. Yet clearly they are inseparable. With these explanations, we may understand a complex object to be a whole of parts, and Husserl proceeds to distinguish two kinds: (i) those which can be cut up into "pieces," which are thus subject to *Zerstückung*; strictly, they are wholes that can be divided into a plurality of mutually exclusive parts; and (ii) those whose parts are essentially dependent upon or "founded in," others, as redness is in extensity. The relation may be symmetrical, as in the case of a spatial configuration and its boundary, or it may be asymmetrical and transitive, as in the case of the intensity, pitch, and temporal duration of a sound. Where such asymetrical transitive relations pertain, concatenations may be formed.

The parts of wholes of the first kind Husserl calls independent objects, or contents, and those of the second, non-independent, inseparable, and sometimes "abstract" contents. The key to this distinction is the way objects can be thought or conceived, not just how they are presented or how we attend to them. Although no object can be conceived in complete isolation, some can be held constant in idea despite unlimited variation of associated or accompanying contents (so long as the variation is not prohibited by a law rooted in the content's essence). Others cannot be so mantained in all cases of variation in their associates, for they are founded in, dependent upon, and inseparable from, certain others. Independent contents are separable; nonindependent are obviously not, they are "moments" of the wholes to which they belong.

The two kinds of whole are not, however, mutually exclusive. A concatenation, or some other sort of association of non-independent moments is clearly not subject to *Zerstückung*, but it may be contained in a larger whole of separable parts, other separable parts of which may (or may not) be similar concatenations (or included wholes of non-independent moments).

There is also another form of inseparability than that of being founded in another content. Some contents are continuous and merge into one another in continuous gradation. This kind of mutual dependence of contents, however, does not prevent separability of parts of the scale or of parts of the concrete object covered by the scale. An extended surface involves spatial continuity but does not prevent separability of the qualities it supports. Different parts, for instance, may be differently coloured; and even where a colour changes by continuous gradation over a spatial stretch, one part is separable from others.

A concrete thing, Husserl contends, is separable from others owing to the discontinuity and qualitative "gap" between neighbouring moments, but its separability as a concretum takes precedence over the separability of its moments (or parts), because the moments of one concretum interpenetrate in a peculiar way with regard to change and destruction. To just what sort of interpenetration he is referring is not very clear. But it does seem to be connected with, or at least to include, the relation of mutual or continuous founding.

Where contents coexist, he says that they form a whole, especially if several of them have a common foundation. When they found one another serially, as stated earlier, they form a concatenation; and some wholes are interpenetrative in respect of some of their parts though merely combinatory with respect to others.

However, Husserl finally limits the term whole only to *those combinations which have a common foundation*[3], and consequently he denies that all wholes have a common form in the sense of a specific "moment" of unity. The "unity" of wholes of non-independent parts is completely accounted for by the relation of foundation, which unifies them more intimately than any assumed "moment of unity" binding independent parts. Only in the case of the latter is the notion of such a special "moment" plausible, Husserl declares, and then it is still provided by and dependent on foundation; for such combinatory wholes are "unities" by virtue of the fact that there is "a content founded upon a plurality of contents, and on all of them together." By and large, the internality of relations between the parts (or "moments") of a whole depends on or is the same thing as their *foundation* one in another (a relation in some cases mutual). In effect, the parts of any whole seem to be internally related in some way, either to one another, or to some content in which, as separable parts, they must all be founded in order to constitute the whole.

Husserl has thus drawn attention to a very significant feature of wholes—that they are such only in virtue of the internality of relations between their parts, involved in mutual, or serial, foundation. That this type of relationship is not uniform and is variously intertwined with that between independent parts, and that dependence and independence may, in different cases, be more or less relative, are points easily conceded. But problems remain for which Husserl offers no solution.

II

Unresolved Problems

First, he insists that separable pieces—independent contents—cannot, in the nature of the case, be founded on each other.[4] This is an analytic proposition. And contents which are founded upon them are fragmentable. Accordingly, all wholes with non-independent parts will be mutually independent and the precise nature of the relation between them is never elucidated. Two adjacent colour-patches in a spatial extent are said to be mutually independent. Each is founded in the extension it colours, and that again in the surface it extends, and that presumably in the solid of which it is a surface, and so on. But each, with its concatenation of foundational relations, is independent of the other. In this way, any coloured extent is indefinitely divisible (*Zerstückbar*) into independent parts. How do they, as such, form any sort of a whole at all? What relation between independent parts binds them into a unity?

This raises a second problem. What is the "content" which is founded on the plurality of independent parts that binds them into a whole? Husserl rejects the notion of any "moment of unity." Unity, he says, is not a real predicate but only a categorial predicate, the implication presumably being that it is futile and mistaken to look for some element additional to the parts which effects their unity. The justice of the insight that wholeness is no additional part nor yet anything over and above the plurality of parts knitted together into a unity may be conceded immediately. It is always the unity *of* the differences and is only unity through their interrelation. But if the parts are *essentially Zerstückbar*, if they are mutually independent, how are they held together? Husserl correctly denies that a mere aggregate any more than a mere likeness or unlikeness is properly called a whole.[5] But if this is so, how do independent contents ever combine into anything more than an aggregate? The answer we are given is that some more comprehensive whole may exist in which all the parts, in themselves independent, are non-independently founded as moments.[6] We find no such example, Husserl tells us, in the field of pure intuition, and here again he is right if he means what Hume affirmed that no necessary (*a priori*) connections are revealed in direct perception. That such comprehensive wholes might be found in empirically real natural cases however, is not ruled out by Husserl's definitions, and, he contends, is indeed demonstrable.[7]

This answer to our question is surprising on two counts. First, it conflicts, is in fact the opposite, of what we were told in § 22. There we learnt that independent contents might, taken together, found another content so that it gathered them into a single whole relative to which they would be non-independent. Now we are presented with the reverse relation; the mutually independent elements must be non-independently founded in a wider whole. But if they were, would not their mutual independence (as asserted in the section)[8] infect the more comprehensive matrix so that it would become *Zerstückbar* correlatively to them? Indeed, if the uniting content were non-independently founded in the separable parts all taken together, would not their separability similarly infect it?

Secondly, empirical natural connections are all the product of transcendental constituting within pure intuition. This, surely, is why, apart from that constitution, we do not find them at the hyletic level. How then do relations of foundation differ in the case of the former from that of the latter? Or if pure intuition is taken to include objects already constituted (as they must be if they are spatially and temporally ordered), why do we not find in it the unifying principles which Husserl describes in this final section?

The third problem remaining unanswered is akin to the last. What sort of interpenetration is it that knits together the parts and qualities of concrete objects and gives them priority over the separable moments of their contents? How are the moments of the concretum intimately fused?[9] The nearest we come to an answer in Husserl's account is the founding of one in another but this, as is clear from what has been said above, is by no means enough to lock together the moments of a concrete thing in the kind of unity its individuality demands.

In the final section of the essay, Husserl finds the causal relation between natural events one which connects cause and effect as non-independent contents and so unites both space and time into wholes, irrespective of our intuitive ability to separate their phenomenal contents. It may well be that he intends this to be only one of many possible examples. However that may be, the result is somewhat sweeping, and the questions we have raised above remain unanswered.

This discussion of wholes has not been peculiarly tanscendental, and the formal definitions and theorems (which I have not thought it necessary to reproduce) offered by Husserl in § 14 are largely expository of the points summarized above. They are presumably intended as the foundation of a possible deductive system, but they give no further promise of insight into the nature of genuine wholes than has already been provided. What we must seek to understand is how wholes with so-called independent parts can be unified, a question on which Husserl sheds no light.

The examples he gives of such parts are invariably spatial or temporal, alleging that any portion of a spatial (or temporal) expanse is detachable from its surroundings in the sense that they may change indefinitely without necessarily affecting it. It is not founded upon its neighbours. As a recognition of the mutual externality of parts in all forms of extension this has justification, and has some plausibility when one talks in terms of colour patches and the like; but if attention is turned to the essential properties of space or time its falsity becomes immediately apparent. A spatial area is wholly dependent for its size, shape, and position upon adjacent (as well as remote) neighbouring spaces and without these determinations it is nothing. A lapse in time, similarly, consists wholly of the relations of before and after, comparative durational extent, and the like, with those periods which precede and succeed it. Its date depends upon them and its duration can be assessed only by comparison with other durations. There is an important sense in which such parts of space or time are "founded," immediately and serially in other parts. Husserl's claim, therefore, that the infinite extension of space and time is solely dependent upon (empirical) causal laws is unfounded.[10] The converse is much more defensible, as Kant's insight revealed.

Even when we turn to qualities filling space and time we cannot avoid a similar conclusion. A colour is not self-dependent in isolation from its surrounding; it varies with contrast and illumination and is affected by colours preceding and following it in an order of changes. This is eminently true also of sounds, as musicians well know. Nor may it be argued that such dependence (or "foundation") is confined only to our sensation and does not apply to the physical substrate. Contemporary physics demonstrates on all sides that the properties of space-time (*e.g.*, its curvature), energy, mass, atomic structure, radiation, whatever physical property you select, are all mutually interdependent in quite inextricable ways, if only because every quantity is relative to the frame of reference in which it is measured, the motion and velocity of which is again relative to every other reference frame. And if appeal is made to invariants and to the primary physical constants, Eddington and Sciama have shown what has been further confirmed by more recent physicists, that these too (and much else in the physical world) are mutually interdependent, and that nothing can be regarded as independent short of the physical universe as a whole.

Husserl, moreover, takes no cognizance, and seems in fact oblivious of organic wholes. He remarks in one place that a hand is part of a body in a different sense from its colour, but does not make clear in what sense. Of course, in his terminology, the colour is "founded" in the hand, making it inseparable from its surface in a way which is not true of the relation of the hand to the arm. But the hand is also non-independent for it can function as an hand only in conjunction with the muscles of the forearm and only if both are supplied with blood and sustenance produced by other bodily organs and circulated by the action of the heart, all of which (the hand included) are activated by the discharge of nervous impulses controlled from the brain. A hand, Aristotle reminds us, is no longer a hand when severed from the body. Husserl might have admitted such examples as empirical and as dependent upon empirical natural laws. But are not empirical laws themselves dependent upon the *a priori* principles imposed upon "absolute consciousness" by the constitutive performance of the transcendental subject, and should that not point to a mutual interplay of relations and a unification of objective wholes more universal and integral than, at least in this essay, Husserl seems to acknowledge?

We must, accordingly, go more deeply into this matter and shall begin afresh in the next chapter to examine the essentialities of relation and system and the principles determining the nature of a whole.

Notes

1. The subject is treated phenomenologically in *Experience and Judgment*, §§ 30–32.

2. *Logical Investigations*, ch. III, § 21.

3. *Ibid.* § 22.

4. *Ibid.* § 25.

5. *Ibid.* § 23.

6. *Ibid.* § 25.

7. Cf. *loc. cit.*
8. Cf. *loc. cit.*

9. Cf. § 9.

10. Cf. § 25 *ad fin.*

Part III

Dialectic

Chapter 8

The Logic of System

I

Relations, external and internal

Dialectical logic is the logic of system, and as all science claims to be systematic thinking, it is the ultimate and genuine form of logic. It does not, however, altogether exclude or repudiate formal or transcendental logic, but by its own intrinsic principle it incorporates them and situates them within the total system which develops as *Wissenschaftslehre*. The demonstration of just how it does so will find its place in the body of the detailed exposition, but the first task is to explicate the nature of system as the true theory of the concept—true because self-substantiating, while at the same time it founds and vindicates its own rivals, each at its proper level in the hierarchy of the dialectic.

System is a structure of elements in relation. We shall begin therefore, with a consideration of relation.

Formal logic acknowledges the existence only of external relations. Even what it consents to call "internal relations" are no different, for it distinguishes between the two as (i) relations between a particular and other particulars external to it, as opposed to (ii) relations between parts internal to some aggregated whole. But all wholes are viewed by the formal logician as mere aggregates; therefore, relations between parts, called "internal," are just as much external to their terms as are those, called "external," between the whole aggregate and others outside it.

Properly speaking, external relations are such as fall between their terms without intrinsically affecting or modifying them, or being affected by their intrinsic nature. Thus, the same terms can persist unchanged in different external relations and the same relations can obtain between different terms. Internal relations, on the other hand, are such as determine and are determined by the nature of their terms, so that any changes in terms or relations are concomitant. This is the case wherever we are dealing with genuine wholes constituted of parts generated by the self-differentiation of an organizing principle universal to them all as the elements of a system. In such a whole, the relations between parts are determined by the organizing principle, because, as it is equally immanent in all the parts, it governs their nature and behaviour, and hence the relations they bear to one another. Thus, in a geometrical figure, like a regular polygon, the number of sides, the angles between them, and the length of the perpendiculars joining them to the centre are all determined by the nature and structural unity of the figure, so that the general nature of the whole is destroyed by a change in any one of the parts or in its relation to other parts, which requires concomitant changes in all the rest to reconstitute the whole on the same pattern and principle. Even more impressively, the energy system, which an atom is, determines and is determined by the number and type of the nucleons, which in their turn determine the number and distribution of the orbiting electrons. Any change in any one of these constituents is a function of the state of the total system and is concomitant with changes in all the rest. The relations between nucleus and electrons are dependent on the combined charges on the particles, and relations between any of these and any other depend on their intrinsic states of motion (their quantum numbers). The whole is a single structured complex field and the constituent particles are features (or singularities) in it, determining and determined by the principle of organization which governs the whole.

It is always possible for special purposes to treat a complex whole of this kind as if it were a mere aggregate of independent parts in external relation. A pentagon may, for certain purposes, be regarded as five straight lines of equal length arranged cyclically end to end. But when it is so viewed, abstraction must be made from the plane figure which the lines bound and the relations between their length, its area, and the angles between the sides. An atom may be considered as just a collection of nucleons of a certain weight (the sum of their separate weights) plus a group of attendant electrons of negligible mass. But then abstraction must be made from their types and charges and states of motion, together with the chemical affinities of the atom. A whole which determines its parts can be treated as a collection of things in external relation only by making abstractions of this kind. Insofar as this is done, the aggregate envisaged can be subjected to mathematical treatment and formal logic comes into play. But if the whole is recognized as an integrated self-differentiating system, relations between its distinguishable parts are seen to be internal, so that mere separation and aggregation of them would destroy its character, and therefore theirs. Where holism prevails, formal logic is inapplicable without falsification.[1] This is because in the course of rigorous analysis the organized structure of the system is lost from sight and with it the essential explanatory principle. Accordingly, other principles of inference must be sought.

If the results of contemporary science are taken seriously we must acknowledge holism to be pervasive throughout the world, and all relations actually obtaining between real existents and their constituent parts to be internal. That this is so is tacitly assumed in the methods of reasoning and research pursued by scientists, who construct systems of evidence so interrelated that none of the facts could be otherwise if any were not as it is; hence their conclusions become cogent. This was precisely the claim made by Copernicus for the heliocentric theory of the solar system, and the reason he gave for advocating it.[2] The principles on which such reasoning is based are what I seek to discover.

In his brief but famous discussion of relations, F. H. Bradley argued[3] that, however conceived, whether as external or internal, they could not be made intelligible. If they are regarded as external, they fall between their terms, and then they fail to relate them or to bring them together. Further, and worse, a new relation must be sought between each of the terms and the linking relation, which, being likewise external, would, when found, simply give rise to the same problems afresh; so relatedness degenerates into an infinite regress. If they are regarded as internal to their terms, either the terms must be resolved wholly into relations, in which case there would be no terms to relate and relations would disappear altogether; or else each of the terms must be internally divided into a portion resolved into relations and another unaffected by them, In that case, however, all the difficulties hitherto encountered are again involved: the unaffected portions of the terms would be externally related and the affected portions internally; and the predicaments of both would be compounded because a new relation must be sought between the two portions of each term, and this relation, whether it be internal or external, would be subject to the same difficulties, so that a new infinite regress, more complex and more vicious, would result. To compound confusion still further, the terms, or that portion of them resolved into relations, will be analysable afresh into terms and relations, all recapitulating the original trouble.

It is clear from this argument that Bradley has adopted (if only for the purpose of criticism) the presuppositions made in formal logic. He assumes that terms and relations are all particulars which either fall outside one another or are subdivisible into other particulars identifiable as terms or relations.[4] Consequently, once again all relations become external, even when considered to be internal, for what are called internal are simply particulars dissected out of a presumed aggregate. Bradley was well aware of the existence of wholes which inform each and all of their parts with the nature of the whole and are constituted nevertheless by the parts, for he appeals to them in his discussion of moral responsibility.[5] But in his treatment of relations, he makes no attempt to consider the implications of such holism, presumably deeming it to abolish relations altogether (although the subsequent chapters of *Appearance and Reality* give little support to this view, and he treats relations throughout as they are conceived by formal logic).

So Bradley concludes that relations are not real and are only apparent, a conclusion which Bertrand Russell found altogether incredible because, he said, the existence of relations was so obvious that no amount of subtle argument could conjure them away.[6] Perhaps there is some truth in both these opinions, but also some error. If relations are elements in wholes or systems, it may well be, as Russell says, that they are indispensable for the definitive elaboration of the wholes; but at the same time it may be the case that relations can exist only within such wholes and in such a way that the whole determines both what the terms and relations shall be, so that they are inseparable from one another and from the principle of organization, and if we try to conceive them as mutually distinct and independent, we inevitably fall into the kind of antinomies that Bradley develops. In that case, relations as conceived in formal logic would be unreal and we should need a completely different approach.

II

Continua and the Overlap of Terms

In what follows, "organization" and "structure" are to be taken as interchangeable terms; also, the difference in meaning of "organization" and "order" is minimal. The former is the more inclusive term, and every form of organization will necessarily involve one or more forms of order, because by its very nature it determines specific relationships between the elements into which it differentiates. Order is usually understood as serial, whereas organization may involve both serial and coexistent patterns, but the latter also entails serial order if (as is, in fact, always the case[7]) transition from one element to another is requisite. It is not necessary therefore, to be over pernickity about using these three terms, ("structure", "organization", and "order") as roughly synonymous.

In a genuine whole, where the parts are adapted to one another in conformity with a universal principle of structure, the terms of all relations overlap. This is because each is a definite specification, in a particular context, of the universal principle of organization determining the *Gestalt*, the configuration, of the whole. If every element in the whole is a particular specification of its universal principle of order, they must all have something in common, yet equally they must all differ (for reasons which we shall later stress). They will, therefore, be overlapping elements in a continuous field. What they have in common will constitute the field and their mutual divergence will be continuous within it. That this must be so and that there can be no breaks in the continuity will appear anon.[8] The continuous field and the universal principle are strictly one and the same. The field is a continuity of the universal quality or character which is being differentiated in the system, be it space-time, energy, matter, colour, multiplicity, or universality and structure themselves. That this is so will become progressively more apparent as we proceed. In fact, when we examine relations closely, we find that their terms always overlap, for relations involve comparison, and terms can be compared only in some respect or other. This "respect" forms the universal matrix within which the terms occur and in respect of which they are compared and related. It is thus the common element within which the terms are distinguished and in respect of which they diverge.

There is always such a continuous matrix in which the terms of a relation are embedded and within which they are in a specific manner mutually distinguished through an intermediary divergence. And because the matrix is continuous, the divergence is smooth and gradual between elements which merge and overlap. But because the terms, to be related, must be distinguishable, they can never be wholly coincident and must always be differentiated by some degree of intervening lapse. They must be at once divergent and mutually interdetermining, giving some colour to (although also undermining) both doctrines of external and of internal relations.

Terms in relation are therefore always features in a continuum, and can be separated only through the intervention of continuously overlapping intermediate terms. To be mutually continuous they necessarily overlap; yet again, to be distinguishable they must differ one from another. Without divergence of some degree they would be coincident and would cease to be continuous. The overlap cannot therefore be total, because if it were, the terms would merge completely and the relation would disappear. So we are led to a definition of continuum as a system of distinguishable elements (terms in relation) which nevertheless overlap in their gradual unbroken divergence. In other words, the parts of any and every continuum, if it is to be a continuum at all, must be both identical and different—identical in the respect in which they are continuous, and different insofar as they continuously diverge and are distinguishable from one another.

Moreover, because they are mutually continuous, overlapping terms, however else they may differ, will always differ also in degree. For example, if *A* is to the left of *B*, it can be so only if *A* is *more*, or farther, to the left of *B* than any intervening point, and only if other points which are mutually continuous intervene. Any other relation you may choose to consider will display the same character of gradation. So it transpires that the terms of a relation are always also degrees in a scale of some sort, though commonly we fail to notice the fact. Further, as the terms must be distinct, gradations within the continuum are equally *distincta*; in short, the relations of gradation and distinction themselves overlap. In summary, then, terms in relation overlap, are distinct from one another, and are grade-points in a scale of degrees of the respect in which they are related.

The overlap of terms in relation is consistently revealed to us in science: in the sharing of electrons by atoms in a molecule, in the sharing of atoms by molecules in a crystal, in the sharing of a catalyst by chemical reactions, and in the interweaving of chemical cycles in living metabolism. Even the relation between points in space is seen as the overlap of regions, when a point is defined, as it is by Whitehead, in terms of abstractive sets.[9] The relation between points in space is, in fact, a clear instance supporting the account we are here giving of relations, for space is a continuum and points are the ultimate elements that constitute it, and the relation between any two of them is distance; that is, the continuous progressive divergence from one to the other. In like manner, the relation between two colours is a function of their respective positions in the colour continuum; that between two numbers is a function of their respective places in the continuous series of natural numbers (with appropriate qualifications for irrational and imaginary numbers) and the relation between two chemical elements is dependent upon their positions in the continuous scale of atomic numbers.

It might be countered that these examples are weighted. What should we say of the relations of consanguinity between biological individuals? What continuum is involved here? Surely it would be the continuous generation of the germ-plasm, the continuity of generic transmission of genes through meiosis and fertilization of gametes. Here the overlap of genetic material is apparent and it is this that determines relations of consanguinity in its different degrees. A more complex case would be the relation of ownership to property, where the continuum involved is strictly historical, being one of legal activity within a structure of social rules and customs which are maintained through continuous changes in time. Here there are not one but several overlapping continua: a society of biologically continuous human beings, a continuum of legal and moral ideas,[10] and a temporal continuum in which all of these are connected.

Two corollaries follow from the description we have so far given of terms in relation: (i) no continuum can be wholly and unqualifiedly homogeneous, and (ii) no series of elements can be absolutely random. "Homogeneous" and "random" are terms that can be used only relatively and neither can be given an absolute sense without cancelling out.

(i) No continuum can be wholly homogeneous because homogeneity consists in having parts that are completely uniform and so indistinguishable, and that excludes the divergence necessary for continuity of relationship. When we call a continuum homogeneous (*e.g.*, mathematical space), it is only with reference to certain characteristics found to be identical throughout all its parts. But, for the reason given, this cannot be so for all characteristics. The parts of "homogeneous" empty space, for instance, must differ at least in position, or else space collapses to a single point; and a single point apart from and unrelated to other points is *nowhere*, and so no point in space. The supposed homogeneity of mathematical space is only an abstraction from the differences still essential to it. If we take it to be real, we become victims of the fallacy which elsewhere[11] I have called the fallacy of spurious homogeneity. Indistinguishable parts are, according to Leibniz' principle, identical. Thus, any absolutely homogeneous continuum would contract to a single point and disappear. This is what would happen to physical space-time without matter and energy, as Eddington explains:

> A region outside the field of action of matter could have no geodesics, and consequently no intervals. All the potentials would then necessarily be zero. . . . Now if all intervals vanished space-time would shrink to a point. There would be no space, no time, no inertia, no anything. Thus a cause which creates intervals and geodesics must, so the speak, extend the world.[12]

Intervals are what distinguish the parts of space-time, and without them there could be no space-time continuum.

The contiguity of overlapping terms thus generates a continuum of serially diverging forms, which, because they must diverge continuously, establish a rule of order and gradation. It is now apparent why organization or system involves order, for every organized system is a structure of terms or elements in relation, and relations are always embedded in a continuous matrix, specifying the distinctions between its parts in serial order.

(ii) Within a continuum, however, series need not always be regular, even though there must always be some degree of regularity. In space, direction can change without being wholly discontinuous, for however abrupt the change may be it always implies continuous rotation between dimensions. But while a series can be absolutely regular, none can ever be absolutely irregular and remain continuous. For absolute irregularity means a total lack of continuity between the terms of the series, so that once again the continuum would be dissolved.

Nevertheless, changes may be more or less random if the divergence of elements runs regularly and continuously for a certain range and then changes direction more or less sharply. But the sequences must be regular for some length between the changes otherwise the continuity will be broken completely and there will strictly be no sequence at all. The regularities may be reduced in length, and as they diminish, so the series becomes more random. But they can never be reduced to zero, for, if they were, continuity of change would evaporate.

No continuum, therefore, can ever be utterly random in its heterogeneity. The necessary diversity of parts can never extend to wholly abrupt changes from one to another without breaking the continuity, and such breach implies a lack of mutual adaptation which violates the rule of order required by the structural principle. Moreover, the intervals of relatively orthogonal continuous variation between changes of direction, the brevity of which is the measure of the degree of randomness, cannot be reduced to infinitesimal length, for in the limit sheer discontinuity is reestablished—in fact, all direction of change vanishes and progression itself disappears with continuity. At most, we should be left with a field of randomly related characterless particulars indistinguishable one from another and so should lapse into homogeneity.

This may be illustrated by the course of a particle moving randomly in space. The randomness of its movement consists in the frequent and irregular changes of direction which it makes; but between any two changes some direction must be continuously and regularly maintained for however brief a duration; and the changes, as we have seen, however abrupt, will involve continuous rotation of direction from one to the next, rapidity notwithstanding. If we now assume that the regularities of direction are reduced so that they tend towards zero, once they reached the limit, each phase of the movement would occupy a single point, and both direction and movement would be lost. For either no contnuous change of position could occur, or it would occur from one point in space to the next and so would be perfectly regular—though strictly speaking this is impossible for there are no separate yet adjacent ponts in space. Randomness, therefore, when it does occur, is always and only relative to serial order, direction of variation being definite in brief stretches between relatively abrupt changes.

From this analysis we may gather that, as randomness is always relative to order, so order is prior to disorder; and the primary form of order is continuous seriality in a heterogeneous but graded scale of overlapping terms. This will be common to every system, for every system is a complex of terms in relation and must therefore be a more or less complex continuum resolving itself into a scale of forms. This can be demonstrated by an examination of the general nature of system.

III

Organizaton and System

Every system is a whole and every whole a system; but its systematic character is a matter of degree, for a whole may be no more than a mere aggregate without further structure. As such, it is a system of a very rudimentary kind, but unless its elements are together and so are interrelated in some way, it could not be even an aggregate. Every system, therefore, is a structure of relations and we have seen that the related terms overlap. Because they overlap, they follow a rule of progression in a continuous order and so present some form of configuration which the rule of order determines. This is the principle of structure determining the nature of the system as well as of its parts and elements. The terms in relation, therefore, are mutually determining and are governed by the pervading principle of structure. Even in a simple aggregate it is in virtue of their mere togetherness that the terms are bare particulars, and, being such, the relations between them can be no other than mere togetherness. Thus, every configuration is a whole such that the principle of structure which makes it one also determines the nature and interrelation of the component elements.

A mere aggregate is, as has been said, a very rudimentary type of system, and one of its characteristics is that it is open ended. However many items are collected together, more can always be added, and the wholeness of the structure consists in the sum so far accumulated. This open-endedness of the system is due to its simplicity and is strictly only repetition of the juxtaposition of units exceeding one. It may be represented symbolically by the arithmetician's formula $n + 1$, where n is any aggregate you care to choose and $n + 1$ simply produces another n. Repetitive structure of this kind can be made more complex to almost any degree and may be of many kinds, from a string of beads to the complicated patterns depicted in M. C. Escher's fascinating engravings. But in every case, the repetition and progression is based on a structure which is relatively closed (*e.g.*, the single bead, the sum, or some more complex pattern) and which is more or less exactly repeated. This closed unit of structure can never be reduced to nothing, however simple it may become, because its disappearance would destroy the entire repetitive series.

Moreover, any continuous series can be such only by virtue of some unitary principle of generation and on the basis of some identifiable unitary component element. Further, the principle of generation invariably involves a cyclical movement which makes the ostensible endless progression constantly self-repetitive and dependent upon perpetual return to its starting pont. Thus, the number series is generated on the principle that the successor of n is $n + 1$, and the progression of the series is a perpetual repetition of the decad, or of some other arbitrarily selected base—a constant return to its beginning. The same is true of the Greek key pattern, which is generated according to a constant principle continuously repeating the characteristic key-like shape. More complicated graphical series, like those invented and depicted by M. C. Escher, fulfil the same conditions. There is always a unitary whole which is constantly repeated. We may therefore, confine our attention to closed systems,[13] for they are basic to every form of structure, whether open or closed, and are the prior condition of existence of any cognizable object.

Examples of relatively closed systems would be: (i) a geometrical figure like a circle, or a regular polygon, or solid, or some more complex arrangement of figures such as a five-pointed star (the tetraktys); (ii) a machine like a bicycle or a car engine; (iii) the solar system, or a spiral nebula; (iv) a molecular structure like a carbon ring, or the double helix of DNA; (v) a chemical cycle in living metabolism, such as the Krebs cycle; (vi) a living cell; or finally (vii) a scientific theory, like Newton's theory of motion. None of these is absolutely closed, because each of them is related to other systems outside it and is therefore dependent for its structure, or behaviour, or both, on external influences. An absolutely closed system would not be related in any way to anything beyond itself. Thus, there can be only one absolutely closed system, which must include all other systems, for however isolated any of the others may be, they cannot, as long as they exist together in space and time or are in any other way related to one another, be absolutely self-dependent. As terms in relation, they belong to some common matrix, to a larger system in which they are liable to overlap in some degree or form.

A geometrical figure is an obvious whole. A circle is not just a curved line but one determined by its constant distance from a fixed point—its centre. This equidistance from the centre of all points on the circumference determines all the numerous fascinating properties of the circle: *e.g.*, the relation of its radius to its circumference, the equality of the angles subtended at the circumference by any chord, the fact that any tringle erected between the diameter as base and the circumference is rectangular, and so on. Apart from the primary principle of structure these properties are absent, and each of them in some way, and in some sense, expresses and involves this principle. The same is true, *mutatis mutandis*, of regular polygons and solids. Irregular geometrical figures are also relatively closed systems, but the principle of organization determining any one of them is more difficult to discern. Nevertheless, there always is one which determines their structure and geometrical properties in the way we have indicated.

The organization of parts in a machine (i.e., a human artifact) is determined by their functions, and each is related in a specific way to the purpose of the machine as a whole. This governs the entire working of the parts and determines how their functions must interrelate. Each part and function accordingly reflects, in its own way and from a particular angle, the purpose of the whole, to which it is accommodated and which requires the mutual adjustment of all the parts in its service.

The solar system is determined throughout by the law of gravitation, which determines the movements of each of its component bodies, their relation to the sun and to one another. This law is reflected and expressed in the shape of every orbit—its governance by the sun as well as its aberrations resulting from the pull of other planets.

Molecules and chemical cycles in similar ways give expression to the physico-chemical laws governing their structure and functioning—basically the laws of quantum physics. The activities of a living cell are determined by and express the self-maintaining auturgy of the living system—its teleonomy. A scientific theory is itself a principle or organization systematizing the observed facts within a specific field of experience. It formulates laws that determine and interrelate the facts, and it interrelates both facts and laws according to logical principles, so as to form a coherent whole. The logical principles are precisely those we are seeking: namely the laws of systematic and coherent thinking. These laws all sound theory must reflect and exemplify. A theoretical system is thus an *example par excellence* of systematic order and its structural principles are the system of logic itself. The proof of this coincidence of logic with system will develop as we proceed.

In every one of these examples, the principle of organization is one of unity making the system a coherent whole, and at the same time a principle of differentiation determining the disposal and mutual accommodation of the parts. Unity of differences is the hallmark of wholeness—unity by virtue of the intermesh of diverse but mutually adjusted parts. A system is essentially a one of many.

A closed system is necessarily and undeniably whole. It cannot be merely or ultimately fragmentary. Any fragment which reveals elements of structure presupposes the *whole* of the structure of which it is a fragment. It is therefore inescapably relative to the whole. Moreover, the whole, or the principle of order, determines the character and structural identity of the part or fragment. For example, a palaeontologist finding a fossil can recognize it as part of a skeleton and can identify the species only from his knowledge of the whole anatomy of the creature, apart from which the fossil would be no more than a number of curiously shaped, or marked, stones.

The whole, with its principle of structure is, therefore, prior to the parts. It is the universal or pervasive influence of this structural principle that makes the distinguishable and diverse elements what they are, that determines their relations to one another, and adjusts each one of them reciprocally to every other. It is the universal principle of which the differentiations are manifestations or (as we shall shortly see more convincingly) exemplifications. Seen from a slightly different angle, this universal appears as the continuous matrix within which, and out of which, the terms in relation that constitute the system are differentiated. To revert to an earlier example, the terms in relation in the system constituting an atom are elementary particles, nucleons and electrons, each of which is a singularity or specific differentiation of and within a complex field of energy. The field is the continuum or matrix, and *qua* energy it is also the universal which is being specified. The principle of organization that determines the whole is the law (or complex of laws) governing the disposition of energy and (or) particles, *e.g.*, Pauli's Principle of Exclusion. The differentiations of this system are particles and the whole atom is a particle; each particle is associated with a field and the whole is a complex field. Each is related to the rest by laws of Coulomb forces and saturation. So each is an exemplification of what the whole is and each a specification of the universal principle of structure governing the whole.

But, on the other hand, this structural principle is nothing, or at best a mere abstraction, unless it is embodied and expresses itself in the multiplicity of the elements comprising the system. No whole exists apart from internal differentiation. As we saw earlier, there are no terms in relation unless they can be mutually distinguished. A merely simple unit is no whole and is not really conceivable;—for unless it is a unit in some structure, it dissolves away into nothing. An isolated point, apart from relations to other points is not conceivable as a position in space at all, and so is not even a point. As a unit in some structure, its character and identity is determined by its relations to the other elements—that is, by the structural principle of the whole; and the internal differentiation of the whole is reflected, or immanent, in it, as it is in every other element. Likewise, a blank undifferentiated unity is not whole and is strictly inconceivable, for unless it has distinguishable parts or elements within it, it has nothing to unify.

A whole, therefore, as a system of elements in relation, a continuum of overlapping moments, is always both unified and differentiated, both one and many, and is always a totality, fragmentariness being inevitably relative to completion. Its unity and multiplicity are mutually dependent and inseparable. Each requires and implies the other in order to be itself. There is and can be no unity without multiplicity and no multiplicity without unity, for it is nothing other than the interdependence of the differentiations that constitutes the unity of the whole. Conversely, the unity of each constituent element is dependent upon its interrelations with the other elements. Its specified position in the whole makes it a reflection or expression of the total structure from a particular viewpoint. To this inevitable microcosmic character of the part I shall return shortly; meanwhile, what I wish to stress is that wholeness and structure imply multiplicity and differentiation as much as, and correlatively to, unity. Every whole must be differentiated, and every principle of structure must be specified or deployed in interrelated differences.

IV

The Self-Differentiation of System

This deployment or explication of a totality is always a discursive movement. The differences must be run through, or run off, while at the same time being held together in unity. The interplay of unity and diversity is a perpetual dynamic activity that is difficult to conceive except as temporal. Yet it is prior to all temporality and process, because it is already involved in any succession or movement. As Kant showed, no succession would be conceivable if each successive item were to disappear and were completely annihilated before the next arose. To be conceivable as successive, the elements must somehow be held together in one as well as run through. This is true not only of our conceiving but of the very nature of successiveness; it is true not only of mental states but of any elements in successive relation. Any succession must be a whole of distinct elements, at once a unity and a multiplicity, and each by virtue of the other. Temporality and movement, therefore, are manifestations of the fundamental logical discursus which is not itself temporal but is basic to all thought, to the conceivability and intuitability of any object, as well as to all motion, or lapse, succession, or duration, in actuality.

A totality, accordingly, must by its very nature be set out or deployed, as it were, bit by bit. Its elements or moments must be discursively run through. For a complex pattern to be coherently integrated, its diversity must be set out and explicated. To apprehend it as a whole of related elements the intellect must, as Piaget has shown, run through its differences in reversible order and grasp them together.[14] The pattern cannot be simply intuited all at once without any discursive, if only implicit, comparison of diverse parts. And the condition is not merely epistemological, not merely a condition of our apprehension; it is a condition of existence of a differentiated totality. It may not seem to be true of spatial patterns that they involve succession, for almost by definition their elements coexist and are all there at once. But this is quite literally an illusion. Relativity physics teaches that even coexistence of diverse elements involves transition from one to another, for all spatial distance is a function of causal transmission, so that all extension involves temporal lapse. Spatial pattern is always traced out and sustained by a series of successive events, which, because of their rapidity, often appear static to the grosser senses. The picture on a television screen is a case in point. Perception itself is grounded in a succession of physiological events, and the coexistent patterns it reveals are built up by successive integrations.[15]

In each partial element, as we have already seen, the whole is immanent, for none has being or identity except in its relation to the rest and by virtue of its conformity to the structural principle governing the whole. While this is the case, however, and for this very reason, the part which expresses the structural principle is only a partial expression of it and is inadequate to the immanent totality because of its partial nature. Therefore, in its own self it demands supplementation. This demand manifests itself as a conflict or contradiction in the nature of the partial element. That nature is determined by the immanent principle of wholeness, yet equally, because of its fragmentariness and finitude, is inadequate to it and so far contradicts it. It is therefore impelled by this very internal discrepancy and conflict towards self-development and self-completion.

The deployment of the totality is, accordingly, a self-deployment. It cannot even begin unless the whole is already implicit and potential in the initial deposition; and once any element is posited, it exerts of its own nature an effort or *nisus* towards self-completion. This expresses itself in a progression from the partial element to what it excludes, the complementation which its partial nature demands, and from that to a union of the two in a more adequate totality. What is thus developing itself is the whole immanent in the part. Any attempt to conceive the latter as independent and self-sustaining will prove self-defeating and fatal. The immanence of the whole in the part moves it from partiality through contradiction to supplementation and augmentation.

At the same time, the partial and inadequate phases cannot be abandoned and lost, but must be preserved in their successors. An ordered series, to be a series, must as it proceeds somehow retain and incorporate in the subsequent phases those upon which they have supervened. Otherwise the series would not be continuous nor any ordered structure come to light. This "sublation" of the earlier in the later is already implicit in the overlap of related terms, for the overlap is obviously included in the subsequent term. As already noted, if each phase of a succession passed away and were utterly obliterated as it passed, no structure or ordered series could emerge at all. The earlier phases must progressively be integrated into the unity of the later; but, as we have been warned, this is no mere progressive aggregation or col-location, because the terms in relation, the elements organized together, mutually determine one another, so that as the progression proceeds the earlier phases taken up into the later are modified and transformed. Later forms are more developed, more complete, more fully articulated, and more thoroughly integrated; they are therefore not just repetitions with augmentation of the earlier forms. As less adequate fulfilments of the universal principle, these earlier forms are superseded. In a definite sense, therefore, although the subsequent phases also express this principle and do so with a higher degree of completeness, they contradict and are in opposition to their predecessors insofar as the latter fail to present the structural principle adequately and are *not* what its essential nature fully requires.

Because the organizing principle determines the nature of every element in the system, each element in some way and to some extent reflects that principle and exemplifies it. Accordingly, in the same measure it is in itself a whole prefiguring the totality to which it belongs and of which it is a specific manifestation. It does and can do so only to some extent, for only in the complete whole is this manifestation adequate. Moreover, wholeness or organization is itself a matter of degree and systems vary in type forming a scale in which the characteristics here being described are less clearly apparent in the more rudimentary sorts of whole than in the more complex and highly developed. In a living organism, for instance, the elements are cells, themselves living organisms, clearly microcosms of the living macrocosm. Almost every distinguishable function in the whole can be paralleled by an analogous function in the part. But at the lower end of the scale this parallelism is much less obvious.

Aggregates may indeed be, and beyond some point always are, made up of aggregates, but it would seem odd to say that a marble in a bag of marbles was a microcosm of the whole to which it belongs, or that it exemplified the universal, "aggregate". In what sense, it might be asked, is the arm of a tetraktys a microcosmic representation of the whole? And how does it "exemplify" the principle of organization determining the five-pointed figure?

Of course, a marble is a whole of a kind, although not of the same kind as the filled bag; and the arm of a tetraktys is an isosceles triangle, which is a geometrical figure, a structure in itself. And, if we are liberal enough in interpreting our principles we may argue that in these cases, too, the whole is made up of wholes that exemplify the same universal. But to argue thus would be to miss the main point of the objection, which is that in a system the parts do not always seem to reflect, each in itself, the whole to which they contribute.

Here a caveat must be issued. Aggregates, so viewed, are abstractions in which important, if not always obvious, features are neglected and overlooked, even when they are not denied. The elements of which I have been speaking are elements of wholes, and it is only as such that they exemplify the principle of order and replicate (in some degree) the pattern of the whole. A marble in a bag is not just a marble in isolation, but one held together with others in a constraining envelope. It registers pressures and exerts resistance, and all these factors taken together do represent the whole structure of the enclosed group, even if only schematically. The triangle which forms the arm of a tetraktys is, of course, an instance of triangularity, but as such it is an instance of a different universal and an element in a different system from what it is as part of the tetraktys. There it is not just an isosceles triangle, but one so constructed that, when its sides are produced and similar triangles are erected on them appropriately, a new and more complex figure results—a five-pointed star. So, each arm of the complex figure must be regarded not merely as a triangle but as an element in the whole configuration, which takes on a new and different aspect within its context. Its microcosmic character is its presage, through the interrelation of its sides and angles, of the more complex figure. This is, indeed, largely proleptic and is hardly apparent to the casual glance, but the system is no more than geometric and cannot be expected to display with much adequacy the full nature of organized wholeness.

It must, further, be remembered that we are not dealing here with abstract universals, but with systems. The instances of abstract universals simply repeat one another. Every marble is just another marble, every triangle a triangle. But each exemplification of a principle of organization differs from every other, and it is by their mutual complementarity that they form a whole. This complementarity is reflected in the very incompleteness of each part and so makes it a rudiment of the totality. Isolated from the system to which it belongs, the part is no longer what it was within the configuration and is then no longer a microcosm nor an exemplification of the principle of order. It may well belong to a different system and express and exemplify that. So Schroedinger argued that an electron ejected from an atom by the impact on it (or absorption by it) of a photon is no longer the same particle as when it was an integral part of the atom, but becomes an element in a new and different energy system.

Systems themselves differ in order of complexity and elaboration; the different types of system (the specifications of systematicity) constitute a scale of graded forms. Spatiotemporal systems are more elementary than energy systems, and energy systems are less elaborate and are on a lower level of the scale than organic systems. Each level includes and adapts to its own requirements the properties of its predecessors; and as we ascend the scale it become steadily more apparent that the elements are microcosmic exemplifications of the wholes in which they occur. Thus we may say of system in general, as well as of every system in particular, that, because the whole is immanent in the part, each part exemplifies the universal principle of order and is a microcosmic premonition of the whole to which it belongs.

For this same reason, as the whole is discursively elaborated, each element or moment, as it is deployed in turn, displays the character of a premonitory or provisional whole, a microcosmic reflection of the macrocosm in which it is component; and the process of exposition reveals itself as a series of wholes, developing progressively from one phase (or revelation) of the ultimate totality to another more adequate and more complete expression of its organizing principle. The all-embracing totality thus differentiates itself as a whole into a scale the phases of which are themselves in some degree wholes, increasing from one stage to the next in adequacy and completeness. It is hierarchical: what Leibniz and Whitehead described as an organism composed of organisms. And the discursive process of its self-deployment (or self-differentiation) moves through a succession of wholes, each a specific exemplification of the universal principle of structure which pervades the entire scale. And as each phase in the advancing progression is more adequate to the nature of the final totality which is its outcome than are its predecessors in the series, the scale is one of degrees of wholeness and integration mounting through the successive specifications of the self-actualizing universal.

This process from part to whole, from inadequate to more adequate, through contradiction and reconciliation, is a dialectical development, the general characteristics of which we are now in a position to enumerate.

V

Summary and Exemplification

(i) Each phase of the process is a provisional whole determined in its specific character by the principle of structure governing the universal totality. As having the ultimate totality immanent in it, it is a specific exemplification of that totality, and (what is only another aspect of the same thing), as expressing the universal principle of structure, it is a specific application of that principle. Accordingly, each phase ranks as a species of the generic concept and all of them together constitute the self-specification of the whole.

(2) Each successive phase is a more complete whole and is more complexly and more intensively integrated than its predecessor. Each manifests the generic principle more fully and more adequately than those which it succeeds. Consequently, they constitute a scale of degrees or gradations of adequation. Moreover, this scale is continuous, so that each phase merges with and grows into its successor.

(3) It follows from all this that the later phases include and supplement the earlier, which are presupposed by them. The progression grows, not simply by aggregation, but by incorporation and supplementation of what has been superseded. Nevertheless, the earlier phases *are* superseded, and the later therefore supervene as negating or contradicting them, especially what is only partial and inadequate in them. Therefore, they appear as mutual opposites, the more advanced cancelling out the less developed phases and making them obsolete.

(4) Yet, the later presuppose the earlier; they are continuous with them and develop out of them. Thus, they preserve in themselves what in the earlier phases was merely potential, supplementing and rounding out what was deficient and reconciling it in a fuller whole with what it had lacked and excluded.

(5) Thus, the immature phases are not preserved unchanged. In the developed phase the earlier heritage is transformed and what in it was merely implicit becomes explicit, what was merely potential becomes actual.

(6) The later phase is the more adequate exemplification of the generic principle and is thus the truest form as yet reached both of what was earlier expressed inadequately and of what has all along, throughout the scale of advancing forms, been progressively revealing itself—the universal structure.

(7) This, however, is always and in principle complete. It cannot be only partially whole (a contradiction in terms). Every partial and inadequate phase or moment in the course of the development is a part, or a phase, or a moment (however it is appropriate to characterize it) only by virtue of the principle of structure immanent and expressing itself in it. That principle is one of wholeness and is essentially complete and adequate to itself.

(8) Accordingly, the dialectical series cannot be indefinitely or interminably progressive. Its progression is measured by the degree of wholeness, integrity, and adequacy that the current phase displays.

Therefore, it is and can only be progressive towards a final culminating consummation.

(9) As this is the realization of everything that has hitherto been implicit and potential in every phase of its development, the consummation, while it is the culminating phase, is also, at the same time and by the same token, the entire process sublated and united in a single reality—the whole fully self-differentiated, the universal fully self-specified and particularized—a complete, explicit, self-maintaining, and absolute individual. Hence, it is both an end and process in one. it is a complete scale of forms, the phases and moments of the self-actualizing universal, and at the same time the final phase of the scale.

(10) Thus, the universal, which is the organizing principle of the whole, manifests itself in each of its differentiations, or specific differences, and in the scale as a whole. In each specific phase of the series it is more fully and adequately presented, its true character being progressively unfolded as they succeed one another. So it is the universal that is the variable running through the entire scale and is thus at the same time the matrix within which and out of which the terms in relation, the various moments of the whole, crystalize. It is the universal that was immanent from the beginning, and has been the directing and governing influence throughout the progression, which is continuously realizing itself more completely throughout the process, and emerges at the end fully fledged as the entire system of successive phases.

To exemplify: energy is matrix and its laws are the principles of motion in the physical world. It manifests itself as curvature in the space-time continuum, as radiant energy, various forms of which are associated with elementary particles, and these combine in the complex field which is the atom. It manifests itself likewise as gravitation governing the movement of matter in space, the formation and the motion of the heavenly bodies, and the structure of the universe generally. And, as modern physics demonstrates, the same physical principles are expressed equally in the microcosm and in the macrocosm, in particular the Principle of Exclusion, which determines the architecture as much of the whole world as of the atoms and molecules it contains, determining their progressive complications.[16] Every phase of the series is a manifestation of energy and in each successively the laws of motion, relativistic and quantum, are more fully revealed, the same principles of order being more adequately realized in more complex forms—in elementary particles, in atoms, in molecules, and in

chemical bonds and affinities between diverse substances, right up to
the complex macromolecules which make possible the self-
reproductive chemical cycles typical of living activity. The whole
physical world reveals itself to the physicist as a scale of forms
throughout which the principle of motion and order is ultimately the
formula determining the curvature of space-time.[17]

Such a scale of forms is itself a totality or structure and every
system resolves itself into such a scale of forms. A structure of this
kind, governed by a self-specifying universal principle, is rightly called
a "concrete universal". By "concrete" I mean whole or completely
specified, and a concrete universal is one which specifies itself (in
Hegel's phrase), "has its particularization in itself".

Earlier we saw that some forms of structure were more rudimentary than others, and, in fact, these forms themselves constitute a scale
from mere aggregation to complex organization, which is the self-
differentiation of the very concept of structure. The principle of
wholeness in a mere aggregate is simple togetherness. The aggregate is
grasped as a whole simply in view of some similar feature among its
elements—a uniformity which warrants their being grouped together.
It is the abstracted quality common to all the members of a class—the
basis of what we may term a class-concept or "abstract universal". This
is the universal of formal logic, and it is at this level of the dialectic that
formal logic operates.

But a systematic structure is not simply a class. It is no *mere* collection of particulars; nor is it simply a common property of its members.
The elements which make it up may have nothing in common except
their conformity to the principle of organization that determines the
structure of the whole—a principle of wholeness that requires difference, and one that specifies itself in a dialectical process of self-
deployment of its differences.

A structure, being a system of elements in relation, everything
which was said above of relations applies to it in detail. The scale of
forms that constitutes it, therefore, is the scale of degrees that links the
elements as terms of its constitutive relations. The continuum which is
the matrix of the relations, and which is unified by the element of identity running through the terms, is one and the same with the universal,
or generic principle of wholeness that specifies itself in the scale, and
the various types of relationship we have identified are all subject to the
features we have observed. These are aggregation, differentiation,
specification, opposition, and sublation. The terms of these relations,

and these relationships themselves as specific forms, overlap, and the continuum in which they are the singularities is heterogeneous and progressive; it is, in short, a dialectical process.

The logic of a dialectical scale, cannot, in the nature of the case, be a formal or symbolic logic because formalization presupposes a collection of atomic particulars as the form of the subject matter to which the logic applies, and that is a direct denial of the structural holism that underlies dialectical progression. Where such holism prevails, the commutative, associative, and distributive laws do not hold, and they are indispensable to formalization.

Moreover, holistic structure is not merely presupposed by dialectic. It is discovered by science and revealed as *fact*. It is revealed as a scale of forms, continuous from physical systems to chemical and from chemical to living, with the emergence in the latter of sentience and consciousness. Here the self-organizing activity, which is discernible from the physical beginnings in Pauli's Principle, centres itself on the self-conscious subject, and the ego, aware of itself as a product of natural development and as a finite entity in the world, has been generated from lower forms through a scale that is dialectical in structure. Further, it is a structure in which the universal principle of the whole, its essential nature, is most adequately revealed and realized in its most fully developed form, that which is in actuality what all the preceding forms are in potency. The human mind, with its conscious self-reflection, is a highly developed form; hence, the ego expresses more adequately than any less advanced phase in the scale, the true character of the whole. The self-reflective subject of consciousness is thus an active manifestation of the universal principle of the entire gamut of nature, it epitomizes and reflects the whole, yet is at the same time, a form in the scale, highly developed at a late stage, and also the expression and self-revelation of the ultimate self-specifying universal. The difficulties besetting transcendentalism have thus been overcome, while the element of truth which it harbours is clarified and confirmed, and its achievements have been preserved in the dialectical conception of the world and of mind.

First, natural forms generate thinking beings; next, thinking beings bring their living activity to fruition in knowledge and action based upon self-reflective consciousness. This discloses in science the nature of the world that has engendered them. Science thus transpires as the truth of that world,[18] and further reflection finally discovers all this to itself philosophically, revealing the logical structure of its knowledge as a scale of forms such as we have been describing[19]—a scale in which the last form is the true and formative principle of all those preceding. This last form, moreover, is the form of the self-reflective knowledge itself—its logic. Logic therefore, does indeed, as Wittgenstein declared, show forth the form of the fact; but the form it shows forth is not (as he maintained) that of an aggregation of atomic simples, but of a dialectical scale.[20] The logical form of knowledge, as of the facts of nature, cannot in the last resort be that of symbolic logic, which at best displays only the form of congregated atomic particulars. Dialectical logic, on the other hand, cannot be formalized or set out as an algebraical calculus, for this reason, and it is hardly surprising that all attempts to formalize Hegel's logic have failed. Perhaps the most valiant has been that of Michael Kosok,[21] but it is unsuccessful partly because of faulty interpretation of the logical procedure, giving insufficient attention to the implications of *Aufheben*, and partly because, even were his interpretation correct, no effective algorithm emerges from the attempted symbolization. Not Wittgenstein nor Russell, therefore, but Hegel provides the model for a logic adequate to science and rational thinking: that is, a dialectical scale of categories which are themselves the principles of structure and the essential form both of the natural and of the intellectual world.

In this ultimate phase, however, form and content are no longer distinguishable. The world is a dialectical scale and so is our knowledge of it. Its form is the self-specification of the universal principle or concept of the whole, and that *is* its content. The content is dialectical and scalar because it is a system, an organized whole, of which that self-specification is the universal form. Logic is, therefore, no mere abstract schema of principles—it is not simply formal—but a concrete theory revealing the ultimate nature of the content of the world, for it is the outcome of the dialectical development, the complete course of which is the world, and is the most adequate expression of that principle of order which has been realizing itself throughout the process. The concept or universal is not merely an abstraction, but is self-specifying, that is, concrete. So it spans the whole scale up to itself as the self-awareness of the scale. It is the logic of nature, of science, of mind, of philosophy and, *ipso facto*, of logic.

Notes

1. It does not follow, however, that mathematics is irrelevant or inapplicable in such cases, but (as Hegel strove to demonstrate) the fundamental

principles implicit in the type of mathematics used differ from the presuppositions of formal logic outlined in the preceding chapters.

2. Cf. *De Revolutionibus Orbium Coelestium*, Prefatory letter to Pope Paul III.

3. Cf. *Appearance and Reality*, ch. III.

4. Critics of Bradley for the most part ignore or fail to appreciate the fact that his analysis follows from the commonly made assumption that relations are either external, falling between their terms, or internal, falling within them. Cook Wilson, for instance, in *Statement and Inference*, discovers, by reference to examples, that relations are not external, and assumes forthwith that he has refuted Bradley, ignoring the fact that Bradley's critique also covers the examples cited. But, although he does not say so, Cook Wilson may have sensed that there is also something about internal relations that Bradley had missed.

5. Cf. *Ethical Studies*, ch. I.

6. Cf. *Our Knowledge of the External World*, ch. I.

7. This is because, as we learn from Relativity Theory, there is no simultaneity at a distance, and time and movement are integral to the very essence of space.

8. Cf. my *Foundations of Metaphysics in Science*, ch. XXII, §§ 3–8.

9. Cf. *Process and Reality* (Cambridge, 1929), pp. 421–423:
Definition 10: A set of regions is called an "abstrative set," when (i) any two members of the set are such that one of them includes the other non-tangentially, (ii) there is no region included in every member of the set. . . .
Definition 13: A geometrical element is a complete group of abstractive sets. . . .
Definition 16: A geometrical element is called a "point," when there is no geometrical element incident in it.
Cf. also *The Concept of Nature* (Cambridge, 1930), p. 92.

10. The idea of ownership, for instance, is continuously linked with those of labour, possession, inheritance, sale and transfer.

11. *Foundations of Metaphysics in Science*, p. 462.

12. *Space, Time and Gravitation* (Cambridge, 1950), pp. 157f.

13. What has been described above as an open-ended system must not be confused with what is called in physics and chemistry an "open system". The latter is the maintenance of a constant structure in a flux of matter and

energy. The sense of "open" here is different from that intended in the text, for what the physicists call an open system I am describing as closed. What its wholeness consists in is the cohesion and constancy of the structure which is maintained, and is not affected by the constant flux of its constituent matter and energy. A living organism is an eminent example of this kind of open system, yet it is equally an eminent instance of the sort of system I wish to classify as closed.

14. Cf. Jean Piaget, *The Psychology of Intelligence* (London, 1950), p. 79.

15. This has been copiously demonstrated both by physiological and by psychological experiment: to draw attention to only a few of many examples, cf. Sir Frederick Bartlett's experiments reported in *Remembering, A Study in Experimental and Social Psychology* (Cambridge, 1967), pp. 23ff.; J. J. Gibson, *The Perception of the Visual World* (Cambridge, MA, 1950), pp. 157–158; *Experiments in visual Perception*, ed. M. D. Vernon (Harmondsworth, 1966), pp. 327–339.

16. Cf. Sir Arthur Eddington, *The Philosophy of Physical Science* (Cambridge, 1939), pp. 176ff.; Sir Edmund Whittaker, *From Euclid to Eddington* (Cambridge, 1949) p. 194. Also D. W. Sciama, *The Unity of the Universe* (London, 1959); Fritjof Capra, *The Tao of Physics* (London, 1975), ch. X; Paul Davies, *God and the New Physics* (London, 1983), chs. 11, 13.

17. Cf. Sir Arthur Eddington, *The Expanding Universe*, p. 101.

18. Cf. *Hypothesis and Perception*, ch. XII.

19. Cf. *ibid.* and *The Foundations of Metaphysics in Science*, pp. 489–493.

20. In his later philosophy, Wittgenstein abandons this atomistic metaphysic and adopts a position similar (at least by implication) to what is advocated in succeeding chapters of this book. Cf. *On Certainty* (Blackwell, Oxford, 1969), 102–105, 117–118, 121–126, 140–141, 225, 234, 247, 410, 603, where knowledge and certainty are said to rest upon the total system of the experienced world.

21. Cf. Michael Kosok, "The Formalization of Hegel's Dialectical Logik," in *Hegel*, ed. Alasdair MacIntyre (New York, 1972).

Chapter 9

Negation and the
Laws of Thought

I

Identity and Difference

In all logic, negation is of primary importance, and the history of philosophical attempts to grasp its nature is a long one. If it is treated as bare denial, as sheer obliteration of what is negated, difficulties arise, both semantic and metaphysical, which have been recognized ever since Parmenides, which were exploited by the Sophists, and which began to be resolved by Plato in the *Theaetetus* and the two dialogues to which Parmenides and Sophist afforded names. In the *Sophist*, Plato identified the negative (or "Not-being") as "the Other," in effect the complement of a finite element in a differentiated whole.

Formal logic overlooks both the difficulties and their historical resolution. It treats negation merely as a logical operator, as a mere striking out or erasure of the negated term, whereas in dialectical logic it is always significant negation: that is, it has positive as well as negative import. In formal logic $\sim p$ simply denies that p is true; $\bar{a}$ simply deletes a., and it has no affirmative force. In dialectical logic this is never the case. To negate is to indicate an alternative, a neglected complement; it is to delineate a determination and to fix a definitive character. Negation is a necessary feature of all systematic

157

structure, without which it has no coherent function, and within which it is the instrument of specification.

Every continuum, we have seen, requires distinction of parts, subject to their continuity and overlap; and distinction involves negation. Its most elementary formulation is "this not that", which corresponds to the figure-and-ground configuration, the minimal object of sensory perception.[1] This configuration is a primitive relational whole to which both terms are integral. The negative does not and cannot function without either, hence its positive as well as its negative force. It does not simply eliminate and leave a sheer void in place of the negated term; and even if it did, that would have some positive significance as a defined empty space. The essential point is that negation differentiates between the elements of a system, or, what we have found to be the same thing, between the gradations of a scale of continuously diverging forms. it sets the distincta in mutual contrast and so makes them contraries. It excludes one from the other and so makes them contradictory opposites. It defines each in terms of the other and so makes them complementaries.

In a dialectical scale the differing degrees in which the universal manifests itself are its specific forms. They are thus species of the genus (or generic essence), and so they rank as distinct elements of the system. As mutually complementary they are contraries.[2] But they also exclude one another and the level of gradation appropriate to one is inappropriate and inimical to any other. They are in this respect contradictories. Negation, which differentiates them, denotes either or both of these relationships. Not-A, as substitute for A, is its contradictory; as complementary of A, is its contrary. It is always both, for as complement it can never be substitute, and as contradictory it is always complement. The substitution of not-A for A is what the Law of Non-contradiction forbids; their complementarity is what the Law of Excluded Middle affirms. The Law of Identity, we shall presently find is dependent upon both of the other two, and not, as is traditionally maintained, *vice versa*.

But the phases of a dialectical scale also overlap. They are degrees in the scale, which is a continuum. What negates any one of them, therefore, also affirms it, as well as its opposite (or complement), for not only are both specifications of the same genus, but, as such, they are mutually constitutive and definitory. Each is indispensable to the other if either is to be what it is. Its negative is therefore an aspect, or moment, of its own affirmative being and has positive implications for its identity.

What exemplifies a principle of order in one way, by that very fact, excludes from that place in the scale any other exemplification. It is its identical self by virtue of such exclusion. On the other hand, the exclusion is two-edged, for the opposed exemplifications determine and define one another and overlap. Consequently, each makes the other what it is. The different identity of each is essential to their determinate series, A is not B (or C or D . . .), and by that exclusiveness is self-identically A. It is the first letter of the alphabet and thus can occupy no other position in the series. But what makes it the first is the fact that all the other letters succeed it in their prescribed order, each in its proper place in the series. It is not B, because it is the predecessor of B; but as predecessor it presages B, and so B's immediate proximity to it is what makes it A. If C were the successor, the preceding letter would be, not A, but B. Hence its identity is determined precisely by its differences, and by its precise differences or, in other words, by its systematic relations to its other(s). The differences, as features of the system, dictate the identities—A differs from B by being before it, and is A, and no other letter, because it comes first. It is this interdependence of identity and difference that makes negation significant and forbids the assertion of a bare and abstract identity excluding all differences, or sheer difference excluding all ground. The essential point is that the ground of both identity and difference is the structure of the relational system to which both belong, and it is the principle of order that determines the identity of the differing terms.

Identity has two forms or aspects, both of which involve negativity. The first is the identity of differences in a system, the identity of the whole, which is entirely constituted by its moments of specific self-manifestations. This identity is not anything apart from the differences. it is not a uniform and unchanging core running through or alongside them. As already explained, the system is the continuum of specific grades by which a universal principle of order explicates itself. The universal is the element of identity and it realizes itself only in its diverse modes or moments. It is thus an identity of differences, an identity realizing itself in and through differences. In other words, it is identity negated and reaffirmed in the negation—negated by its numerous particularization, and reaffirmed as the whole which is specified in them.

The second is the identity of each moment or specific form. This is determined by the universal principle of order, through the interrelation of its moments, which it governs. The identity of the part (the phase or specification), therefore, depends on what it excludes and on

what excludes it—on its relation to its other. It is negative relation to
self, or identity through difference from its neighbours in the scale. Its
identity depends on its position in its context and is a function of the
diverging series of terms in the continuum. In short, it depends on
what it negates and what negates it. This is the significance and the effect of the overlap of terms in relation and of graded phases in the scale
of forms. Once more, identity is inseparable from difference and has a
negative moment.

As every phase in the scale is a provisional whole premonitory of
the ultimate totality, it must be evident that both forms are really but
two aspects of one relationship: that between the universal and its particulars. It is the identity of the whole as manifested in and through the
parts and their interrelation within it as the scale of degrees of its self-
specification. The principle of structure, which unites the whole and
constitutes its identity, equally identifies the parts in their relation to
one another. The universal, or generic essence, which realizes itself
and is immanent throughout the scale, and which sustains the continuity of the manifold in which it is embedded, is the element of identity.
It evidences itself in the overlap of terms and phases and, as principle
of order, determines the specificity of particular gradations in the scale
of its self-manifestations.

Identity is, accordingly, the inner aspect of diversity and is expressible only in terms of difference. It is, so to speak, the by-product
of negation. The Law of Identity is but an obverse assertion of the
Laws of Noncontradiction and Excluded Middle, and all three are
merely abstract statements of the principles, in generalized form, of interrelation in a system, without which none of them has coherent
significance. The reciprocity of identity and difference is not to be
denied; each is equally necessary to the other, but the indispensability
of negation to both is what needs to be stressed.

All that we have said above is anathema to the formal logician.
Identity in and through difference is to him blatent contradiction which
he shuns. Yet the contradiction is of his own making, if only inadver-
tent and repressed. He takes what are really moments in a whole, what
are in truth overlapping phases in a scale of forms, to be separate, independent, and abstractly identical particular entities. For him, each
"thing is what it is and not another thing"—a truth only valid under conditions he is excluding—and he gives the negative no positive force.
But there can be no bare, absolute, and independent identity and the
attempt to maintain a doctrine in which A is A without qualification or

external reference leads to contradiction and absurdity. A world of atomic particulars might seem to warrant such doctrine, and that perhaps is why it is advocated by formal logicians. Yet even such a conception of the world is subject to dialectical stirrings, for a collection (or aggregate) of atomic particulars is itself a form of system, although it occupies a very humble rank in the scale of structural complexity. Consequently, even the attempt to identify the particular finite atoms as mutually independent and exclusive involves the definition of each in terms of its relation to the rest. The attempt to maintain their independence, in short, tacitly rests upon an appeal to their interdependence, and contradictions unavoidably arise—the very contradictions which their mutual separation is designed to avoid.

To assert that A is A where there is no difference at all between the referent of the first symbol and that of the second is to make no significant statement. But if there is some difference, the identity is rooted in the system to which the differences belong. For example, if the first A is "the evening star" and the second is "the morning star", clearly there is a difference, namely in the times of appearance. To identify *these* would involve contradiction. But the interrelation of the movements of the planets and their positions in the solar system at different times enable us to identify these two appearances as of the same planet, Venus. It is an identity in differences, which is determined by the system, and without the system the statement, "The evening star is (the same as) the morning star" would be either meaningless or contradictory. The identity of the planet, Venus, is likewise dependent on the system. It can be identified only with reference to its peculiar motion (itself a system of different positionings) and (or) to its successive distances from the sun and the earth (another, or the same, system of differences), and (or) to its differences from the other planets in the system—its place in the succession of planets according to their distances from the centre; or else, by its internal properties, which constitute a system in their mutual relations. Without any such reference, Venus cannot be identified, and the statement, "Venus is Venus" is, as Hegel avers, a silly tautology without assignable meaning.

Only distincts can be identified. "A is A" requires at least two As; otherwise, the proposition is unproponible. Unless some distinction is made, it is impossible to say or to know what is being identified with (or as) what. "A is A" is a proposition, and if it is to have meaning, the terms must be different as well as identical. "A" by itself is not a proposition; and if I identify A without formulating any proposition, I must still recognize it as something distinguished in a context (as what I have met before, or as what may be thus and thus defined and described). Without distinction of some sort, not even immediate perception is possible, and then the identities are such only in mutual contrast. In Hegelian language, identity is always "negative identity with self", implying and uniting distincts. A single undifferentiated and indistinguishable content is no content and cannot be identified. To be identified it must be distinguished from what it is not, and if it is identified in different contexts *they* cannot be the same. Accordingly, as a statement of bare identity, A is A contradicts itself, for unless each A is distinct from the other, the formulation of the statement is impossible, yet if they are distinct and are understood as excluding all difference, it is contradictory.

"But in reality," it may be countered, "there are not two As; there is only one thing to which two symbols refer." The identity of any one entity, however, is subject to the conditions set out above—it is what it is only in its context and is defined only by its relations to its other—to deny which would be to destroy it. So each of the two symbols must equally refer to A in relation to not-A, yet for the statement to be significant, the reference must be different in each case, contradicting the bare identity that is being assumed. The reference of the two symbols cannot be utterly the same or else they cannot be two distinct tokens. There can be no relation if there is only one term, and to identify two implies at once some kind of distinction, while to repeat without implicit difference is to sacrifice meaning. There must be two temporal phases, or two spatial aspects, or two different appearances, or two inseparable moments of what is essentially one, that are being indicated by the repetition of the symbol, and identity is asserted in this difference. But if identity is held to be wholly devoid of difference, two distinct terms cannot be thus sheerly, absolutely, and abstractly identified without contradiction.

If the internal self-identity of A is thought of as pure uniform sameness, it is a homogeneous continuum, which we have already found to be an incoherent concept. The uniform sameness of distinct elements is a contradiction, and within such a uniform field whatever is singled out and identified as A must be identical with anything else that may be identified in the field; that is, with not-A. A and not-A are thus identified and the Law of Noncontradiction is violated. If this is denied, then within the field there are no distincta, and so it is not a field, not a continuum, and it collapses (as we saw earlier) into non-

entity without identity of any sort. If, on the other hand, *A* is taken to
be internally differentiated, its identity will be the unity of these differences and will not be mere sameness. Their diversity will contradict
the assumption of abstract self-sameness, while at the same time the
identity of each of the differences will be subject to the same conditions. Any such differentiation, as we have demonstrated, resolves
itself into a scale of forms, which are overlapping gradations; so they
will be both identical and different, as determined within the system.

II

Dialectic and the Law of Contradiction

Identity is thus always identity of differences, or identity in difference, or identity through difference and to insist that it is not is at
once to become embroiled in contradictions. This is not because the
Law of Noncontradiction fails to hold or because it has been
repudiated—quite the contrary. If the law did not hold, no such contradictions could emerge. It is because it does hold and because contradiction is inadmissible, blank identity is an untenable idea. What is
at fault are not the Laws of Identity and Noncontradiction but the manner of their interpretation, their misconstrual as holding in abstraction
from system and in isolation from the negativity that gives them
legitimate meaning.

Dialectical logic is far from abandoning or abjuring the Laws of
Thought. It affirms them in their mutual interdependence as the in-
cidents and consequences of systematic structure, which is fundamental to them all. They are aspects and products of negativity, which is
the differentiating principle of structural wholeness, and unless they are
observed the coherence of the structure disintegrates. The coherence
of the system is the mark of its wholeness and is the foundation of all
consistency within it. Consistency based on bare, abstract identity is
inconsistent, because, as we have seen, bare, abstract identity proves
on analysis to be either meaningless or a contradiction. Accordingly,
the common belief that coherence depends on the consistency of propositions conforming to some abstract law of identity is a mistake. The
converse is the case: that consistency of propositions depends on their
coherence, their mutual support and implication.

The applicaton of the Laws of Thought in dialectical logic is not
difficult to recognize. What each element in a system is and does is

determined by the principle of organization that fixes its place in the structure. Conversely, the nature of each element determines its position, and both are functions of that same principle of organization. If the attempt is made to maintain (or assert) one element in isolation from the others on which it is so intimately dependent—or if it attempts to maintain itself in isolation—the principle of order, which makes it what it is, is at once both denied (in the attempt) and yet tacitly asserted in the identity of the selected element. A contradiction is thus immediately generated by the neglect of the reciprocal determination of the system.

Alternatively, assert one element (*A*) in the place of another (*B*) and at once the principle of order which determines both and their interrelation is implicitly affirmed yet explicitly denied, because *A* is then related to its neighbours on a different principle (while being maintained as *A* on the original principle), or else it is construed as *B* on the true principle, while still being identified as *A*—which contradicts it. *A* is thus affirmed in a context where it could not be *A*. This is not because *A* and *B* sheerly exclude each other, for they are mutually determinant and internally related, but because this very interdependence forbids their mutual transposition. Their identity is identity within the system and it involves diversity and negativity. Contradiction is the assertion of identity without the system, either of a dependent moment in isolation, or (what amounts to the same violation of principle) by transposition of mutually dependent moments irrespective of context. Self-consistency, therefore, depends on the structural order, and if it is understood narrowly to demand sheer self-identity in total abstraction from all differences, it degenerates into self-contradiction, not because the laws of thought do not hold, but because they are laws of systematic interrelation without which there could be neither identity nor difference, neither consistency nor contradiction.

The persistent and incredulous may still object: "Even if we concede that the nature of things depends on their place in the system and that they are defined by what they are not, this could not be so unless every position in the system where identically what and where it is and differed from every other precisely for this reason." But the system is not a kind of scaffolding or framework fixed independently of its constituents, and they are not attached to it, as it were, from the outside. It is nothing apart from its elements, for it is the universal principle of organization expressing and revealing itself only in the interdetermining reciprocal action and relationships of its particulars. Without these there can be no "fixed positions" in the system, nor could the crucial points even in an external framework be identified apart from their own mutual relations. However the system is conceived, the relations between its elements are continuous and the terms overlap, and only in reference to this overlap can the Laws of Thought consistently be interpreted and understood. In the logical system, identity and difference, positivity and negativity, are concepts in overlapping relation, and the law that *A* is *A* and not not-*A* indicates a structural whole in which identity and difference merge in their *Wechselbestimmung.*

True self-consistency is the recognition of the identity in and through difference governed by the principle of order constituting the system. It requires the following out of the dialectical process of self-specification of the concrete universal. It is only in terms of this organizing principle that one can determine what is and what is not consistent, what is and what is not contradictory; and it is only with reference to the context that consistency and contradiction have specifiable meaning.

It is not, however, to be forgotten that system, structure, organization, and order are all features of the self-specification of the concrete universal, which always takes the form of a dialectical scale. It is nothing static or fixed, but is a continual and continuous discursus, within which there is a constant interplay of contradiction and consistency, varying according to the context and the level of dialectical development to which they are relevant. So that what seems consistent at one level of abstraction develops contradictions when viewed more concretely, and what is contradictory in the lower phase can be reconciled in the higher.

III

Criticisms and Misconceptions

Misconception of the function of negation and contradiction is the root of widespread misunderstanding and faulty interpretation of dialectic, among its defenders as well as among its detractors. The former are mostly Marxist theorists who base their arguments on the wrong reasons or, at best, on half-truths. Lenin advocates dialectical logic in preference to formal on the ground that the latter is based on the Laws of Identity and Noncontradiction, which hold, he says, only of static and unchanging subjects but are violated by the phenomena of motion and life (hence Zeno's paradoxes). Formal logic, he therefore maintains, can be used only in relation to the immobile and inanimate, while dialectical logic, which rejects the Laws of Identity and Noncontradiction, recognizing the inherent contradictions in the nature of things, is the true logic of movement and life. In this there is but half the truth, for as we have seen movement and life are not the precondition of dialectic, but are forms of its manifestation or expression in spatiotemporal existence. Dialectic is prior to movement, as it is to time and change, and it establishes the Laws of Identity and Noncontradiction, so far from rejecting them. Marxist philosophers, however, follow Lenin persistently; and their opponents attack them by declaring first that motion and change do not violate the Law of Contradiction, and secondly that to reject the traditional Laws of Thoughts subverts all reasoning and renders all discourse impossible.[3] Both sides, however, argue beside the point, while each clings to half the truth. Both err in asserting that dialectical logic repudiates the Law of Noncontradiction, which is in fact as essential to it as it is to formal logic.

The source of these errors is now fully apparent. Both sides are wrong, the first because they confess to a sin that is not committed and excuse it for the wrong reason, the second because dialectical logic, rather than violating the Laws of Thought, establishes their true foundation by demonstrating the proper function of negation and the interdependence of identity and difference. The formal logician rightly contends that violation of the Laws of Thought renders discourse incoherent and impossible, but fails to see that for that very reason dialectic, which elaborates the conditions of coherence, establishes the fundamental laws more firmly than formal logic itself.

Karl Popper provides a flagrant example of this failure in his essay, "What is Dialectic?".[4] His misunderstandings and misrepresentations of Kant, Hegel, and Marx, and generally of the nature of dialectic, are so gross that, but for the great authority that Sir Karl Popper's name carries, refutation would be supererogatory. Only the untutored and unphilosophical, ignorant of the writings he criticizes, whom Popper confesses he prefers as his audience, are at all likely to be deceived by the criticism he offers. Sir Karl proceeds throughout on the presuppositions of formal logic that we have laid bare above and which dialectical logic supersedes. He understands the Law of Noncontradiction in its abstract and inadequate sense, and then castigates Hegel and Marx for allegedly tolerating and even advocating contradiction and for asserting its ubiquitous presence in thought and reality. This is, of course, crude misrepresentation. What Hegel (and also Marx) assert is the prevalence and ineradicability of negativity in system and the inevitable contradiction involved in efforts to maintain as absolute what is only partial and finite. Sir Karl attempts to refute them by showing that contradiction has deleterious effects on thought and discourse, which nobody should wish to dispute; but his demonstration that from a self-contradictory proposition any and every proposition can be deduced (even so far as it is defensible) rests on the doctrine of material implication and the assumption that propositions are atomic and intrinsically unrelated. It is, therefore, altogether irrelevant. In any case, Sir Karl is flogging a dead horse, because, as I have shown, self-contradiction is no more tolerated by dialectical than by formal logic, and it is this alleged toleration on which the whole of Popper's argument revolves. Clearly, he has not the slightest inkling of the nature and relevance of significant negation or of the mutual implications in system of complementaries, contraries, and contradictories. Thus, he derogates legitimate examples of dialectical relationship without understanding them, and lumps them together with illegitimate examples like that which he quotes from Engels ($x \text{ x } -x = x^2$).

Popper has an unfortunate habit of putting between quotation marks, in proximity to the names of those he criticizes, statements that are not theirs, giving the impression that he is quoting them, when he is in fact misrepresenting them.

Kant is alleged to have maintained that the world is mind-like, because, as we experience it, the mind has imposed upon its sensuous material its own form and principles of order—"a world digested, a world formed by our own minds." But Kant nowhere says that the world is mind-like, nor ever asserts, as Popper maintains that he and his successors do, that this is why the mind can know the world. Kant does argue that we can experience objects only because and so far as our minds impose categories and schemata upon the manifold of sense: but what the world is like, apart from the way in which it appears to us, he declares we cannot know. We do form ideas about what goes beyond our experience. Kant calls these ideas of reason, but thinks that their validity is not scientifically substantiable. He does barely suggest that, for all we can tell, the unknown cause of *a posteriori* and of *a priori* knowledge may be the same. But Popper's representation of Kant's position is distorted and misleading.

When Sir Karl comes to Hegel his misconceptions and misrepresentations are far worse. He attributes to Hegel what he calls a "philosophy of identity", whereas that was the title applied to Schelling's doctrine, and accepted by him, but adversely criticized by Hegel, who rejected it as one-sided. Popper quite falsely attributes to Hegel the contention (again in quotations marks) "that contradictions do not matter" and that therefore Kant's critique of reason need not be taken seriously. What Hegel does say is that Kant's critique applies quite rightly to the understanding, which does fall into contradiction; but, he maintains, Kant erred in applying it to reason. Reason, Hegel asserts, is able to reconcile the oppositions in which the understanding persists, by seeing the opposites in their proper mutual supplementation and interdetermination. Popper, of course, cannot accept this, because he remains blinkered at the level of what Hegel identifies as the understanding. He alleges, further, that Hegel declared the world to be mind-like (as Kant supposedly did) and that because reason tolerates contradictions, so the world also harbours them. But Hegel said none of these things.

Oddly, Popper shows more sympathy for and approval of Marx, such as is hardly to be expected of the author of *The Open Society and its Enemies*, and he attributes all Marx's worst errors to the influence of Hegel. But to allege that Marx held the mind to be material because he accepted the view that the world was mind-like and the world is basically physical, is a parody too ludicrous to be entertained. Geoffrey Mure once said of *The Open Society and its Enemies* that in it "Professor Popper has thrown all scholarship to the winds." Here again, in this essay, he has done likewise, in extraordinary contrast to his admirable work on the philosophy of science.

This is no place for an extended exposition of the theories of Kant, Hegel, and Marx, which if faithfully given would immediately reveal the half-truths and misrepresentations in Popper's polemic. Therefore, no further trouble need be taken to refute his criticism.

On the other hand those who seek to defend breach of the Law of Noncontradiction because motion and life do not conform to it are doubly mistaken; first because statements about movement and life do not violate it, and the facts of motion and change involve contradiction only because they are continuous processes of its overcoming—the process from imbalance (contradiction) to equilibrium (consistency); and secondly because the limits of formal logic are not what these apologists allege. True it is that dialectic is the appropriate theory of change and development, but it is not restricted to the dynamic and flowing, for it also makes room for coexistence and fixity. In neither case is the Law of Noncontradiction inoperative; and the limits of formal logic are set by the degree of its abstraction and not by its alleged applicability solely to the unmoving.

It is this indulgence by the formal logician in abstraction that violates the Law of Noncontradiction and not perverse toleration of absurdity by the dialectician, for it is a law fundamental to dialectics, one which holds and has proper significance only in a systematic context where pregnant meaning is given to both identity and difference in their mutual overlap. In abstraction from such systematic background, these terms do indeed contradict themselves. But to say this would itself be futile if the Law of Noncontradiction did not hold. It is very true that contradiction plays an important role in dialectic, but its significance is not in conflict with that which it has in formal logic. Neither the formal nor the dialectical logician should wish to deny that contradictions do in fact occur and that they are the mark of defect, whether in argument or in the structure of the real. Both formal and dialectical logicians seek to avoid contradiction in discourse and in action. In natural processes, contradiction is always an obstacle and an irritant; their persistent tendency is to prevent or to overcome it, and the urge of living activity is to eliminate it. The aim of reason is to remove contradictions just because they involve incoherence and conflict. But formal logic never reveals the ground of contradiction, alligning it merely with tautology as its opposite number, while dialectic elucidates the rational basis from which negation and contradiction derive their significance and importance.

Notes

1. And is also the form of incipient judgement.

2. In the traditional square of opposition contraries are universal and subcontraries particular. The former cannot both be true, the latter cannot both be false. But the reason why it may be false both that "All S is P" and that "No S is P" is that one or other of the subcontraries may be true. They are,

therefore, the genuine complementaries. Contrariety is an essential property of particulars, for they are mutually alternative instantiations of their universal. Strictly the universal has no contrary except the entire range of its particularization.

3. For a review of the dispute see A. A. Jordan, *Philosophy and Ideology* (Dordrecht, 1963), pt. IV, chs. 13–15.

4. *Mind*, XLIX, 1940. Reprinted in *Conjectures and Refutations* (London, 1963).

Chapter 10

Categories of
Perception

I

The Form of the Facts

The formal logician claims that his logic is free of metaphysical entanglements, but the claim cannot be sustained. We, on the other hand, insist that all logic has metaphysical implications, and that dialectical logic especially is inseparable from metaphysics—is, in fact, a metaphysic in its own right, because the structure of the world is itself dialectical, and human consciousness and knowledge are the dialectical outcome of natural processes. They are, therefore, forms in which the universal immanent in the processes of nature is more adequately and truly expressed than at the levels of physical and biotic existence. This is why science is the truth of nature.[1] Knowledge is not simply a representation—a sort of mirror image—of the natural world, though in some sense and to some extent, as will later appear, it is representative. It is the actual product and actualization of the potencies inherent in natural processes. As such, it is a more complete and adequate revelation of the true character of the natural world. For the dialectical series is essentially teleological, and the outcome is the explication and the truth of the preceding process. Knowledge, therefore, is the proper essence of its subject matter, not just the image of it, but the actual presentation in conscious form of its true reality. This, however, does preserve and sublate the actual form of the object and so recapitulates, at a higher level, processes that have gone before. Knowledge is thus at the same time representative, not as a copy of nature, but as its fruition and the developed form of its universal structural principle.

The recognition of this fact awaits the development in knowledge of that self-reflection that reveals, in its own activity, the immanent universal, which has specified itself and is still being specified in the dialectical scale. This reflective self-revelation in knowledge is its philosophical phase, in which logic is precisely the theory of the concept, or concrete universal; and as this is the sublation and the essential expression of the universal immanent throughout the scale, it is at once both logic and metaphysic. It is the theory of the structure of thought, of knowledge, and of the world all in one. We must expect it to review, therefore, the earlier phases of the scale, but to do so in the guise of thought-categories. As was said before, logic, just because it is the dialectical continuation of the cosmic process, reveals, or shows forth, the form of the fact, and that form is a dialectical scale. At the level of logic it is a scale of categories, which have been operative, unreflectively and often unrecognized, at lower levels.

These categories, however, embodied as they are in natural processes, have already been extracted thence by perception, which apprehends objects unreflectively as structured according to their principles. They are further put to use in more reflective form by the sciences whose employment of them is overt and deliberate. It is upon such forms of knowledge and their structure that logic reflects. What it recapitulates, therefore, is not directly the forms of nature, but these mediated by perception and science. A mediation which it sublates in its own dialectic. The principles of the earlier phases of knowledge are finally set forth in pure categorial form, the peculiar form of logic, as specifications of the concrete universal, for the explicit theory of the concept and its self-specification is logic.

The whole with which logic is concerned is the system of knowledge which gives meaning to every element of our common experience. Its task is to distill out of this the organizing principles (or universals) that determine its structure; and as it is one system, these principles are intrinsically interdependent, each being a specific differentiation of the universal principle governing the whole. We have seen that the structure must be dialectical and we have seen why. Our next step is to give some indication of the general course of the dialectic, as well as of the details of its specification.

But the system of knowledge is knowledge of an objective world acquired through the experience of an individual conscious of himself as a member in and product of the world he knows. Knowledge, therefore has (as it were) two dimensions. It is a level of experience that has developed through an evolutionary process, itself dialectical, from natural and unconscious rudiments; and it is also a developed system setting out the structure of the world of which it is the developed product. As both are dialectical in form, end and process, form and content, overlap and ultimately coincide as an identity of opposites. This has already been demonstrated in Chapter 8.

Knowledge, however, is in the nature of the case not all on one level of sophistication or of systematic articulation. It begins with perceptual immediacy, is elaborated systematically as science, becomes further reflective as epistemology, and still more refined as a series of logical categories. But in consequence of its dialectical form, each phase recapitulates (or sublates) its predecessors. Dialectic, therefore, is not only the logic of developed thinking, but also that of the less systematic levels in perception and common sense.

II

Being and Becoming

The first categories with which logic must concern itself are those of the most elementary forms of cognition; for, it is cognition as it emerges from sentience and the physiological activity of the organism, that reveals in consciousness the structure of the natural world. And the most elementary phase of cognition is sense-perception. The prior phases, even if classifiable as mental processes, are precognitive. Whatever is perceived has sense quality of some kind, so the categories of quality are those that first claim our attention. They are the categories of the immediately presented and intuitively grasped. The first of these categories is being.

That bare nothing cannot be thought was recognized by Parmenides at the dawn of Western philosophical speculation. To think nothing is not to think, and the very act of thinking reveals itself as being—*cogito ergo sum*. The act of thought is the self-evidence of being; and "nothing" can only be conceived in relation to it as an op-posited object. Thus it becomes "something" and ceases to be nothing. Consequently, being is the first category of cognition, as Hegel main-tained. But, as he further insisted, mere being, without discriminable character, is no identifiable object. It has no content and is altogether empty, identifiable in effect with nothing. Each of these categories in its very conception turns into its opposite, and their reciprocal transfor-mation is no more nor less than the activity of thought itself, which, in conceiving either, posits both in their mutual contrast and interchange (compare Fichte's *Wechselbestimmung*).

Being is thus a dynamic and not a static concept, and in its dynamic opposition and interchange with nonbeing it issues as Becom-ing. That, in its very nature, is the unity of being and nonbeing—the coming to be of what is not, and the ceasing to be of what was. Neither is independent of the other, for what comes to be does so through the passing away of its opposite. What we are describing here is not just the movement of thought, but equally that of its object, as has been demonstrated by contemporary physics, to which we shall turn in a moment.

Being is at once a universal concept, the most general and abstract, and also the designation of the universal object of cognition. So it is concept and object in one. And the transition from being to nonbeing and from nonbeing to being as becoming, in attaining stable dynamic equilibrium (for they are equivalent and coordinate) generates, or, as it were, precipitates, the distinguishable objects (determinate entities). This, too, is confirmed in the new physics, as we shall presently show. Being, nonbeing, and becoming, then, are the primary categories both of cognitive awareness and of the real.

Whatever is, must be somehow qualitied, and whatever has quality must be. At the physical level, qualities need not be (and, in fact, seldom are) perceptible. They may be such features as charge or spin, more appropriately, perhaps, termed states than qualities of the en-tities they characterize. But at the cognitive level, what has no quality is not perceived, is cognitively null. Altogether abstracted from qualitative character, being is utterly indefinite, and as such is in-distinguishable from—in fact, is—nothing. But whatever is distinguishable, is so only in virtue of its distinction from something else, from an other. It is so in virtue of negation and contrast, or demar-cation from what it is not. This identification in terms of difference is the logical discursus noticed earlier (in Chapter 9), a perpetual two-way reference from being to its negation (nonbeing), from is to is not . . ., which is the emergence or becoming of something definite. This logico-epistemic discursus among the first categories of being is revealed in nature in the physics of elementary particles, as well as in the psychological character of the percept.

In contemporary physics, energy and matter, field and particle, are equivalent; and in relativity theory, energy manifests itself as curvature of space-time, which is the universal field. What previously was regarded as the void (nothing) is now identified and interchangeable with being (energy and matter). "The field theories of modern physics," writes Fritjof Capra, "force us to abandon the classical distinction between material particles and the void."[2] W. Thirring concurs:

> The field exists always and everywhere; it can never be removed. It is the carrier of all material phenomena. It is the "void" out of which the proton creates pi-mesons. Being and fading of particles are merely forms of motion of the field.[3]

Physicists have found that virtual particles can come into being spontaneously out of the void in a vacuum, and disappear again into it, without the presence of any other strongly interacting particle, so that "the relation between the virtual particles and the vacuum is an essentially dynamic relation." Thus, being and nonbeing are identical for modern physicists, and their dynamic relationship is a becoming that spawns particles (determinate entities). "In the quantum world of potentiality, everything is becoming." So writes Edward Harrison.[4]

Even before the discoveries of modern particle physics, earlier scientists of our era expressed similar ideas, if in rather different language, establishing the same categories as valid of the physical reality as we shall find essential to perceptual thinking. This is what they say:

> We may picture the world of reality as a deep-flowing stream; the world of appearance is its surface, below which we cannot see. Events deep down in the stream throw up bubbles and eddies on the surface of the stream. These are the transfers of energy and radiation of our common life, which affect our senses and so activate our minds; below these lie deep waters which we can only know by inference. These bubbles and eddies show atomicity, but we know of no atomicity in the currents below.[5]

This is the imagery of Sir James Jeans, but others are less poetical and more technical:

> Imagine a sub-aether whose surface is covered with ripples. . . . Individual ripples are beyond our ken; what we can appreciate is a combined effect—when by convergence and coalescence the waves conspire to create a disturbed area of extent large compared with individual ripples but small from our Brobdingnagian point of view. Such a disturbed area is recognized as a material particle . . .[6]

Thus Sir Arthur Eddington; and Werner Heisenberg writes in yet more technical language:

> The final equation of motion for matter will probably be some quantized non-linear wave equation for a wave-field of operators that simply represents matter, not any specific kind of waves or particles. This wave equation will probably be equivalent to rather complicated sets of integral equations, which have "Eigenvalues" and "Eigensolutions," as the physicists call it. These Eigensolutions will finally represent the elementary particles . . .[7]

At the physical level, the energy matrix corresponds to what, at the logico-metaphysical level we are calling mere being. Its ceaseless and complex wave motion is becoming—a pulsating oscillation from being to non-being, as wave-motion vibrates from one pole to its opposite, resulting in irreducible quanta of action. These enfold upon themselves in the form of super-posed waves producing wave-packets, which behave in the general field as elementary particles. And so we get determinate entities.[8] Further, continuously increasing complexifications take us up the whole scale of natural forms, from atoms and molecules to crystals (periodic and aperiodic) and living cells, until we reach that high level of integrated organic structure and activity which is the living creature, registering in feeling the impinging causal influences of its surrounding world.

(2) Just as the form of integration of physical activity (energy) organized as a complex field or a consortium of elementary particles is (in the first instance) the hydrogen atom; just as the form of unity in which molecules combine is the leptocosm of the crystal; just as the form of unity of chemical cycles in a cell is the metabolism of the organism; so the form of unity of physiological activity fully integrated in a living being is sentience.[9] this is the most primitive phase of men-

tality as it emerges from the level specifically describable as physiological. It is the form of unity of the organic processes at a high level of integration and an intense level of activity.[10]

Sentience or feeling is the pervasive characteristic of mind, which persists at all levels and throughout its dialectical development. It is the matrix of all mental process—its "proximate matter" (to use an Aristotelian concept). But it is not yet cognition. Like the prior phases, of which it is the formal unity, and which are all dynamic processes, sentience too is a form of activity. It is the organism's activity as felt—the active registration of the impingement upon it of its environment, its own reactivity to it. As such, it is internally diversified, but as felt it is a unified totality within which the differences have yet to be delineated. This requires ordered selection, differentiation, contrast, and interrelation of qualitative distincta. The activity by which sentience thus differentiates and organizes itself is a specialization of its own functioning, namely the discursive activity of attention, which singles out particular qualitative elements and sets them in context. The organic needs and impulses are its initial guides, causing it to focus on particular sense-contents in turn and to set each against a felt background, organizing the sentient field into a figure-and-ground structure, which is the minimum requirement for cognition, or perception.[11]

It is not easy to define psychologically or to identify the physiological counterpart of attention, but it cannot be regarded as a merely mechanical process of sorting and singling out. Although it has a character analogous to a searchlight directed and focused upon an object, and although terms appropriate to light are often used to describe its effect, it is no mere illumination, because it is *cognitive*. It does not merely reveal an object, it grasps and assimilates it. In fact, it virtually creates the so-called datum, for apart from its selectivity no cognizable object exists, only the indiscriminate conglomerate of primitive sentience. Attention is no merely passive unveiling, but is an active comprehending of the discriminated elements in their mutual relation. Accordingly, it is (or involves) incipient judgement. The datum it creates is a "somewhat" in contrast with another (somewhat else), and this contrast is cognized, or apprehended. It is an awareness, not simply of the single datum, but of that in relation to its background, or other. It is the apprehension and inchoate intellectual articulation of a structured whole.

The principles of organization on which the sentient matrix is thus perceptually ordered so as to constitute objects of cognition are categories or concepts. Apart from such organization, primitive sentience is noncognitive—as Kant expressed it, "intuition without concepts is blind" (though "intuition" as he meant it, is something less primitive than mere sentience). The pure, indefinite, confused mass of feeling is qualitatively utterly indefinite. It is the mere "manifold of sense" of which Kant remarked that it is "as good as nothing." It is likewise the equivalent of what Hegel called pure being and which he, too, identified with nothing. It is only in the discursus of mutually contrasted contents, of "this" distinguished from "that," a figure on a ground, that perception of an object arises—perception of something definite in contrast to something else.

This contraposition of figure and ground, of the object centered by attention against a less distinct background, or, within attention, of contrasted qualities and levels, is a cognition entirely dependent upon the mutual mediation of the moments. It is a dynamic process of comparison and contrast, an activity or motion which is not improperly identified as becoming. The object comes to be for consciousness in this movement, and without it (as copious physiological and psychological evidence testifies)[12] no object is cognized. The object (or if one relishes the term the "datum") is created by attention,[13] and attention is the concentrated focus of the discursive activity.

Here then we discern the primary categories of perceptual knowledge: (i) being and nonbeing, (ii) becoming, the discursion between the first two, which generates (iii) a definite something in contradistinction from an other. That these categories are Hegelian should surprise nobody, for contemporary physics, experimental psychology, and physiology have proved Hegel right. The evidence from these sciences has shown that the very object of perception is generated through a process of organizing (a) the physical, and (b) the sensuous field.[14] In part, it is an unconscious physiological process, recapitulating the physical, and in part a subconscious psychological one involved in the activity of attention, which selects, distinguishes, and contrasts elements in the field. And the logical categories it exemplifies are those listed above.

What Hegel called "becoming" is a discursus of opposite moments in unity; the opposites, in the first instance, are being and non-being. This answers to what we have been describing: the discursive activity of the processes operative in attention mediating a "datum" ("this") with its other ("that") in an otherwise indiscriminate field, which, without the discursus is blind—a being that is at the same time nothing. What becomes (comes to be) is a definite object, made definite through the discursion of positive and negative moments, being and nonbeing, the one and the other. The concept of becoming and the discursive contrast between one determinate object and another provide us further with the categories of change, alteration, and movement,[15] concepts to be subsumed later under higher categories, of the advance to which we have yet to speak. Apart from the logical and epistemological reasons for adopting Hegelian categories here, the physiological and psychological are compelling, to say nothing of the merely physical. If there are some who avert their eyes in pain from anything associated with Hegel's philosophy, they do so at this point only at the cost of ignoring the evidence of contemporary experimental science.

Objection may be raised that all this, however interesting, has nothing to do with logic; and physics, physiology, and psychology, whether or not they give support to Hegel, are irrelevant. Any such objection, however, would be quite wrong-headed. The categories thus revealed are concepts, and concepts are the subject matter of logic. The concepts, moreover, by their very meaning and content, necessitate one another in dialectical order. They are, in fact, differentiations of *the* concept, which is not abstracted from particulars falling under it, but is the concrete universal, dialectically related to its particulars which are the products of its own self-specification. The particulars, at the percipient stage, are the qualitative elements of sentience registering the physiological processes, which are sublated and raised to the mental phase by the discursive activity: the activity of the immanent whole (the organism) specifying its inner principle of unity. The categories are, therefore, not merely categories of perception but equally of its object. "Being" is a concept, but it is also the subsistence of the sentient field registering and evidencing that of the physiological and biological influences impinging on the organism. Becoming, likewise, is a concept; but it is also the activity of ordering the sentient field and these impingements to constitute a perceived world. and this activity is itself a dialectical and evolutionary product of the dynamic present at every level of reality, from the indeterminate matrix of the physical world, presupposed (rather than discovered) in the observed phenomena and adumbrated in various ways by the physicists, up to the stage we are now discussing. It is a dynamic apparent in each new complexification: in the wave-packets identified with elementary particles, in the "vibrations" of atoms and molecules, and in the ceaseless activity of protoplasm.[16] This dynamic is dialectically transmitted from each phase to the next and the forms it takes at one level are sublated in higher levels, until it emerges as human thought and knowledge.[17] Mere being, at the physical level, corresponds to the energy matrix, and becoming is that process which, in Sir James Jeans' words, "throws up bubbles and eddies", or by self-enfoldment in wave-packets, generates elementary particles, determinate entities, positive and negative in mutual correlation. The same dialectical relationships are found at the levels of life and sentience, of which last the categorial forms are those we have listed above. What was immanent throughout the gamut of natural forms is here being brought to consciousness, in which these categorial forms reveal themselves. The logical structure thus reveals the form of the facts recapitulating that of the experienced world.

Husserl's phenomenological analysis of the substrate object prepredicatively evident against the horizonal context of the *Lebenswelt* exemplifies these elementary categories. But Husserl presents the *Lebenswelt* as implicitly an already sophisticatedly elaborated structure imbued with ideas from science and determinate thinking. He also regards the substrate object as an individual body in space given as a whole in sensuous intuition. Even if we accept as intelligible this sensuous self-givenness, dependent as it must be on the implicit discursus of perceived relationships with the background of the *Lebenswelt*, we are at once involved in categories more complex and dialectically advanced than being and not-being. An individual body is the substrate of qualities yet to be explicated, while itself it is discriminable from its surroundings only by qualitative contrast. It is body, thing, spatially situated, and, as Husserl proceeds to explain, spatially moveable and variable to present different aspects from different points of view. In his phenomenological description there is a whole gamut of logical categories indescriminately presupposed and already operative. Accordingly, instructive and illuminating though it is, it will not serve as a strict dialectical unfolding of logical forms.

It is not sufficient to perform an *epochē* which leaves the developed and sophisticated awareness of a world phenomenally unchanged and then to describe it as it stands. The categorial forms implicit in that awareness must be extracted and analysed. The most primitive are those of pure quality, which emerge through the selective, contrasting (and so negating) activity of attention, discriminating determinate elements within the diversified unity of sentience. This presents a "prominence" (in Husserl's terminology) distinguished from and against an indefinite background, both of which are determinate just in so far as they perpetually define and negate one another in a continuous logical movement of reciprocal definition. This perpetual discursus between opposites is the becoming of the determinate object, which must be determined still further in various ways and at subsequent dialectical levels before it can be identified as "thing" or "body," or related to other bodies in space and time. Thus, long before we get to the stage of phenomenological description of a *Lebenswelt*, we must attend to the elementary concepts of being, not being (or being-not), and becoming—the generation through discursus of the primitive object in contrast with its other.

From the start, then, there is an activity of organization discriminating "this" from "that" and defining A in terms of not-A, to produce a determinate object or quality. Negation is the logical operation which is here at work, the determination of a finite object by what it excludes. But the determinate object does not, and cannot, stand alone. It cannot exist or be cognized by itself and in isolation from its other. The true concept is the whole system which is progressively specifying itself, and those categories, the particular concepts in which it is exemplified, are provisional totalities at specific levels of abstraction. At the stage we have so far reached, the system, apart from which the character of any particular object cannot be discerned, is that of object-in-relation-to-context. It is the system that negates the negativity of the partial, finite, being, converting it into a positive definition—the negation of the negation, or the supplementation of the negated. This is the category that Hegel calls *Fürsichsein*, being-for-self, and that has proleptic significance prefigured in the account given above of cognitive attention. But, prior to that, the physical being of atoms, crystals, solar systems, and galaxies displays the same character of holism. Each is a system in which the existence, nature, and movement of particular constituents (elementary particles, atoms, molecules, planets, stars, etc.) is derived from their spatiotemporal and physical relations in the structure of the system. The organic interdependence of parts and processes in the self-maintenance of a living system is also covered by this category of intrinsic determination. None of these examples is completely self-sufficient, however; in none of them is the system self-cognizant. Its holism still operates blindly, and the dialectic, in consequence, presses onward.

III

Quantity, Number and Formal Logic

So far we have spoken only of qualitative differences, which are minimally necessary to qualitative discrimination. The concept thus far has specified itself as being and nonbeing, quality determined as particular qualities in mutual contrast, and individual qualified objects, or determinate structure requiring further and more specific determination. But the precise delineation of an object requires also quantitative determination. This is already implicit in the qualitative distinctions, for they must have extent and intensity as yet unspecified, and these must be made explicit in the continued course on the one hand of objectifying the subjectively felt content of primitive sentience, and on the other of differentiating the indeterminate matrix of the world. Quality, therefore, implies and demands the specification of quantity.

But the quantitative determination is not feasible without the conception of a unit. Quantity is magnitude and cannot be assessed except in numerical terms. Size is indeterminate and relative, and can be made definite only by the enumeration of unit values. Here, then, is another folding in upon itself of the dialectic (now at the logical level) by which it recapitulates in a new way the categories of its earlier stage. Mere quantity, like mere being, is indiscriminate and indefinite, it is only as quantized in units that it become specifiable.

The concept of unity, however, is already implicit in the qualitative configuration, and is derivative from the unity of the individual whole. That is one; but as self-sufficient and all-inclusive it is not a one among many, and so is not countable. The countable must be a set, or *Menge*, of self-contained units, each distinct and self-dependent, yet unlimitedly reduplicable. Each unit must be not only one, but one among indefinitely many. The qualitative whole is, moreover, self-sufficient and self-contained only qualitatively; it still lacks quantitative determination. Although, as qualitatively self-contained, it is not one among many, it is nevertheless one *of* many. It is a whole of differences, and the multiplicity which is its opposite moment is its own internal differentiation. As so contrasted with its internal particularization it is taken abstractly and as indifferent to the qualitative characters of the particulars. So regarded, it lies outside or beyond its concrete particulars and is the abstract universal. This contrasts with the "set" of particulars which fall under it, as one to many, but in the process it has degenerated into simply another particular.

When abstraction is thus made from qualitative diversity, the universal is posited as a simple uniform identity under which a number of equally simple and uniform similar particulars are subsumed. It becomes at once unit and sum. It is unit (as Frege saw) as determining what is to be counted, and sum as the class, or set, of its particulars; and the subsumption under it of the particulars gives them the status of its extension, determining the number which belongs to it. This is the concept as presented by Frege and it generates the idea of number.

Here the notion of unity is supplied by the universal or concept, for it is the unitary moment; but as a one embracing many, as the concept under which the particulars fall, it is also a *Menge* or set. The number of the set, we saw when discussing Frege, is the common property of all sets of the given magnitude. Here concept and extension are both entirely indifferent to quality. It is the abstract concept that provides the notion of unit and which defines the unit (as Frege insists); and, as making up the numerable extension of such a concept, the units enumerated are qualitiless particulars in external relation. Their number is the extension of the concept of all concepts with quantitatively similar extension. This is the notion of an aggregate of bare particulars that are, consequently, numerable, and where it prevails mathematics and formal logic operate legitimately and successfully. The relevance of formal logic is thus restricted to a specific aspect or mode of thought (and of reality), which is but one moment, however pervasive, of the concretely real.

Any whole or complex may, as we noted earlier, be regarded for specific purposes as a mere aggregate of unit elements. All that is required is abstraction from the qualitative aspects mutually determined by their interrelations in the system. When such abstraction is made and the object is taken as an aggregate of units, relations become external, both the relations between the units and the relations between the aggregate itself and any other which may be contemplated. So far as qualities are considered at all they are simply particulars, related once more externally or contingently to the objects in which they inhere; and these can be classified, collected into sets, determined by their contingent similarities. Facts can then be defined as the inherence of qualities in objects, or the relation of objects one to another or in groups, all of which are contingent and variable *ad libitum*, each being the case or not being the case without in the least affecting the rest.

Such facts are expressible in propositions either of the form S is P, or of the form a R b, or, more generally, ϕx. So regarded propositions are atomic, their truth-values are mutually independent and can be discovered only by inspection of the facts. The propositional calculus and the all the structures of symbolic logic may subsequently be erected on this basis.

Whenever the subject under investigation can profitably be treated in this manner symbolic logic is of immense value and power, and at this level of the dialectic of knowledge it holds its proper place and relevance. Here everything claimed for it by its proponents holds good and it ranks as a special science in its own right—or perhaps, more correctly, it ranks as a special, very generalized branch, of mathematics.

As nobody would dream of calling in question the importance and efficacy of mathematics in its proper exercise and application, so nobody need doubt the use and legitimacy of symbolic logic in its proper sphere. It is the logic of quanta, and of the abstract universal, of external relations, of sets, and of calculation. The categories appropriate to it are pervasive, like all categories, so that everything, the whole world, can be thought of in their terms; and the efficacy of formal logic has a corresponding all-pervasive character. For, as Hegel told us long ago, every category is a provisional definition of the Absolute. But it is *only* provisional and to take it (short of the Absolute itself) as final, when it is palpably and self-confessedly abstract and one-sided, would be a fatal error.

Quantity in its various aspects, with the corresponding view of the concept as an abstract universal, is an indispensable phase in the dialectic of the system of knowledge. Like every other phase, it is a necessary and persistent aspect of the whole, and its specific character is pervasive and is never wholly lost. It is carried up into subsequent phases, but there it is transformed in its integration with opposing moments. For the whole is *not* a mere aggregate and the relations between its moments are not merely external, but are themselves systems at successive levels or degrees of dialectical concretion. The quantitative system, the aggregate, is one of these, at a relatively elementary level, but it is far from being the last, and is not even the highest among the categories of immediacy. Accordingly, to make formal logic final would be to neglect the major and most highly elaborated phases of the totality which it is the task of dialectical logic to develop, while to reject formalism altogether would be to ignore an essential and ineradicable stage in that development.

The concept we have reached is that of magnitude or quantity, a conception of being, the variability of which makes no difference to its quality. It is dialectically the opposite of quality, for each excludes the other while nevertheless presupposing it. As there can be no quantitative assessment of bare nothing, quality is still tacitly presupposed in quantity, though suppressed. It may be what it will, quantity is indifferent to it. And quality requires quantity for the precise definition of its limits, on which it depends for its intrinsic character, although in its specific quality the quantitative aspect is again suppressed. They are, therefore, both abstract concepts, both moments of a more concrete concept that is yet to be developed through their union.

The subcategories of quantity as set out by Hegel need not be discussed in detail. It has two aspects: it is both discrete and continuous. It is thus both extensive and intensive. All these aspects are present in number, which is discrete and extensive as aggregate or sum, and intensive as a precise unity or object to which a proper name can be given—"one", "two", "three", etc.[18] It is also continuous, generating compact series, the intervals between the members of which are indefinitely divisible. As it displays these features, quantity is the appropriate category under which space and time are to be treated, for they eminently display the same aspects of extensivity, continuity, and discreteness. But space and time are not strictly logical categories; they are rather physical or psychological (perceptual) counterparts of the logical categories.

Determinate quantity is the quantum, and this, in the form of number, is again dependent upon its relation to other defined quanta for its determinateness. So it becomes rational number or ratio. This is quantum expressed as the relation between two precise quanta or numbers, and, having its related moments within itself, is analogous to the self-contained whole of quality. In this phase quantity has a qualitative aspect expressible as proportion, which is apparent in the qualitative contrast between geometrical figures, so important in architecture. In concrete objects, this qualitative quantity manifests itself, for instance, in tonal harmonics and in the hue of colour mixtures; but in such phenomena the culminating category of immediacy is being anticipated, namely that of measured quality, or quality as the expression or manifestation of a correlative quantity. This is the combination and reconciliation of the opposition between quality and quantity in which both categories merge. Thus, temperature varies with the quantity of heat per unit of volume, colour with wavelength, and tone with frequency of vibration. More complex expression of this category is to be seen in phenomena such as the relative brightness of illumination that produces alteration in the absolute appearance, in apparent variation of tone in the resolution of musical intervals, and, in general, the determination of the qualitative appearance of things by quantitative relations and equilibria. In physics, this category is at work in the resultant of interrelated forces, the equilibrial states of energy systems, the proportional combination of chemical elements, and in countless other quantitative relationships manifested qualitatively in the related phenomena. Just one example from biology is the relation of area to volume which is of such vital importance in the growth of plants and animals, determining their physiological and active capabilities and so their viability and capacity for survival.

The sketch given of the dialectic of the perceptual whole shows it specifying itself as being and nonbeing in the discursive interchange of becoming, which generates a determinate something in contrast with an other, and so develops the qualitative *Gestalt* of the perceptually immediate qualitative system. But this gives only one aspect (the qualitative) in which the other (the quantitative) is implicit and which posits itself in contra-distinction to the first by indifference to its specific quality. Quantity specifies itself in the opposing forms of discrete quantum and continuous extent, an opposition resolved as determinate quantum, as unit and sum. In numerical ratio, quality returns to quantity and the two combine in the measured relationship of qualitied quanta and their concomitant variation.[19]

Notes

1. Cf. *Hypothesis and Perception*, pp. 375–377, 383–384. *The Foundations of Metaphysics in Science* and its sequel attempt to develop the above theses in detail. To recapitulate the argument here, even in summary, is hardly appropriate.

2. *The Tao of Physics* (London, 1976), p. 245.

3. "Urbausteine der Materie," *Almanach der Österreichischen Akademie der Wissenschaften*, vol. 118, p. 159.

4. *Masks of the Universe* (New York and London, 1985), p. 125.

5. Sir James Jeanes, *Physics and Philosophy* (Cambridge, 1942), p. 193.

6. Sir Arthur Eddington, *The Nature of the Physical World* (Cambridge, 1928), p. 211.

7. Werner Heisenberg, *Physics and Philosophy* (London, 1959), p. 68; cf. *ibid.*, p. 60; *Philosophical Problems of Nuclear Physics* (London, 1952), pp.

103, 105. On all this, cf. my *Foundations of Metaphysics in Science*, ch. IV and pp. 126–127, 146–147.

8. A more recent description of this emergence of the particular from the general dynamic matrix has been given by David Bohm:

> To generalize so as to emphasize undivided wholeness, we shall say that what "carries" an implicate order is *the holomovement*, which is an unbroken and undivided totality. In certain cases, we can abstract particular aspects of the holomovement (*e.g.*, light, electrons, sound, etc.) but more generally, all forms of the holomovement merge and are inseparable.

Wholeness and the Implicate Order (London, 1980; Boston, 1983), p. 151.

9. Cf. *The Foundations of Metaphysics in Science*, ch. XVI.

10. Cf. Susanne Langer, *Philosophical Sketches* (The John Hopkins Press, Baltimore, 1962), ch. 1; *Mind, An Essay on Human Feeling* (Baltimore, 1967), vol. I, ch. I.

11. Cf. *The Foundations of Metaphysics in Science*, p. 326; R. G. Collingwood, *The New Leviathan* (Oxford, 1942), 4.5–4.54; K. Koffka, *Principles of Gestalt Psychology* (London, 1955), ch. IV.

12. Cf. W. Russell Brain, *Mind, Perception and Science* (Blackwell, Oxford, 1951), p. 14; D. O. Hebb, *The Organization of Behavior* (London, 1949), pp. 21–26; Floyd A. Allport, *Theories of Perception and the Concept of Structure* (New York, 1955), p. 612; K. Koffka, *Principles of Gestalt Psychology, loc. cit.*; M. D. Vernon, *The Psychology of Perception* (Penguin Books, Harmondsworth, 1962–1968). Sir Frederick Bartlett, *Remembering* (Cambridge, 1961), ch. II.

13. Cf. R. G. Collingwood, *The New Leviathan*, 4.5–4.54.

14. Cf. K. Koffka, *Principles of Gestalt Psychology*, ch. IV; G. W. Harris, "The Reticular Formation, Stress and Endocrine Activity," *Reticular Formation of the Brain*, ed. H. H. Jasper, L. D. Proctor, *et al.* (Henry Ford Hospital International Symposium, 1958), along with other papers in the same volume.

15. Cf. Aristotle's treatment of change and motion, which he analyses in terms of opposites: potentiality and actuality, and contraries. *Physics*, III, i.

16. *The Foundations of Metaphysics in Science*, ch. XXIV, 1.

17. Cf. *The Foundations of Metaphysics in Science, passim*, and *Hypothesis and Perception, loc. cit.*

18. Cf. G. Frege, *Grundlagen*, §38, pp. 29–31 above.

19. For more detailed discussion of this part of the dialectic, see my *Interpretation of the Logic of Hegel*, bk. II, pt. I, ch. 2.

Chapter 11

Categories of
Reflection

I

Common Sense

The categories so far traversed are those in terms of which what is immediately presented is apprehended; they are the categories of the perceived world which constitutes the whole which they specify. It is a qualitied whole discriminated into mutually contrasting and defining qualities quantitatively delimited and delineated. Perception, however, does not remain at the merely immediate level, but spans a considerable range of cognitive awareness steadily increasing in sophistication. In its more immediate phase, quantitative differences are largely implicit and the structure of objects is apprehended in relatively crude outline with only very elementary quantitative evaluation. Things are perceived vaguely as large or small, heavy or light, hard or soft, and so on, without any effort at exact measurement. But at quite an early stage in the development of experience, contradictions inherent in the cruder forms of apprehension become a stimulus to reflection introducing into the ordinary common sense awareness of the world more advanced forms of the categories of quality and quantity. These higher categories, as it were, leaven the lump of perceptual common sense and raise it to the level of understanding.

189

Measurement becomes necessary in practical situations, where manipulation and construction of existing entities requires a modicum of precision. It is usually such practical activity that stimulates further reflection and impels thought to a more advanced stage than that of mere perception. What is large in one context is small in another (as Socrates in the *Phaedo* points out) and contradictions arise from vague assessments of immediate impression which must be removed by the more precise means of measurement. Even these will not in all cases suffice, and more advanced categories typical of reflective thinking are called forth. Neither does reflection occur nor remain at a single level. Its first phase may roughly be called "common sense," a broad term including perceptual consciousness and low-level reflective explanation of immediate cognition. It is, in fact, too vague a term to do more than indicate an intermediary phase between naïve apprehension and scientific investigation. It is, moreover, never clearly distinguishable from these two forms of cognition. What we refer to as common sense is an unsystematic and often confused (and inconsistent) mixture of interpretation in terms of folklore, mythology, and religious belief (as primitive explanatory hypotheses),[1] and scientific explanation, usually outdated.

What Husserl designates *die Lebenswelt* corresponds in large measure to this level of consciousness. It is, also, what he sometimes identifies as "the natural attitude." It provides the "horizon" of everyday perception and the matrix from which reflection and science emerge. Reflection is a critical assessment of common sense notions, and science is the systematic attempt to make precise the categories by which observed facts can be interpreted. But its findings are made public and are absorbed back into common sense, permeating and restructuring the *Lebenswelt* of what we call the educated outlook.

II

Common Sense and Newtonian Science

Thus, our own contemporary common notions of the world are, for the most part, those of Newtonian science along with older concepts, which Newtonian science inherited from the middle ages and from ancient Greece, and incorporated into its own conceptual scheme (such as atomism, substance, cause, and the concepts of Euclidian geometry), preserved but not unaltered by the new setting in which they became enmeshed. These Newtonian categories were tabulated and philosophically "deduced" by Kant at the end of the eighteenth century. That they contain Aristotelian overtones is not surprising, because, while Kant's categories and Kantian terms have meanings which are not always quite the same as Aristotle's, the earlier categories developed and were continuously modified during the middle ages and are sublated in those of seventeenth century science despite revolutionary changes. Hegel included what are known as the dynamic categories among those of reflection, in what he called the Doctrine of Essence, and they are still the categories of common sense.

The categories of reflection develop logically (*i.e.*, dialectically) from those of perception, and we have already seen the implicit presence of the former in the latter. The interplay of something and other already implies the distinction of identity from difference, the operation (as has been shown) of negation, which is recognized on reflection as positivity and negativity. The ground of this distinction, as we have seen, is the pervasive system in which the distincta are mutually related. Reflection, henceforth, elaborates the interrelation of ground and consequent in successive dialectical stages: for example, as thing and its properties (the category of material thinghood), matter and form, whole and parts (at the level at which the parts are seen as an aggregate, Husserl's wholes subject to *Zerstückung*), substance and attribute, cause and effect, action and reaction.[2] All these are nowadays common concepts used, consciously or unwittingly, by the educated layman as interpretive principles in his common experience.

Identity and difference are the two inseparable moments of the systematic background of experience and of every discriminable element within it. This general "horizon" provides the ground or structure of conditions which issue in the existent as its consequent. The things so existing display themselves each as a network or concatenation of qualities and properties, and these again are distinguished as matter and form. Each is analysable further as whole and parts, and they are aggregated together into more comprehensive wholes. It is these categories of which Husserl gives a phenomenological account in the works noticed in earlier chapters. At every level, reflection distinguishes form from content and affects to treat each separately while confessing that they are but aspects of the same thing. Where it considers movement and action, it distinguishes the inner force from its outer expression, which again are but inseparable moments.

At a further stage of concretion, the thing with its properties is converted to substance and attribute, and the outer expression of an inner force to the effect of a cause. The whole structure of interdependent entities is then viewed as a dynamic system of interacting causes, of substances in reciprocal action and reaction.

What reflection sees as correlatives it nevertheless tends to treat as separable, still dealing in abstractions, though at a higher level than that of perception. So the categories of perception are sublated in and reappear as the categories of reflection: being and not-being as affirmative and negative aspects of identity and difference; quality and quantity as form and matter in its various manifestations; ratio and measure as the interactivity of substances and their mutual causation (as in proportional combinations of chemical elements), which again sublates the prior categories of force and expression, thing and properties, matter and form.

In general, these reflective categories are those of a mechanistic science, of atomism and materialism. But they are not the categories of contemporary science, which has given up mechanism and materialism and is based on new and more developed principles. The older categories remain the interpretive principles for the common sense view of the world and for that philosophy which is, in its several forms, effectively the philosophy of common sense—contemporary empiricism. We have seen that its fundamental tenet is the atomicity of facts and propositions, and in its epistemological theories, the category of material thinghood is frequently explicitly cited. It conceives wholes as aggregates and their parts as additive, and its tendency is constantly towards a less and less compromising materialism. None of these ideas, however, are in harmony with contemporary science as inaugurated in the early years of the twentieth century by Max Planck and Albert Einstein. The categories of contemporary science, nevertheless, are still those of reflection and should fall within the sphere which Hegel distinguished as the logic of Essence.

This is not the place to enter into a detailed commentary on Hegel's Logic, but something may be said here about the final phase of the Doctrine of Essence, for it seems to me that the categories of contemporary science belong there, as if expanding or diversifying Hegel's last category of Essence beyond the point that in his day was conceivable. Hegel brings the Doctrine of Essence to a conclusion with the major category of Actuality and its subcategories, into which all the prior categories are absorbed and in which they are transformed as moments of a reality which determines its own manifestations. It is the unity (identity) of essence and existence—the *Ens realissimum* of the Mediaevals and that which in all later philosophies ranked as actual reality. In Hegel's logic it marks the transition to the Doctrine of the Concept and the Idea. It is the substantial, concrete reality of which the universal principle of structure is self-specifying in its phenomenal manifestations. It is what I have called elsewhere a "polyphasic unity," a whole displaying itself in many different phases in which alone it is actualized.

III

Contemporary Science

The concepts of contemporary science fall as subcategories under this category of Actuality. They are concepts of discursive unification, of unity in and through differences. In present day physics, the entire universe is viewed as a single whole, and its physical contents as the various ways in which the principle of organization, immanent throughout, specifies itself into the diverse physical entities that make up the whole. Atomism has given place to what might be termed "energism", and mechanism and materialism have been abandoned. Matter and motion are no longer separable, the distinction between them having become purely relative. The particle is a wave-packet and its properties (velocity, position, spin, and the rest) are conjugate quantities expressible in and deducible from a mathematical equation. Substance has been transmuted into the space-time continuum, in which different frames of reference correspond to different sections and rotations of axes. It is the metrical field in which special electro-dynamic and gravitational fields correspond to various degrees of curvature—a sea of energy in which superposed waves behave as particles and standing waves correspond to their movement around the nucleus of an atom, itself a single complex field of energy. In relativity theory, force and its expression, cause and effect, have given place to geodesic motion; reality, as opposed to appearance, is replaced by the invariants among systematically related projections of nexūs of events. In quantum theory, the forces of attraction and repulsion have been resolved into mathematical relationships between the quantum numbers of like particles by the Principle of Exclusion, and saturation forces are non-dynamic features of the structure of the atomic or molecular system concerned. The whole is no longer conceived as an aggregate of parts,

but rather as a totality specifying itself as a dynamic correlation of inseparable moments.

Such revised concepts of whole and part, in which the whole
determines the parts and is no mere collection, have been well
established in numerous branches of science and at every level of
natural form. M. Gaston Bachelard[3] has effectively shown how in contemporary physics the more complex, or what he calls the "organic,"
serves to explain and to resolve the contradictions that arise from the
more simple, and not *vice versa*. For instance, in spectroscopy, at first
the spectrum of the hydrogen atom seemed to provide the simple unit
from which all others could be compounded in a series corresponding
to atomic numbers. But aberrations and anomalies in the spectrum of
helium, at first ignored, had later to be explained and resolved by
quanatum theory in terms of fine structure and the more complex
organization of heavier atoms. Again, in chemistry, valency was
originally thought of as a property of the atoms of the separate
elements, but under quantum analysis it has turned out to be a property accountable only in the light of the structure of the compound. B.
Cabrera (quoted by Bachelard) writes:

> Valency is something more complex, of which the origin is the
> stability of the new dynamic configurations of superficial electrons
> produced as a result of the mutual perturbations of the atoms in con-
> tact. It is evident that the details of that configuration and the degree
> of its stability depend on the structure of the intervening atoms, so
> that, strictly speaking, valency is not a property of each element in
> isolation, but of the group of atoms bound together.[4]

That this priority of the whole to the part, the complex to the simple, the universal to the particular, holds at the organic level is so obvious that it hardly requires illustration. The properties of enzymes and
of proteins generally depend entirely on the configurations of their
component amino acids, as do those of nucleic acids on the structure of
their macromolecules. The activity of substances in living processes
are all regulated homeostatically to serve the norms imposed by the
organism's systematic solidarity, by its needs and the conditions of its
survival as an organic whole. Each cell is an organic system and the
multicellular organism is a differentiated system of such systems. The
behaviour of organisms is similarly regulated to attain ends serving to
maintain the integrity and coherence of the system and to reproduce it,
reproduction itself being a form of self-maintenance.

Not only is the organism a whole internally determining the structure and behaviour of the parts, but it lives in symbiosis with other organisms in what biologists call a biocoenosis or ecosystem, and this may be as small as a drop of water or as large as a lake; it may be a forest tree or a whole forest; a sea or a continent. In fact, the entire planet is such a system. Nor can this be isolated from the effects upon it of the sun and the collective influences from outer space. The whole structure and envelope of the earth constitutes the organic environment without which life could not have come into being, nor living beings persist in existence. It is a single organic whole uniting organism and environment in an integrated biosphere.

Actuality is thus the integrated whole of the universe specifying itself as the self-differentiating space-time unity of the physical world which evolves to the self-differentiating biocoenosis of the biosphere, through a chemical process exhibiting the same principles of holism. This is how the world is conceived by modern sciences using a constellation of categories that go beyond those of classical physics and pre-evolutionary biology.

This holistic conception of actuality is already implicit in the category of reciprocal action, for the world of things or "substances" reciprocally determining one another does constitute a whole of interdependent parts. Once that is recognized, the dominance of the organizing principle over the constituents and their interrelations, and over the processes of interaction, becomes apparent, and interpretation seeks to explain the latter in terms of the former.

The categories of contemporary science, accordingly, are those of holism and evolution, such as cannot be the foundation of any formalized logic, for the presuppositions of formal logic contradict and exclude them. They are categories implying internal relations, which cannot be formalized. But this disqualification of formal logic does not apply in the same way to mathematics, which, as eminent mathematicians, from Poincaré to the present day, have insisted, is not a purely analytic science[5] (as was alleged by Wittgenstein) — in the sense of "analytic" adopted by formal logicians. There are undoubtedly some branches (at least) of mathematics which are synthetic and capable of expressing the structure and internal relationships of genuine wholes. To mention but one example, Pauli's Principle of Exclusion, which is essentially an expression in mathematical form of the necessary quantum relations between elementary particles, proves to be a fundamental principle of organization not only at the purely physical level, but equally at the chemical and organic.[6]

The categories of contemporary science are creativity and integration, field and complementarity, self-enfoldment and self-specification. They are the subcategories of concrete actuality. The creative continuum by its self-enfoldment produces nodules (superposed waves or particles) that contrast with its continuous uniformity, but are harmonized with it by mathematical equivalences displaying the complementary of matter and energy: e.g., $e = mc^2$. Thus the universal matrix is self-specified in the opposing forms of radiant energy and elementary particles. The same categories are further exemplified as the process continues in an unbroken series of natural forms of increasing complexification, atoms, molecules, crystals (periodic and aperiodic), viruses, protista, and multicellular organisms. They are all exemplifications of the one actuality and each is an actuality exemplifying the same subcategories. Throughout there is a principle of self-differentiating activity that is progressively becoming more characteristically expressed.

The final subcategory of actuality in Hegel's logic is reciprocal action. This is the integral unity of substance differentiating itself into its attributes through causal processes in thoroughgoing reciprocity. Such a unity is dynamic, for the causal process is incessant and is saved from the interminable finitude of external determination by the return upon itself which reciprocity entails. It is thus self-determinant and concrescent in and through its own process. This coincides with, or better, emerges as, the process designated by Whitehead "creativity", a process of reciprocal "prehension" by actual entities in a thoroughly interrelated and interacting universe of actual occasions, whose drive is toward concrescence, both within each individual entity and as a whole (in the "consequent nature of God").

The concrescence of each individual entity is directed by its "mental pole," and is an integrative (or synthetic) activity uniting all physical prehensions (the physical pole) with "eternal objects" in "comparative feelings," and achieving "satisfaction" in a "superject," which is transmitted to the subsequent phase of universal concrescence in the creative process. The precise nature of eternal objects is obscure in Whitehead's philosophy. He compares them to Plato's "ideas."[7] But if they are understood as the idealization or conceptualization of the physical totality prehended, they serve to mediate the precise transition from physical to mental for which Whitehead seems to be striving, and from actual to conceptual, which Hegel postulates. I have deliberately used Whitehead's special terminology to underline the continuity between the Hegelian categories of Essence and contemporary *Denkbestimmungen*, derived, as are Whitehead's concepts, from reflection upon modern physical theory.

These notions can be resolved further (as Whitehead does somewhat obscurely) into field and complementarity of its moments. The field is the complex of prehended occasions and its moments result from their integration by the prehending process, which, on the one hand, remains a fluid process, and, on the other, is the concrescence of the individual entity.

As historic routes of actual entities, reticulating and combining in nexūs, effect further complexifications, the self-enfoldment[8] of the process engenders organic unities with minds, conscious of themselves and their environment through the specification of their sentient experience (feeling) into an objective world. These are the transcendental subjects of Husserl corresponding to the Hegelian Concept, into which, in his system, Actuality is transformed (as the rational whole become aware of itself—*für sich*). It is the explicitly self-conscious unification of "mental" and "physical poles" (for Hegel, of subject and object), which, in being aware of itself, is *ipso facto* aware of the whole prehended universe. It is not merely one pole of each actuality, although it is also that in its quasi-embryonic forms, for it has been implicit in every phase heretofore; and for that very reason it is what actuality becomes dialectically when the organic is further integrated in sentience, so that the "mental pole" becomes the explicit awareness of the unified totality that has been immanent all along in the physical and the biotic. Mind is the self-enfoldment polyphasic unity become aware of itself, expressing and specifying itself in consciousness, first as perception and then in theoretical systematization, the categories of which are next to be considered. These are the logical categories proper, the categories of theorizing and scientific method, as opposed to the concepts in terms of which empirical science constructs its models.

Notes

1. Cf. Bruno Snell, *The Discovery of Mind, The Greek Origins of European Thought*, (Oxford, Blackwell, 1953); Francis Cornford, *From Religion to Philosophy, A Study in the Origins of Western Speculation*, (London, 1912).

2. The precise dialectical relationship between these categories is set out by Hegel in his Encyclopaedia Logic and in *The Science of Logic*. Cf. my *In-*

terpretation of the Logic of Hegel. The object of the present discussion is not to repeat this exposition but to suggest its extension to cover contemporary science.

3. Cf. *le nouvel ésprit scientifique* (Paris, 1932–1966), ch. V.

4.   C. Cabera, *Paramagnetisme et structure des atomes combinés, Activation et structure des molecules,* 1928, p. 246.

5. Cf. H. Poincaré, *Science and Hypothesis* (New York, 1952), pp. 12–13; G. J. Whitrow, "On Synthetic Aspects of Mathematics," *Philosophy,* XXV, no. 95 (1950).

6. It is interesting to note that in much of the mathematical formulation of Quantum Mechanics the commutative, associative, and distributive laws are not applicable.

7. Cf. *Process and Reality,* pt. II, ch. II, §§ ii and v.

8. Here I have borrowed terms from Pierre Teilhard de Chardin. Cf. *The Phenomenon of Man* (London, 1960).

Chapter 12

Categories of
Systematic Thinking

I

The Concept, Theoretical and Objective

Logic is the theory of the Concept, and the Concept is the one systematic whole come to consciousness in the mind. The common notion that there is an indefinite number of concepts, unrelated in any systematic way except fortuitously as they happen to belong to some special scientific field, is an inheritance from formal logic, which treats concepts as abstract characters attaching contingently to loosely aggregated groups of particulars. The Concept as system, however, is one and only one, even though it differentiates itself into many different forms, which are indeed concepts, but which are nothing other than its own specifications and diverse particular exemplificatons. In the first instance it is the world theoretically conceived, so that the theory of the concept is first the theory of theory as such; but it is not confined to pure theory if only because theory is the concept of the *object*, and, as knowledge or truth, it is the true and explicit form of what the object actually is in itself. In short, the Concept as science is objective knowledge. Yet it is also and at the same time subjective as the ordered experience of the knowing mind. Furthermore, as knowledge, it is the subjective aspect of informed practice in which it is objectified both in conduct and as realized purpose (or "objective").

Our first concern will be with its theoretical aspect, but we must at no stage lose sight of the equally objective validity of categories that may seem *prima facie* to be merely theoretical. We are about to examine the categories of systematic thinking, but we have all along been considering categories, and every category is a concept, and every concept is an implicit foreshadowing of the Concept that is now before us; each and all of them have the characters which we shall find it displaying. Every concept is a universal specified in particular forms which constitute an individual system, and every system is a phase in or moment of *the* system which comes to consciousness of itself as Concept proper.

II

Conceptual Moments

The Concept is, in the first instance, the universal principle of organization determining the structure and activity of the system as a whole. But, in the second place, as a merely abstract principle of order, the Concept is nothing actual apart from its particularization and is realized only in its self-specification. Its particular instantiations, however, are no alien importation; rather, they are the efflorescence of its own necessary self-development. Thirdly, the self-specified whole is the individual reality, the coalescence of universal and particular in the fully self-realized system. Further, the universal specifies itself as and through a scale of forms, each of which is a provisional whole and so is, in its own right, both universal and particular and, therefore, at its own level, individual. The three primary moments of the concept interpenetrate and are in thoroughgoing reciprocity.

Without order and structure, there is no object of cognition nor anything definite to objectify. The primary condition of perception is structure, both in the object and in the process of apprehension. As Plato remarks in the *Sophist*, "Whatever comes to be, comes to be as a whole";[1] and whatever is cognized involves organization, concomitantly in the sensuous or psychical field and in the objective context. This omnipresence of structure is the concept in its universal aspect; and, because structure is impossible unless it is a unity of differences, it is at once both universal and particular, realized as an individual self-differentiated whole.

In scientific knowledge, the theoretical element is the universal. The theory is the conceptual schema, the structural principle or system of principles, organizing the field of experience to which the theory is relevant. It is the fundamental law, or system of laws, governing the field. But, as such and without embodiment in examples, it is purely abstract—mere theory—the reality and confirmation of which resides in its application to observed fact, its specific differentiation.

On the other hand, observation itself is not a mere blind manifold (the purely sentient level is precognitive and is not yet perception), but is impregnated with theory. Perception is always interpretation of primitive sentience in the light of a background of ordered knowledge, a conceptual scheme of some kind, and at some level of sophistication, however elementary. There is thus ubiquitous interdependence of universality and particularity in perceptual and scientific knowledge.

The intermesh, however, is seldom if ever perfect, and when it seems so it is only within relatively narrow limits. Incoherencies are apt to reveal themselves under closer inspection, and, when the limits are exceeded within which harmony appeared to reign, disparate systems come into conflict. To resolve these conflicts, new adjustments are necessary in the conceptual schemata, with consequent modification of the perceptual content. Thus, the development of knowledge proceeds as the deployment of a scale of forms—a succession of conceptual schemes, or theories, each supplanting its predecessor, which, as supplanted, ranks as error; yet each developing out of its predecessor, preserving in new guise what in the superseded theory was sound and viable. The series then constitutes the specification of the universal (in alternative theories), each phase of which is, at its own level a self-specifying universal. At every stage knowledge is, in Kant's words, "a whole of connected and related ideas (*Vorstellungen*)",[2] a system of theoretical systems, a universal particularized in lesser universals, each and all actualized in the world of perceived objects.

The advancement of scientific knowledge is thus characterized by two main concomitant processes: one is that of specifying, in observed fact and experimental result, the currently proposed schema—the working hypothesis provisionally adopted. The other is the supersession of accepted theories, because of internal contradictions, by more coherent and more comprehensive theoretical principles. Universal and particular interrelate in both processes, for current theories attempt and profess to link up into a fully comprehensive system. They fail just so far as their self-differentiations reveal internal contradictions, and (or) bring them into mutual conflict; and it is to resolve such conflicts that new principles of systematization are conceived and investigated by application to observed and experimental situations.

The two main procedures, therefore, alternate and may be further subdivided: (i) Accepted theories reveal anomalies in the course of application and development. The specification of the universal leads to internal conflict or to contradictions arising from incompatibility with other specified universals which bear essential relation to the matter under investigaton. (ii) To remove these anomalies, new hypotheses are proposed progressively modifying the prior theory. (iii) The new hypotheses are tested by developing their implications and examining them in experimental situations, until (iv) a system of mutually corroborative evidence is built up in the light of which either the hypothesis under investigation must be affirmed, or else the entire system of fact which has been established would have to be repudiated. If contradictions persist, of course, the hypothesis is rejected and a new start must be made.

III

Scientific Judgement

The activity by which evidence is marshalled is that of scientific judgement, the process of identifying the universal in the particular and specifying the polyphasic unity of the universal in its various phenomena. It constructs a system of evidence (observed facts) in which the universal principle is exemplified. It is the sustained and progressive interpretative process by which the evidence is assessed in the light of the system (that is, of the accepted and proposed hypotheses), and the hypotheses in the light of the evidence. Evidence is provided by observation, so our first task must be to consider the nature of observational judgement.

Observaton is perception, and first we may pause to consider the perceptual judgement in its pre-scientific phase. In the first place, no percept is an isolated individual; it is always minimally and in general a figure against a background, and the background is also, in varying degrees and in graded continuity, diversified. The whole involved in perception, then must be specified in further percepts. Each object is a "this-not-that," a differentiated unity and a unity in difference, and it involves and requires identification in terms of its differences. In perception all this is implicit, but action informed by perception is discriminatory in a way which makes the articulate nature of the percept explicit. Thus, the laboratory rat discriminates the rewarding from the unrewarding passages of the maze on subsequent encounter. At the human level, the hand goes automatically to the doorknob without explicit judgement distinguishing the knob from the door or the door (as such) from the surrounding walls. One form of such discriminatory action is speech and the discrimination is made explicit in language by means of judgement, its elementry forms being "this is so and so", "this is not such and such", the affirmative and negative forms indicating the differentiated and opposed elements in the articulated system.

Secondly, perception (or observation) is always of definite and recognizable objects and, as such, requires interpretation of sensuous experience in terms of ordering principles. It is always the interpretation of "the given" at once in relation to a structured context and in the light of ordered knowledge previously acquired. Hence, even prior to science, there is no observation without interpretation any more than there can be interpretation without observation—because interpretation is simply appeal to the conceptual scheme ordering the experienced phenomena.

A judgement of perception is thus the identification of a presented object in the light of an ordered system to which it is referred, or the subsumption of such an object, when identified, under a universal interpretative principle, or the setting of objects in relation according to such a principle:

(i) "This is a book"	(identification in light of the order of the world as experienced, in terms of common classificatory systems, and other such principles of order commonly accepted).
(ii) "The book is red"	(subsumption under a quality, distinguished within the colour series, and from other diverse qualities, in the light of the above system).

(iii) "The book is on the desk"   (setting in relation with objects
                                     identified in accordance with the
                                     foregoing principles and ordered
                                     within the spatial schema).

In each case, a negative counterpart distinguishes the positive content affirmed from what defines and delimits it. It is a negative with a positive significance of its own, interlocking with its contrary in mutual determination.

A judgement of scientific observation is a more complex and sophisticated version of the simpler and more direct judgement of common perception. The latter is more direct because mediated by less complex and systematic background knowledge. The former, although immediate for the trained scientist, is mediated nevertheless by the whole of his expertise, so that what the scientist perceives is missed by the layman. The geologist will observe the folding of the strata where the layman sees only a confused mass of rock, the scientist will note the striation of the rocks and the position of boulders, evidencing effects of glaciation, where the laymen will fail to observe anything to the point. Thus, observation and theory determine each other, are mutually interdependent, and operate in continuous interplay. The one represents the particular, the other the universal moment, yet each involves both at once, for the universal is gathered from the observed particular and the observation interpreted, and in fact cognized, in the light of the universal.

The process is two-edged, and its moments interact reciprocally. For instance, in Harvey's research the hypothesis that the heart's action was in systole (and not, as previously supposed, in diastole) implied that it functioned as a pump and that its valves would be so constructed and disposed as to prevent blood from returning into the veins when it contracted, and from being drawn in from the arteries when it expanded. It also implied that the valves in the veins would impede the flow away from the heart. Harvey describes his observations in judgements which interpret them in the light of his hypothesis, and shows them to be mutually corroborative, so that the facts confirm the hypothesis. The judgements build up a system of fact organized by the hypothesis coherently and without contradictions (such as had emerged from earlier theories and were enumerated by Harvey in his criticism of the Galenic tradition.)

The development of the system is reflected in the forms of judgement in traditional logic. The categorical judgement reports observation, "the book is red"; but that is itself an interpretation and implies an order, which, if the judgement is to be substantiated, must be further and more explicitly displayed. This is done by stating conditions as the explanatory system dictates and is set out as a hypothetical: "If it is clearly illuminated and is not seen in reflected light, it is red." A further specification of the system delimiting the phenomenon more exactly is effected by a disjunctive judgement: "(In such and such circumstances,) it is either red or orange." Returning to the scientific example of Harvey's investigation, we find these forms clearly exemplified: categorical in the report of observation, hypothetical in the deductive process from hypothesis to consequent, and disjunctive limiting the possibilities which necessitate the conclusion. For example, "The arteries, when opened, are found to contain blood only and never air." "If both ventricles contract and dilate simultaneously, neither blood nor air can be forced through imperceptible pores in the septum." "Either the blood circulates or the quantity passing through the heart in a given time (half-an-hour) could not equal the total contained in the body."

Such development is necessitated because the system being articulated in thought always runs out beyond the limits of what is expressed in the categorical judgement. That states only one element, stresses only one aspect, focuses on only one feature of the complex totality. The negative is the beginning of movement toward the whole, for it moves from the one moment to its others and draws attention to the contrast of complementary aspects. But at the level of the categorical, the statement is always partial, truncated, and incomplete. It is true only in a slight degree, for what it omits and fails to specify, when brought into the limelight, modifies, if only by explication, its intrinsic meaning. To elicit the truth, therefore, even such truth as can be encompassed in a categorical statement, its implications (as an element in the system) must be developed further. Thus, planetary orbits are elliptical, but only if observed and calculated in a galilean frame. If calculated relativistically, a precession of the perihelion is disclosed which qualifies the accuracy of the original statement.

Even when such modification is less dramatic, it always occurs,[4] so the "truth" of the categorical statement always demands expansion in terms of the conditions upon which it depends, and so it unfolds as a hypothetical; and that again is further determined and defined in the disjunctive, which sets out more explicitly the contrasting distincta of the system.

Such classification of judgement form may be further subdivided according to the degree of systematic thinking involved. The simple judgement, "This is red", expresses a bare perceptual registration of a simple quality. A slightly more elaborated form is crypto-relational. "A red decor has a warming effect." Here the systematic ground of connection is not clarified and attachment of the predicate to the subject is based on casual experience—one constantly finds it to be the case. But the connection is not simple or immediate. Hidden associations are indicated with the glowing warmth of a fire, and psychological propensities are tacitly invoked the explanation of which is not offered or even contemplated. On this level are statements derived from common experience whose truth (so far as it is true) it cannot further explain, *e.g.*, "A fruit diet is healthy."

More systematic investigation of such connections expresses itself in universal judgements such as, "All natural foods are health giving," but these almost at once resolve themselves into conditionals of various kinds.

"If it is a natural product, it will contain such and such proteins and vitamins." And the system of scientific knowledge that provides precise grounds for universal and particular statements proceeds to unfold itself.

IV

Scientific Inference

In this way, we become committed to explanation, which requires appeal to an elaborate system of concepts and we move from judgement to inference, which are never really separable, every judgement, even of perception, being in principle the result of an inference, implicit or explicit. Scientific inference is, therefore,[5] no more nor less than the explicaiton of what is implicit in scientific observation.

Just as the process of judgement is double-edged, so that of inference is twofold. It consists of the discovery in the observed facts of principles of order, concurrently with the deduction of new facts from the principles surmised, and it is therefore both inductive and deductive at the same time—inductive so far as it moves from the particular to the universal, and deductive so far as it descends from the universal to the particular. But in either case, the other is also involved, because the particular, interpreted always in terms of a universal system, embodies the universal, and the new universal being developed specifies itself, in the very process of development, in particular instances. This double process is well illustrated in Harvey's work. The facts as he received them from his predecessors gave pointers to his hypothesis: the lesser circulation discovered by Colombo and the valves in the veins revealed by Fabricius, together with the contradictions involved in the Galenic theory that the heart acted in systole. From this it followed deductively that obstruction of an artery would deprive a limb of blood, while obstruction of veins would cause blood to accumulate in the extremities. These inferences prompted Harvey's experiments with the tourniquet on the human arm which produced the phenomena he expected.[6]

It is commonly held that while there is a logic of confirmation, there is no logic of discovery; and, if this means only that no rules can be prescribed for insight and no algorithm that will generate new theoretical constructs, the view is incontestable. It is, however, just as true of everyday problem solving as it is of scientific discovery, for no logic can provide a mechanical process for substantive reasoning and all constructive thinking requires insight into systematic connections for which formal logic can give no rule. Archimedes' grasp of the relation between the volume of water displaced and that of a body immersed in it could not have been dictated by any logical precept. Nor could pure formal logic direct a schoolboy faced with the problem of calculating the time taken to fill a bath with water from two taps running at different rates while the wastepipe is left open. For insight into the way to tackle such a problem logic has no directive rule. Not even mathematics is exempt from this demand for insight. Poincaré is quoted by Bachelard as saying that while Descartes offered mathematicians (given patience) an infallible method of discovery in place of the accident or genius previously required, later mathematicians so reformed it that only profound knowledge of the truths of mathematics and their mutual accord suffice for discovery of solution to a problem.[7]

Accordingly, rules of a calculus, whether of arithmetic or any other, can never serve as premises or as any part of the reasoning involved in solving problems or discovering scientific laws. Nobody can solve a chess problem simply from a knowledge of the rules of the game, even if that knowledge is a prerequisite to any solution. Calculation operates according to rules, but calculation is not reasoning and serves at best as a prop or scaffolding to assist the activity of thinking and discovery. If formal logic is confined to algorithms, it can give no assistance to thinking proper. It is, therefore, futile to seek rules for discovery or any formal calculus that will substitute for, or even represent, human inventiveness.[8]

Nevertheless, it does not follow that constructive reasoning has no logical or systematic form, for as Poincaré implies, the required insight is into the nature of a systematic structure, and the structural pattern stamps its imprint on the inferential thinking that leads to discovery. For scientific hypotheses (*pace* Sir Karl Popper) are not mere conjectures, and even if they were, conjecture is never wholly blind or arbitrary, but is prompted by clues to the structure of the facts which experience and acquired knowledge provide. This is the starting point of inference which is the medium and the means of discovery and without which there could be no scientific thinking. If such inference is to be valid and sound, moreover, it must proceed on logical principles of some kind. Scientific hypotheses, so far from being blind conjectures, are always guided by and developed from earlier theories—the very ones they may come to supplant; and, as each successive theory is a principle of systematization ordering a province of experienced fact, the line of scientific advance is from one systematic whole to another in a dialectical scale. The principles of inference are, accordingly, dialectical.

Inference is a development and an extension of judgement; the principle of its validity is simply consistency, which we have already found to be dependent upon coherence and the structure of the system. Judgement specifies the universal, and inference continues the process in its double-edged inductive-deductive discursus. Judgement subsumes under a presumed universal principle (an adopted working hypothesis) the particulars of a given area of experience or experimentation. Inference then proceeds to draw from these subsumptions conclusions as to their compatibility within the proposed system. When they are not compatible, contradictions arise causing strains in the system, which must then be revised. For example, adopting the hypothesis that the orbit of Mars is a circle, Kepler subsumed under that principle the Tychonian observations. In the ensuing construction, he found in two cases a discrepancy of eight minutes of arc. The inference from hypothesis (or universal principle) to specification (particular instance) thus broke down. An analogous incoherence is involved in the argument that because most vertebrate aquatic animals are fish, the whale is a fish, for it would imply that the whale breathed through gills and laid eggs. The resulting contradiction impels us to a reorganization of the facts under a readjusted hypothesis—in Kepler's case, a modified shape for the orbit; in the factitious example of the whale, a readjustment of the system of classification. The inference moves from one set of systematic relations, through contradiction,[9] to a new system, and is thus a dialectical movement. But the dialectical form does not prescribe a rule of procedure; that must be extracted from the nature and construction of the subject matter itself, in the form of a hypothesis. As Locke maintained, God did not make man barely two-legged and leave it to Aristotle (or Frege) to make him rational. Seeing the connection between premises and conclusion is not a matter of applying the rules of a calculus.

1. DEDUCTION. That a scientific theory is a system few are likely to deny, but the kind of system contemplated by formal logicians is what they call a deductive system, "pure" if the science is an exact science, "impure" or "mixed" if it is an empirical science. A formal deductive system begins from undefined (primitive) terms which are the basal reference for all definitions. This accords with the presupposition that the primary elements of any subject matter to which it may be applied are bare particulars. Terms, both undefined and defined, are combined into formulae, certain of which, the initial formulae, are underived, and from them others (theorems) are derived by transforming the formulae as required in accordance with stated (allegedly arbitrary) transformation rules. A system of this kind, of which the elements are uninterpreted symbols, is called a calculus, and interpretation consists of substituting for the symbols of the calculus terms representing elements in exact or in empirical science. When that is done, the formulae correspond to propositions, and the transformation rules represent rules of deductive inference. A science is then held to be a deductive system in which higher level hypotheses are deduced from the axioms (corresponding to the initial formulae of the calculus), and lower level hypotheses from the higher, in a linear series. In such a system, lower level theorems follow from higher level theorems and higher level theorems from axioms, never *vice versa*, although in a different system with a different axiom set, what were axioms in the former system may appear as theorems (or theorems as axioms). The most obvious character of systems such as these is that inference is linear and unidirectional.

In a formal calculus, the rules of transformation are such that derived formulae must be equivalent to those from which they have been transformed, and when translated as a deductive system their truth values must be the same. By the rules of formal logic, therefore, antecedent and consequent in any deductive inference are always equivalent, and the deduction is purely analytic, giving rise to no new substantive information.

It is obvious that empirical sciences cannot be pure deductive systems of this sort, and it is doubtful whether exact sciences can be either. In empirical science, the conclusions reached by inference from hypotheses always claim, and their purport always is, to give new factual knowledge. Nor is this new knowledge simply what has been freshly observed by direct perception, but is either a prediction of what will be observed, or a new law having universal validity and stating connections between types of phenomena such that conjunctions previously observed (but hitherto not understood) are elucidated, and future conjunctions are anticipated. The allegation that any such results can be obtained in a formal deductive system by substituting empirical terms for variables, or by adopting empirical laws as axioms, or even by using empirical statements of initial conditions as premisses, must be false, for none of these manoeuvers should enable us to derive by pure formal deduction conclusions which go a step beyond the premisses, however empirical or nonempirical they may be.

Moreover, no factual science can begin from undefined primitive terms, because terms referring to perceived phenomena always have meaning determined by their context (objects are recognizable only in relation to a context) and by funded prior experience already conceptually schematized. They are thus always, to some extent at least, definable; their referents are never bare particulars, but always specify a universal at some level so that the universal principle of order is immanent in them.

Further, definitions in a formal deductive system are held to be arbitrary and stipulative. In an empirical science, this can never be so, for the reasons already adumbrated. The terms defined must have empirical reference and, observation being always theory-laden, will always apprehend them with more or less determinate meaning structured by the operative conceptual scheme. Definitions, therefore, must always be "real" definitions; they must state as accurately and succinctly as possible what the definiendum is in terms of the concept which gives it significance and the characters distinguishing it from other specific forms. Aristotle's insight is more reliable here than the doctrine of modern logicians. Definition must be *per genus et differentiam*.

Similarly, axioms may not be arbitrarily formulated, as is generally maintained by formal logicians (even though they frequently qualify their assertion by the phrase "for convenience"), because whatever truth they can claim is dependent on the structure of the reality to which they apply, and they are usually general statements of its organizing principles (*cf.* Newton's Laws of Motion). Apart from that structure nothing apposite could be deduced from them, and (as we have seen) no tautological deduction would have any scientific value or significance; nor could any "convenience" be served by axioms arbitrarily devised in disregard of the structure of the subject matter of the science. Accordingly, any fundamental principles states as axioms, though they may serve as premises from which hypotheses can be deduced, will always be derived from the funded and already structured background of knowledge which gives meaning to their terms, and are always subject to confirmation and entrenchment by the coherence of the inferences resulting from them.

The definitions and axioms of an empirical science, therefore, already contain systematic implications, the development of which is the deduction from them of the theorems, or hypotheses, of the science. Such deduction is, in fact, nothing more nor less than the tracing out of the systematic connections between the elements of the subject, as these follow from the principles of structure stated in the axioms. But the axioms, as we have seen, are already impregnated with empirical meaning and have been derived from analysis of the structure of established knowledge. They are thus, as Aristotle taught, the fruits of inductive reasoning. In Newton's phrase, they have been "deduced from the phenomena"; and what in turn is deduced from them are new phenomena, whose empirical confirmation establishes the truth of the axioms. The procedure of the confirmation is, we shall find, as much deductive as inductive, so that inductive and deductive movements are mutually intertwined in all scientific inference, which is not linear and irreversible, for what is deduced from the principles may also serve as premises from which the truth of the principles themselves follows. How this occurs we shall presently see. Meanwhile we may note that the system built up by the predominantly deductive movement of inference is a body of organized fact ordered in accordance with a conceptual scheme, in which the coherence of the deduced results establishes the truth of the principles.

The objection will probably be raised that if we use axioms or first principles as premises and then appeal to the results of our deductive

reasoning as confirmation of the axioms, we argue in a circle and simply beg the questions we are supposed to answer. Indeed the reasoning
of science is double-edged, but any circle involved is not vicious. In
fact, it is not so much circular argument as spiral ascent. In some sense,
what we seek to discover is already implicitly known, and what scientific research does is to make it explicit.[10] The explication thus includes and confirms its own starting point, without simply repeating it,
but by raising it to a higher power of illumination, by enriching its content within a wider context and by means of a more varied interpretive
schema. The principles set out at the beginning are hypothetical, and
their function is to organize the experienced facts. The success with
which they do so, as borne out in observation, confirms them as the
right principles.

A clear example of the interrelation of axioms and definitions with
prior knowledge is provided by Newton's *Opticks*, where definitions are
anything but arbitrary, have explicit reference to light as it is experienced, and are just clarificatory statements of its general character and
the systematic treatment it is to be given in the treatise. Thus, "By rays
of light I understand its least parts, and those as well successive in the
same lines, as contemporary in several lines," is the first definition.
The second reads: "Refrangibility of the rays of light is their disposition
to be refracted or turned out of their way in passing out of one
transparent body or medium into another . . ." These are plainly empirical statements requiring familiarity with the concrete subject matter
to be understood and drawing for their intelligibility upon the funded
and already to some extent organized knowledge of the object to be examined. Similarly, the axioms are statements in precise form of already
discovered facts: "The angles of reflection and refraction lie in one and
the same plane with the angle of incidence." "The angle of reflection is
equal to the angle of incidence." "The sine of incidence is either accurately or very nearly in a given ratio to the sine of refraction." These
statements are neither arbitrary nor self-evident, but, in effect, they
report the results of previous investigations. We need not quote them
all, but we may observe that, first, they serve as ordering principles of
the province of facts to be examined, and, secondly, Newton is able
and proceeds at once to deduce from them the new *fact* that light from
a body focused through a lens will form a picture of the body where
the rays converge (Axiom VII). The systematic connections of the
facts under examination, in which the ordering principles of the whole
are immanent, are being set out and are implicit in these definitions

and axioms. They are further specified in Newton's diagrams guiding the proof. And it is this structure that forms the ground and provides the thread of connection in the inference.[11] The result is fresh knowledge not explicitly contained in the premisses; hence, the reasoning cannot have been purely analytic.

In the *Principia*, Newton sets out an empirical science as a deductive system, beginning with definitions and axioms and proceeding to theorems deductively proved, just as Euclid sets out his geometry. But it is patently obvious that the definitions and axioms are derived from experience, and Newton does not hesitate to appeal to "experiments" in their support:

> Hitherto I have laid down such principles as have been received by mathematicians and are confirmed by abundance of experiments. By the first two laws [axioms] and the first two corollaries, Galileo discovered that the descent of bodies varied as the square of the time (*in duplicata ratione temporis*) and that the motion of projectiles was in the curve of a parabola; experience agreeing with both, unless so far as these motions are a little retarded by the resistance of the air.[12]

As the definitions and axioms are all empirically derived, so the theorems proved from them all have empirical reference. Between them they develop the structural form of the facts and phenomena with which the science is concerned. The principles are all derived from phenomena (more properly, from earlier hypotheses established by Newton's predecessors), and the conclusions are all deduced from the phenomena. The deductions are simply the development of the systematic connections discovered in the phenomena. In these respects, therefore, deductive as Newton's procedure undoubtedly is, both in the *Opticks* and the *Principia*, it is at the same time inductive, the coherence of the results, both in terrestrial and celestial mechanics, establishing the principles as much as the principles necessitate the results.

Whereas formal logic strictly segregates deductive from inductive inference, so that only the latter is supposed capable of producing new information, in actual scientific reasoning the two are so fused that new facts can be "deduced" from what is already known by virtue of the organizing principles enunciated as axioms and immanent in the premisses. The point is that fact and theory, observation and concept, are always so intimately blended that, in virtue of the theoretical principles, empirical conclusions, which, without being tautological, are necessary (not just probable), can always be derived from an apposite body of evidence. In short, inferences are possible the results of which are synthetic *a priori*—by which is meant no more than that, though factual, they are universal and necessary within the conceptual system. Let us consider another example.

Given as initial conditions a Wilson cloud chamber set in a magnetic field and bisected by a lead plate, and in the cloud chamber the vapour trail of a particle fine in texture penetrating the leaden barrier and curving above it to the left for five centimeters, it is possible to deduce, on the strength of prior theory and observation, the mass and energy of the particle and the charge which it carries; and so to conclude incontrovertibly that it is a positron.[13] This is because observation of such a vapour trail in such circumstances is interpreted in the light of theory as of a charged particle behaving appropriately in a magnetic field. Theories of electro-magnetism and of ionization organize the relevant phenomena in such a way that from certain of their properties others can be read off or calculated. Before the work of Dirac and Anderson, the theory of elementary particles was incompletely organized. It admitted of only two or three kinds of particles, one positively charged (the proton), one negatively charged (the electron), and one uncharged (the neutron); thus, the appearance of a vapour trail characteristic of an electron but behaving as that of a positively charged particle was anomalous and contradictory. Development of the implications of the partial system, however, mathematically by Dirac and experimentally by Anderson and others, permitted the deduction from a combination of theory and observation of the existence of a positively charged electron. No purely analytic deduction could have produced this result, for where every formula or proposition is equivalent to the one from which it has been transformed no advance in knowledge can be made. Yet the result emerged equally from the mathematical theory and from the experiment. The conclusion was as much deduced from the observed phenomena as within the mathematical theory (from Dirac's relativistic wave equation for an electron in a magnetic field), because it was calculated, as indicated above, from the direction, curvature, length, and thickness of the vapour trail as prescribed by hitherto established theory. This calculation *necessitated* the conclusion to a positive particle with the mass of an electron. So the system was enlarged and modified to include both antimatter and matter, requiring positive and negative forms of all particles, the neutron being a combination of both. The process is from a less inclusive system, through contradiction, to a more comprehensive structure in which the contradiction is resolved. Moreover, the reasoning is deductive and the conclusion necessary although many of the premises are derived from observation, and observation confirms the mathematically derived conclusion of Dirac. So we have a fusion of inductive and deductive movements, and, so far as the inference constitutes an advance in knowledge, the movement is plainly dialectical.

The deductive aspect of the reasoning, while it is not purely formal and analytic, does not violate the rules of formal logic in as much as they are relevant; and this need not surprise us because, in the dialectical ascent, the earlier categories are incorporated and preserved, though modified, in the more developed forms. The precepts of formal logic, we saw, belonged to categories of quantity, which have been sublated in the subsequent advance. There is nothing to prevent our stating any step in the scientific argument in syllogistic form, should it suit our purpose, or as a formal implication. We might say:

> All vapour trails curving to the left in a magnetic field are of positive particles;
> this vapour trail curves to the left;
> therefore, this is the track of a positive particle.

Or we might write:

> For all x, if x moves to the left in a magnetic field, x is a positively charged particle.

But it is unlikely that any physicist would think such formulations worth while as anything more than statements of the obvious. And the use of calculi to determine the values of the relevant parameters is not only permissible but indispensable. Yet, again, mathematics is not confined to calculation and mathematical reasoning is not all purely analytic. In fact, Poincaré has maintained that that too, at base, is synthetic *a priori*,[14] and is essentially constructive. Purely formal calculi do not exhaust the scope of scientific inference, which accomplishes far more than formal logic can account for.

2. INDUCTION. The nature of scientific inference may now be approached from the opposite direction. The traditional theory of induction assumes that particular facts are perceptually intuitable independently of theoretical interpretation, and that from their constant

conjunction we can and do infer to general laws affirming their connection. But when the legitimacy of this inference is called in question, the doctrine is qualified and maintains only that we may conclude to a probable connection, or predict the recurrence of the conjunction with some degree of probability, warranted by the frequency of our experience of it in the past. Scientific laws are thus held to be only empirical generalizations with varying degrees of probability, in most cases very high.

Setting aside all controversy about the validity of this form of reasoning, we may confidently assert that it is not widely practised by scientists of note. The sort of evidence they seek to establish their hypotheses is not the mere repetition of similar conjunctions, and it is seldom, if ever, that they arrive at hypotheses by empirical generalization, if by that is meant enumerative induction. The hypotheses arise out of earlier theories, adjusting and reforming them to account for anomalies; and their confirmation proceeds by a different route from that alleged in the traditional theory.

In the first place, particular facts cannot be cognized directly by mere sense observation, for what is to count as evidence is only recognized as such in the light of some theory, without which it tends at best to be misinterpreted or overlooked, if it is perceived at all. The facts as perceived are already theoretically loaded. They are not merely particular but have universal implications, elements of structure which the scientist is seeking to reveal and develop—implications which prompt and legitimize inferences. The repetition of like characters may serve as a clue to the existence of systematic relationships, and, when it appears, the scientist treats it as an indication of essential connections to be more closely investigated. They are established by the construction of a body of evidence, consisting not of similar but of diverse facts—as diverse as possible—each of which supports the hypothesis under test from a different angle, proving that the hypothesis is indeed the enunciation of the principle that unifies and orders the facts and explains their interconnections.

In each step of this process there is a deductive movement: (hypothetico-deductive) from the hypothesis to the experimental test, and again in the demonstration of the hypothesis from the final interconnection of the evidence. If the hypothesis is true, certain observations should be possible and may be sought; if the observed facts interlock in their support of the hypothesis, so that to deny it would entail denying a whole body of evidence, then the truth of the hypothesis follows of necessity. Thus, in Harvey's exploration of the activity of the heart, if his hypothesis is true the action of the heart must be in systole, and he observes that when it contracts it is pale in colour and hard, whereas when it dilates it is deeper red, flaccid and limp. The presumption is then that in diastole it contains more blood which is driven out when it contracts. There is here a double deductive inference: one from the hypothesis to the expected observation and one from the appearance of the heart to the movement of the blood. Harvey confirms the second conclusion by piercing the ventricle and observing the forcible emission of blood as the organ contracts. Again, if the hypothesis is correct, diastole in the arteries will correspond to systole in the heart, and this is tested and observed in the same fashion. The lesser circulation through the lungs may also be deduced from the hypothesis, and Harvey (being aware of the work of Colombo) verifies the assumption by appeal to comparative anatomy, noting the transfer of blood from the right to the left ventricle in creatures which have no lungs and in the human embryo. Moreover, the position and construction of the valves permits the flow of blood in only one way. From the systematic interrelation of these facts, deduced from the hypothesis as well as observed, and deduced from one another as observed, Harvey infers with cogency that "(the blood) cannot do otherwise than pass through continually."[15] This conclusion is at once both a deductive and an inductive inference—deductive as following necessarily from the evidence, and inductive as gathered from the mutually corroborative observations.

The same kind of inferential movement is detectable in Lavoisier's procedure. First, the contradictions in interpretation required by the Phlogiston theory set him to investigate another hypothesis suggested to him by the work of the English pneumatic chemists. The discovery by Guyton de Morveau of the constant conjunction between augmentation of weight and the calcination of metals indicated that something might be absorbed from the air. But this "induction" did not confirm the hypothesis, it only prompted further, more systematic, investigation in search of a binding connection. If some part of the air is "fixed" during combustion and calcination, it follows deductively that its absorption and its amount should be detectable during these processes. What is needed is appropriately designed apparatus to detect them. Accordingly, Lavoisier designs a series of elegant experiments to measure the absorption and emission of gas during combustion on the one hand and reduction on the other, deducing from the question to be answered and the nature of the processes investigated the required nature and arrangement of the apparatus. The results of these experiments are found to supplement one another and to form a close-knit system of evidence from which the hypothesis follows, and each of the results can be explained only by that hypothesis.[16]

The appeal to observation and experiment is not an appeal to direct intuitive apprehension of bare particular occurrences or conjunctions constantly repeated. It is an appeal to structured situations carefully designed to test different aspects of the consequences deduced from the hypothesis. Each experiment is inspired by theoretical considerations, and each result interpreted in the light of an organized arrangement of apparatus and processes. It is, in fact, a deduction in its own right: if, during calcination of mercury in a crucible confined over water in a bell-jar, the level of the water rises, something, some portion of the air in the container, must have been absorbed. The amount can be measured and compared with the corresponding increase in the volume of the air during reduction. The ensuing inference (from these, along with numerous other experiments with different substances and of varying design) is that some part of the air is "fixed" by the calcining metal, or the burning substance. This is *inferred*, not observed; for all that can be observed are changes of colour and texture in the substances, water levels in certain vessels, readings on a scale, the behaviour of a balance, and the like. The nearest approach here to what may be called induction is the mutual corroboration of observations (all of them theory-laden and all of them involving some deductive inference). They are, moreover, observations of quite different facts, including those negative instances (Laviosier attempted to get similar results from heating charcoal unmixed) marking the limits within which connections hold. Induction from such diverse observations is interwoven with deduction, both from the hypothesis and from the structure of these facts, at every step. The inference is always made on the basis of an ordered system of facts, the principle of order in which is the hypothesis being established.

No inference is possible except on the basis of a system of relations coherently ordered, and its movement is not through tautological transformation of sentences but from the known to the unknown, whether "deductive" or "inductive." My thesis is that, as revealed in the examples cited, it is, always both, even if one aspect is sometimes more apparent than the other. What is previously known is already to some extent organized, and the process of inference is the dialectical development of its implications. When "deduction" predominates, its primary premisses are statements of the principles of structure in the system to be elaborated (as in Newton's *Principia* and *Opticks*), and as will presently be illustrated more at length, they are always derived through an inductive dialectic from earlier hypotheses which have been (in being developed) superseded. When "induction" predominates, the structural principles serve as a conceptual schema in the light of which observed facts are recognized and interpreted, and which the observations are seen systematically to specify. Induction without deduction would be blind; deduction without induction would be empty.[17]

Scientific inference is thus a unity of two opposed movements of reasoning, deductive and inductive in type, and its outcome is a systematic theory of the object of its investigation, in which the observed facts are coherently organized in such a way that other facts, as yet unobserved, can be predicted with accuracy and assurance. The elaboration of the system by this constructive movement, whether set out, like Newton's *Principia*, in deductive form, or built up through a series of experiments, as by Lavoisier, is the specification of the universal principle, in the first case stated as a law, in the second, entertained as an hypothesis. The judgement that identifies universal and particular is thus developed into inference which reveals its ground and elaborates the system upon which it rests.

Let us pause for yet one moment to look more closely into the procedure of this deducto-inductive process. The investigator begins with presented data which are already partially organized, and what he seeks is the principle and disposition of a larger system. The partial organization is evident first in the common assumptions of perceptual habit, and secondly, in the more explicit acceptance of prior theory. Its partial character is betrayed by the contradictions attendant upon attempts to interpret the available evidence. The first step is inductive in its general direction and is a search for elements of structure, which, in the first instance, are revealed by identities (or similarities) running through differences. These may well (and usually do) take the form of constant conjunctions of certain characters—giving colour to the traditional theory of induction—but relevant differences are not only occasional and fortuitous but are essential to the success of the pursuit of structural principles. Beginning, then, from a partial structure, a rule or principle of organization is sought that will, when applied and developed, lead to the completion of the system.

One very simple example is provided by Sir Frederick Bartlett in his experiments on thinking. The subject is required to complete an arrangement of words, of which a fragment is given, by selection from a random group. The fragment consists of the two words, written one below the other:

ERASE
FATE

To solve the puzzle, the subject has to note that the initial letters of the words are in alphabetical order and that the words differ by one in the number of letters they contain. Here are elements of structure. The given sample is so small that no constant conjunctions are evident, but supposing that several pairs of words had been given as examples, it would have been noticeable that in every case the initial letters were in alphabetical order and that the words differed by one in the number of letters: e.g.,

ERASE   HO   CAT
FATE   I   DUTY etc.

The relevant differences are in the length of the words in each pair and the variety of initial letters (differences which nevertheless preserve the identities). The rule of procedure now is to arrange words in alphabetical order so that each differs in length from its predecessor by one letter. From a list of sixteen words, the solution emerges as the following column:

A
BO
CAT
DUTY
ERASE
FATE
GET
HO
I

Kepler's search for the Martian orbit is a more serious scientific example of the same pattern. He was presented with a mass of readings taken by Tycho Brahe of differing positions of the planet at different times, and he inherited from his predecessors the hypothesis that these could be arranged in a circular orbit about the sun. All the positions are different, but the differences are assumed to be relevant to some (as yet undiscovered) geometrical shape. Adopting the rule that the orbit is circular, Kepler was faced with a discrepancy in two cases of eight minutes of arc, and he was constrained to look for a new rule. Omitting his successive failures, we have next to observe his discovery of an identity. Having assumed that the orbit diverged from the circle to become oviod, forming a *lunula* on each side, he discovered an equality between (i) the greatest width of the *lunula* and (ii) the secant of the angle subtended at its midpoint by the line joining the sun to the assumed centre of the orbit. This provided a rule or formula describing an ellipse, into which he found all his observations fitted.[18]

Unless interpreted in terms of astronomical theory, Tycho Brahe's observations would have been meaningless. They were useful to Kepler only because he interpreted them in the light of the Copernican hypothesis. So interpreted, they formed the empirical matrix in which he looked for elements of structure. Using his assumed rule for the orbit, inherited from Copernicus and the Peripatetics, he worked duductively, the rule being his inferential guide. He found it unsatisfactory, but he never wholly abandoned it, modifying it progressively until he reached a version which gave coherent organization to the facts. The circle, by addition of an epicycle (also circular), first became an oviod, and that subsequently was changed to an ellipse, of which the circle is but a special case (in which the foci coincide). Thus the continuity of development is maintained through successive oppositions in a series of systems each a transformation of its predecessor.

The essential nature of reason being order and system, the prevalent assumption of reasoning is the efficacy, in whatever is under scrutiny, of a principle of order. The primary aim of investigation is to discover this principle and to affirm it (explicitly or implicitly) as a law or rule governing inference from the data at hand to hitherto undisclosed elements and relationships within the system. The process is a single inferential movement with two aspects, one predominantly inductive in character seeking to detect elements of structure in the presented material. The other predominantly deductive: the principle of order, once determined, affords a rule for deducing the particulars, and so for developing the complete system which is implicit in the principle of structure, deduction by which features are revealed which were formerly unknown.

V

Scientific Advance

We spoke earlier of two concomitant processes through which the advancement of knowledge takes place, the specifying of the universal (hypothesis) and the development of the system so specified into a fuller and more comprehensive whole. Thus far we have devoted most of our attention to the first, with but few passing allusions to the second. The two, however, are not separable or disparate processes, for each is an aspect of the specification of the universal concept, and the first is always a stage within the second. The whole of connected and related concepts that constitutes knowledge is a system of sciences, and each science is a system of theories. The first of the above-mentioned processes is that of establishing hypotheses; the second is that of making the whole conceptual scheme coherent. Obviously, each is necessary to the other, and the same logical structure permeates them both. Establishing hypotheses depends on the coherence of the evidence, and for no other reason is a theory found acceptable than that it successfully organizes the experienced facts. This is usually described as agreement between fact and theory, but we are now aware that there is no fact apart from theory and no theory ex-cogitated *in vacuo*. The "agreement" sought, therefore, is much more aptly described by Locke as agreement between our ideas, with the proviso always that the ideas are concrete interpretations of experience by concepts. When this is such as to render experience whole and to unify it systematically without conflict, the interpretation (*i.e.*, the theory) is accepted as true. It then takes its place as a subsystem in the total conceptual scheme, the system of systems covering the entire range of empirical knowledge which is properly called the scientific world view.

But knowledge is not a static system, set out and fixed once and for all. It is a constantly growing and developing conception of the world, the progress of which, as remarked above, is a succession of conceptual schemes ordering experience. These develop one from another to constitute a dialectical scale, and this is evident within each theory: (i) we have seen how Kepler's hypotheses concerning the Martian orbit follow this dialectical course, from circle to ovoid produced by an epicycle and from that to an ellipse, (ii) taking another example at random, the idea of atomic structure developed from the notion of a hard massy particle to the hypothesis of a rotating array of negative charges in a spherical positive region (due to J. J. Thompson). The assumed solidity of the former atom contrasted sharply with the conceived fluidity of the latter. Then came the Rutherford model with its positive nucleus and orbiting electrons; but this, according to current concepts, should have radiated away its available energy so that the electrons collapsed into the nucleus. So, with the help of Planck's quantum, Bohr's atom superseded, and the continuity of radiation in the first theory was countered by the discontinuity in the second. The first two opposing theories are reconciled and combined in the third and the contradiction in the implications of that again is resolved in the fourth.

Within each science there is the same sort of process. No sooner is a hypothesis established than it is further specified, and in the course of its wider application conflicts may be revealed, either within its own province, or with related theories. These conflicts stimulate further research, the hypothesis is modified in the effort to remove them, new hypotheses are evolved and tested, until the coherence of the system is once again restored. If the anomalies are inconspicuous, they may at first be overlooked, or if they are not serious, minor adjustments may be sufficient to remove them; but when they accumulate and become an obstacle to the progressive articulation of theories, a crisis arises which demands complete reorganization of the system. This is what has been aptly called a scientific revolution. It is, however, never a complete break with prior theory, and revolutionary though its out-come certainly is, it is nevertheless brought about by continuous development of earlier ideas.[19]

That the source of a new hypothesis, however revolutionary, is the state of prior knowledge may be copiously illustrated from the history of science. Copernicus adopted the heliocentric hypothesis from Aristarchus of Samos, who arrived at it after a long and continuous development of cosmological ideas going back to the Pythagorean belief in a central fire round which the heavenly bodies revolved. Harvey conceived the idea that the heart acted in systole only after the current belief that it functioned like a bellows had proved incoherent, yet, after all, a bellows works much in the same fashion as a force pump, and what Harvey did was simply to put blood in place of air and "fuliginous vapours." Darwin's conclusions developed from the sugges-tions of his grandfather, of Buffon, of Geoffroy St. Hilaire, and of Lamarck. Every innovation in science can be traced back to earlier concepts and is dictated by the need to remove the contradictions that have arisen from those earlier theories. And innovators, almost without exception, preface the exposition of their own ideas by listing the con-tradictions involved in those of their predecessors. Harvey prefaces the description of his own discoveries in *De Motu Cordis* by a critique of the Galenic theories detailing the contradictions implicit in them;

Lavoisier waxed eloquent about the inconsistencies of the Phlogiston theory, and Einstein and Eddington about the incoherencies of the notion of an aether.

The new theory, when it arises and is finally established by its success in reorganizing the phenomena harmoniously, appears as a rival to the old and stands in opposition to it. This is because it resolves the earlier contradictions. Nevertheless, it has developed out of its predecessor and preserves within it the elements of truth previously implied. The heliocentric cosmology, even after it had abandoned the belief in circular orbits, revealed the true basis of the earlier conviction that the heaven revolved in a circle about the earth at the centre; *i.e.*, that the earth revolved on its own axis. Newton's Laws of Motion remain valid in relativity theory, not only as a special case where distances are small and velocities low, but also because the Galilean frame of reference remains the starting point of reasoning and calculation for relativity. Accordingly, the history of scientific advance is a dialectical progression of conceptual schemes ordering experience, each specific to its period, each developing out of its predecessor, yet each opposed to it as the correction of its errors, while yet preserving (though transformed) the elements of truth of the earlier theories. It is, in consequence, a succession of theories each representing a higher degree of adequacy or truth than its predecessor.

Notes

1. *Sophist*, 245d.

2. *Critique of Pure Reason*, A97.

3. Cf. *Hypothesis and Perception*, pp. 139–154; William Harvey, *De Motu Cordis*.

4. In the instance given the whole Newtonian system is shown to be true only conditionally. But the logical principle involved is the same, for the categorical judgement is itself a system in miniature, which is conditionally true on the ground of the wider system in which it inheres and into which it develops.

5. Cf. *Foundations of Metaphysics in Science*, pp. 412–415; *Hypothesis and Perception*, ch. VII.

6. Cf. *Op. cit.*

7. *Cf. Gaston Bachelard, Le nouvelle ésprit scientifique*, ch. VI, § iv.

8. Cf. Kant, *Critique of Pure Reason*, A 133, B 172:

> And thus it is evident that indeed the understanding is capable of instruction and can be provided with rules, but judgement is a special talent which cannot be taught but only exercised. Hence it is the specific (talent) so-called mother wit, the lack of which no school can supply. For although rules galore borrowed from the insight of others may be offered to and, as it were, imposed upon a limited understanding, the ability to use them aright must belong to the pupil himself, and no rule which one may prescribe to him is an assurance against misuse in the absence of such a natural gift.

9. It may be alleged that there is no contradiction in asserting that a whale has gills and lays eggs, but this is specious. If these terms are understood as they should be in their proper context the very idea of a cetacean becomes a texture of contradictions.

10. The Greeks knew as well as Copernicus that there was some rotational relation between the earth and the heavenly bodies. The advance of astronomy developed the interpretive principles implicit in the perceived facts so as progressively to make them more coherent, modifying successive hypotheses until, with Aristarchus, the heliocentric hypothesis emerged.

11. Cf. Sir Isaac Newton, *Opticks* (Dover Publication, New York, 1952), pp. 1–17.

12. *Principia*, trans. Motte, ed. F. Cajori (University of California Press, Berkeley and Los Angeles, 1966), p. 21.

13. Cf. *Hypothesis and Perception*, pp. 189–196.

14. Cf. *Science and Hypothesis, loc. cit.*

15. *De Motu Cordis*, ch. VII.

16. Cf. *Hypothesis and Perception*, pp. 167–178; A. L. Lavoisier, *Traité Elementaire de Chimie* (Paris, 1789; Brussels, 1965); M. P. E. Bertholet, *La Revolution Chimique: Lavoisier* (Paris, 1964).

17. What has been said above of scientific inference in the empirical sciences, seems also to be true of mathematical reasoning, at least if Henri Poincaré is to be believed. Mere calculation is certainly purely formal and analytic as the categories of pure quantity require. But mathematical reasoning is not simply calculation and so far as it is concerned with relational systems it is constructive in the manner alleged above. It is both deductive and inductive at once, even though mathematical induction is not of the form attributed by the empiricist tradition to empirical induction. Proof by recur-

rence, which is what mathematical induction is, Poincaré declares to be synthetic *a priori*, and the indispensable foundation of all mathematical reasoning, however analytic. "Mathematicians therefore", he writes, "proceed 'by construction' . . . For a construction to be useful and not mere waste of mental effort, for it to serve as a stepping stone to higher things, it must first of all possess a kind of unity enabling us to see something more than the juxtaposition of its elements." (*Science and Hypothesis*, p. 15).

18. See J. Kepler, *Astronomia Nova* (Prague, 1609); *Werke*, ch. III (Munich, 1937).

19. Cf. my *Hypothesis and Perception*, ch. VII; "Dialectic and Scientific Method", *Idealistic Studies*, vol. III, p. 1 (1973); "Epicyclic Popperism," *British Journal for the Philosophy of Science*, vol. 23, 1972.

Chapter 13

Objectivity

I

Three World Views

The concept, in its three moments or aspects of universality, particularity, and individuality, thus specifies itself through judgement and inference into systematically ordered knowledge of the world. The dialectic of reason has run from the unity and universality of the concept, through its differentiation in judgement, to the inferential construction of a system unifying its differences in their mutual interplay. the various sciences as they have developed have tended to become more and more interlinked and united until today there is unbroken continuity between physics, chemistry, biology, and psychology, which is again continuous with the social sciences. So a world-view arises which, in virtue of its coherently ordered comprehensiveness and systematic character, claims objectivity and truth. Throughout the history of science this has been the case; even when the individual sciences seemed to be more disparate, some dominant idea has always tended to unite them into a single system. And as one scientific revolution has succeeded another the world-view associated with the earlier theories has been replaced by one coordinating the new views which have superseded.

The outcome is the conception of an objective universe ordered as the sciences dictate. It is objective in that the system of sciences which constitute it is explicit and concretely organized knowledge, but it is also subjective in that it is consciously known, so that the opposite aspects are identified in it. World-views are thus theories of the objective universe which are the truth of that universe as so far achieved, because they are its dialectical outcome. It is a "truth", however, which becomes modified as knowledge advances, and it is to that extent only relative to the historical epoch in which it is current. This does not make it wholly and finally relative, nor does it preclude the validity of an absolute truth, because in and through the current theory the absolute truth is developing itself, and each successive world-view is a specific version, or moment, of that truth. The drive of the process is always toward greater coherence and unity, and it is to this absolute that all theories and all *Weltanschauungen* are relative. Neither does this mean that the nature (let us say) of the physical world changes with our opinions about it. We are speaking of the universe as a whole, and the theories about it are its own dialectical product. At the dialectical stage which they represent, therefore, they are the specific moment of its objective truth.

Up to our own day there have been three major conceptions of the universe: the hylozoic, held by the Greeks and Medieavals; the opposite conception, the mechanistic world of Newtonian science; and the modern conception, which reconciles the mechanism of the second with the vitalism and teleology of the first.

Properly speaking, the idea of nature arises only as the concomitant of science, for it is the idea of the world as a single structure of interrelated bodies and events determined by uniform laws, the indispensable presupposition of scientific thinking. Accordingly, we find the idea of nature coming into being in the Western world concurrently with the scientific thinking of the early Ionian philosophers from Thales onward. First, the nature of things—what determined their mutual disposition and activity—was conceived as the stuff of which they were made, and the unitary, systematic relations among them were maintained by regarding this substance as one and pervasive. All things were held to be water, or air, or fire, and their diversity was explained as the differentiation of the one fundamental stuff (or nature) according to a single principle of change (for example, rarefaction and condensation). Hence the idea of nature became extended to the general way in which things are constructed, interrelated, and mutually affected. Scientific treatises were those "on the nature of things", and they explored precisely these features of the experienced world. Finally, the world as a whole, as a system of interrelated entities governed by universal laws, came to be thought of as a single individual—Nature—frequently personified and conceived as ubiquitous, omnicompetent, and all-inclusive.

The Greeks conceived the world as a living organism, constantly changing and in motion, which, however, they could make intelligible to themselves only in terms of a permanent, unchanging, eternal form, which yet was the source of all change—an unmoved mover at once both final and efficient cause. (This Aristotelian concept developed, of course, from earlier variants, of which Plato's Idea of the Good was the most significant). Because the eternal form was final cause, the world was conceived teleologically, as a scale of forms each striving to actualize a higher form. The ultimate form must therefore be the final object of desire toward which all things purposively tend. This nisus is lodged in a material thing, the matter of which is the potentiality of becoming informed. Matter, as such, is crassly unintelligible and is the presupposed condition of the deficiency of finite existents from the pure translucence of the intelligible form. But all matter is infused with soul, which is the source of all motion and change and the seat of the nisus to the actualization of form.

The Greeks found no hiatus between matter and mind but saw them as continuous phases of one scale of degrees. For the Presocratics it was a material scale, the soul always belonging to the purest or most unmixed grade, be it air with Anaximines and Diogenes of Apollonia, fire with Heraclitus, or "the thinnest of all things", the *Nous* of Anaxagoras. One must not regard these ideas as "materialistic", because the matter of the Presocratics was living matter and the soul was its purest unadulterated form. In a sense, all matter was simply downgraded soul. With Plato, soul floats loose from the body and is "akin to the forms", but yet not one of them; while for Aristotle, the two concepts are combined and the soul is the proximate form of the body, and the passive intellect is the place of forms, so that continuity between matter and form is preserved. Objectivity, accordingly, is a notion not yet explicit in the Greek mind, although its chief ingredient, universality, is their main discovery. Pythagorean numbers (σχηματκ) translated into Platonic forms (εξδη) are the progenitors of the objective truth in modern thought.

This is not the appropriate place to expound or to criticize in detail this conception of the universe, although it is immediately apparent that it holds conflicts implicit in it. For example, the dualism between matter and form is never wholly or satisfactorily overcome, and the soul remains an ambiguous entity which is somehow neither yet also somehow both. Aristotle comes nearest to solving the inherent problems, but he fails in the end by his inability to demonstrate how God, as pure form, can be both immanent in and transcendent beyond the world. He asserts both immanence and transcendence while insisting equally on the absence of all matter in God, and so he is committed to the sheer transcendence of the unmoved mover, to the detriment of his entire system.[1]

The hylozoic world-concept is not, however, a mere error, but is an embryonic form of a truth yet to be derived from it. Indeed there is much in it to which our own age has returned, although in a more sophisticated version. The Greek philosophers were the first to conceive of dialectic and to construct systems, knowingly or inadvertently, as continua of graded forms. Their grasp of the real as teleological was a sound insight, as was also the evolutionary notion of the world discoverable in Anaximander's speculations, in Empedocles', and in Aristotle's. The objective world as they conceived it was not simply subjective to them, but was the essential basis on which later science was built; and that, for all its apparent rejection of much which now seems fantastic, has preserved fundamental and important elements of truth.

In the detail of Aristotle's system, although in essentials it prevailed for centuries as the most advanced scientific theory, there were further contradictions, especially with respect to his theory of motion. These sorely troubled the Medievals and led eventually to modifications introducing ideas precursory to inertia and finally ushering in the Copernican and Galilean revolution. The detail of the history need not be repeated here.[2] Some of its consequences have already been noticed above, consequences following from the ensuing world-view as that of a mechanical universe, "objective" in the sense of being external to consciousness, leading to an unbridgeable gulf between matter and mind, and an intractable separation of facts from values. Here we found the origins of the problems in the practical and social field which mankind is facing today.

But mechanism in physics suffered a decline in the late nineteenth century with the successive failures of attempts to give mechanistic accounts of electro-magnetic phenomena. The physics of the twentieth century, in contrast, has abandoned both mechanism and materialism,[3] replacing forces by space-time curvature and viewing the occurrence of matter as a singularity in the metrical field. The effect of the change has indeed been revolutionary but the full philosophical implications of the revolution have not yet been widely recognized.

The most far-reaching result both of Relativity and of Quantum Theory has been to reverse the logical order of explanation of phenomena. Instead of tracing back events to the external relations between separate and mutually independent particles, contemporary physics locates and identifies particles in energy systems or fields, which exist if at all only as integral wholes. Structure has become prior to particularization, so that if either the position or the velocity of a particle is sought in isolation, the other becomes indeterminable. Further, in the microcosm, Pauli's Principle of Exclusion determines the nature and behaviour of particles in terms of the energy system in which they are included. Particles in Quantum Theory are no longer thought of as mass points so much as clouds, or, as they are often described, superposed waves—and waves are structural entities dependent upon the overall structure of the field. The same subordination of constituent to system is apparent in the atomic nucleus, in the interrelation of the nucleus and its "orbiting" electrons (viewed as standing waves), in the structure of molecules and the chemical bonds that determine it, and in what Henry Margenau calls the "cooperative phenomena" of crystalline solids.[4] In the macrocosm, according to Eddington and Dirac, space-time structure of the universe as a whole determines all the fundamental physical constants; and the mass of the universe, the cosmical number, the ratio of electrical to gravitational forces between proton and electron, as well as their respective masses, all prove to be essentially interrelated.[5] Other physicists, notably David Bohm, E. A. Milne, and D. W. Sciama, have demonstrated the essential unity of the physical universe in other but no less impressive ways.[6]

Such priority of the whole to its constituents is both in the nature of things and is epistemological; it is epistemological because it is also ontological. To explain and describe the entities of the world, they must be referred to the structural wholes to which they belong and they can be made intelligible only by so doing. And this is because they only exist, are distinguishable, and have the properties they do have as inseparable features of a structural whole. Priority of whole to part is what I shall call "teleonomy," borrowing the term from Jaques Monod,[7] but modifying its sense in the direction of holism to avoid his commitment to that of its older surrogate, teleology. Monod attributes purposiveness to organisms, while insisting that every detail of their structure and activity is physico-chemically accountable. Their peculiar character as living systems he describes as teleonomic because it is so designed as to produce an invariant end-result.[8] But that result is nothing more nor less than the maintenance and reproduction of a specific kind of system by reference to which alone their constituent processes become intelligible, and which determine what those processes are and how they interact. It is thus their holism which is teleonomic, and purposiveness proves to be but a subspecies of teleonomy. That it is wholly explicable in physico-chemical terms is hardly surprising since contemporary physics and chemistry are, as I have argued, themselves teleonomic.

Contemporary science also reveals a scale of complexifications, unbroken and continuous, from the physical entities that have already been mentioned to the macromolecules of protein and nucleic acid. These are the constituents of the cytoplasm and the nucleus of living cells. Biochemistry provides the links between inorganic substances and processes on one hand, and metabolic and physiological processes on the other, and these again are continuous with psychological. At every stage, the teleonomic character of the entities and their behaviour is unmistakable, and as the complexification increases so the teleonomy becomes more marked and more explicit. The scale, moreover, is hierarchical. The more complex wholes include the less complex and transform them into beings with the character demanded and determined by the nature of the higher totality.

Where teleonomy prevails, the whole is prior to the part and the ultimate explanatory principle is that which governs the organization and integration of the total structure. And as wholes develop in a continuous hierarchical scale, it is what emerges at the end, the most comprehensive, coherent, and articulated form of structure, that most adequately realizes what is potential in its predecessors on the scale. Explanation cannot therefore be reductive. Reduction will not merely fail to explain, it will even falsify; for it is the outcome of the scale, the end-product of the series of complexifications, which provides the key to the details, the previous stages, the relatively simpler phases, as well as to the structure of the scale as a whole. Hence reductionism always involves the genetic fallacy. The true nature of the real is to be sought in its most mature and developed forms rather than in its basal and primitive elements, though this, of course, is not to say that the basic elements do not implicitly reflect the nature of the totality into which they are integrated and out of which they are analysed. Quite the contrary, they are determined by that totality both in their character and their behaviour.

II

Subjective and Objective

It follows that, if by "objective" we are to understand the most complete and concrete, the most fully coherent and self-sustaining reality, we must expect to find it much more adequately expressed in the most complex and developed forms of the scale than in the elementary, purely physical forms. And the most developed are the mental, the fully purposive, the actively teleological, the conscious and intellectual, in short, the *personal* forms. According to the true bent of twentieth century scientific thinking (as yet but dimly recognized), objectivity does not lie in any barely self-external, mechanical world excluding all life and mind, but rather in self-conscious personality, an awareness realizing itself intellectually in a coherent and self-sustaining comprehension of the nature of the real, and realizing itself practically in the achievement of values that express its own nature as actualized in that comprehension.

This is a complete subversion of the seventeenth century world-picture, which is not surprising because it is the product of an intellectual revolution. Nevertheless, the seventeenth century was not utterly wrong. The physical universe is a mechanism of sorts; but what mechanists fail to see is that a machine is a whole with systematically related parts which do not remain unchanged in isolation. All the same, this phase of knowledge has its virtues. It insists on clear distinctions and precise reasoning, which are necessary to any exact science, even though it is prone to the accompanying vice of too rigid separation of mutually dependent parts which cannot maintain their identity in isolation. Hence the fatal separation of "subjective" from "objective" that has landed us in our present predicament and which today cries out for correction. This the contemporary scientific developments can offer. We are no longer presented with a self-enclosed mechanical world excluding mind, set over against the observer like a specimen in a bottle. Nature can now be seen as the process of generating the consciousness of itself as the mind of a developed organism, which is itself a phase in the process.

The new concept of objectivity is supported by a careful examination of scientific method. Acceptance of a scientific theory depends upon consilience of hypotheses and the convergence of evidence upon which all the best informed and best qualified experts agree. The established theory has been reached through a series of hypotheses

234   Part III. Dialectic

following one another in a developing scale. The objective view is the
most concrete and self-complete, that in which all sane persons agree
and on which all good evidence converges. It is the outcome of intellectual development, not just a separate and independent external
world.

The world-views are the objective (individual) forms of the fully
particularized universal. Each is the whole, yet each is again only one
moment of the whole—one specific world-view—and the last sums up
and includes the entire process through which it has been generated,
conceiving the universe as an evolutionary process from the most
elementry physical forms moving through successively increasing
chemical complications to living creatures which become aware of the
world in which they live, develop intelligence, and excogitate scientific
conceptions of the universe along with the history of their own culture
and intellectual life.

Nor is science with its history the whole story, for by turning in
upon itself yet again the dialectic fulfils itself further in philosophical
reflection upon all that has gone before in a whole range of
philosophical sciences reaching a further level of self-awareness embracing the whole dialectical system. The endeavour of science to comprehend the world always involves a further effort to unify experience
and to substantiate knowledge claims. First, science must presume
that the world is intelligible and can therefore be explained
systematically. This means that every explanation offered for any
phenomenon must be deducible from some unitary principle. Consequently, all science rests on a conceptual scheme defining the ultimately real to which everything can be traced back. Science and
metaphysics are never wholly separable or divorced. For the Greeks,
they were the same thing and so persisted into the Middle Ages. In the
modern period, though they have come to be treated as separable, they
have never really been so. The seventeenth century leaders of science
were all, each in his own way, metaphysicians, and their metaphysics
and their science were always intrinsically related. As Collingwood has
shown, science rests and must rest upon some absolute presuppositions which together, as a system, constitute its metaphysical foundation;[9] and Kuhn, likewise, has maintained that what he calls the
"paradigm" governing the science of any period involves conceptions of
the ultimate elements and fundamental nature of the world.[10] I have
tried to show in detail how science builds up a world picture and how
the conspectus of the findings of the whole range of sciences gives us a

metaphysic, such as, in unison with dialectical logic, I have been developing in these pages.[11]

Secondly, the claim of science to objective truth always involves and stimulates questions about the nature of truth and knowledge and so gives rise to epistomology, whether as a separate investigation or as one forced by the development of scientific thought upon the scientist himself. The development of Greek science in the fifth and fourth centuries B. C. gave rise to the scepticism of the Sophists and prompted the logical and epistemological enterprises of Plato and Aristotle. It is not insignificant that the former identified his speculations as dialectic. The epistemologies of the seventeenth- and eighteenth-century rationalists and empiricists, culminating in Kant's *Critique of Pure Reason*, were the direct result of reflection upon the science of their day. In our own day, scientists have themselves turned epistemologist—Planck, Einstein, Eddington, and Heisenberg are outstanding examples. Nor have philosophers been able to cut the umbilical cord altogether. Logical Empiricism derives its genealogy directly from what it takes to be scientific methods. Husserl's *Crisis* and his logical writings give testimony to the same self-enfoldment of reflective thought, and Merleau-Ponty's theories arise directly out of reflection upon empirical psychology. In short, science burgeons out dialectically into philosophy; objective knowledge generates the reflection upon itself which discovers the principles of objectivity; and that has been the subject matter of the present essay.

The objectivity of knowledge, its truth, is its comprehensive systematic coherence. It is coherence not only within itself but also with the world from which it has dialectically emerged, and so it is also in correspondence with the actual whole. The system of knowledge is itself specified as a scale—perception, understanding, science, and philosophy—and each of these has a similar form. Especially philosophy is dialectical in its procedure (even when it professes not to be and repudiates dialectic),[12] whether as philosophy of nature or of mind; and in its most self-reflective form of logic it is specified as a dialectical scale of categories repeating and repeated in the form of the whole. Thus, in showing forth the form of the fact, knowledge corresponds to the natural world, and in bringing the *scala naturae* to fruition as a coherent system of experience and knowledge it constitutes its truth. For the world is the dialectical totality, self-specified in and as a scale of forms, of which the system of knowledge is a late phase; and we have seen that in such a scale the later phase is the more adequate expression of the universal immanent and particularizing itself throughout the whole gamut. The later phase is thus the truth of all the prior phases, and being immanent in them is in a different sense prior to them. Moreover, it sublates and holds them transfigured within itself, being the explication and actualization of what in them was only implicit and potential. It is this later phase which, therefore, is called "objective," because it is more explicit, more articulated, more systematically integrated, and so more concrete than the phases from which it has developed and which it has superseded. So we say that scientific knowledge is more objective than casually perceived appearances, and we identify the objective world as that which science discovers, rather than that which common opinion imagines. "Objective," therefore, does not mean merely "extra-mental," for what is mental is much more complete and more complexly coherent than anything merely mechanical or simply physical. On the other hand, what is merely perspectival and limited is what in one sense can be called "subjective." It is what the objective supplements and makes complete. The "subjective" in this sense is confined to one special viewpoint and is, in consequence, only partial and provisional. That is why objective science is never the product or property of any one individual exclusively, but is forged by and belongs to a community of savants and ultimately to the total community of mankind.

III

Theory and Practice

A community or social whole, however, is much more than a scientific community of experts, nor could the latter exist without more widely varied and embracing social relationships. Mind is not solely theoretical in its pursuits and could never be theoretical if it were not also practical. The same, of course, is true in reverse. Its practical activity is always informed and so is only the other aspect of its inner experience (whether mere sensation at the lowest level, perception at the instinctive, or explicit knowledge in developed and rational conduct.) Theoretical science does indeed grow out of reflection upon experience, but that experience is just as much practical as cognitive. It is cognitive in and by means of its practical activity, and practical as the outer expression of its cognition and in reaction to what it perceives. Science, especially when experimental, is essentially practical, and both theoretical and experimental science frequently (if not always) arise out of activities directed to the more efficient maintenance of human life, with the devisal of practical means to increase human competence in everyday pursuits. For example, Archimedes' screw and the suction pump were both tools for everyday use and the products of scientific ingenuity.

And just as the common activities required for the supply of human needs call for social cooperation, so do the devisal and use of practical inventions. So, likewise, does the pursuit of scientific investigation. All three are intimately connected, and each have both theoretical and practical aspects involving sociality and community of effort.

Within the social whole, the scientific community, conducting research, discussion, and collaboration in investigation, is but one form of social activity, dependent on and implicating many others. Completely objective knowledge, therefore, cannot be confined to the natural sciences, but must include those intellectual and practical activities in which other values develop than those of theoretical truth and integrity. These other social activities are those which give rise to economic, moral, artistic, and religious consciousness and the standards of value which they disclose. Theoretical knowledge develops in a milieu of social practice with which it is integral and into which it passes over as technology. Theory and practice are two aspects of a single concrete objectivity in which theory is objectified as practice. In both aspects, it is socially organized and the joint outcome is civilization—a social order in which practical ends are envisaged and clarified in the light of theoretical reflection and the means to their realization provided by technical application of developing science. A community or ordered social whole is thus a union of subjectivity and objectivity, developing ultimately into that philosophical comprehension which is the complete realization of the conceptual whole and which illuminates practice as a total way of life, bringing the entire scale to consciousness of itself and pointing to a transcendent consummation symbolized in religion.

IV

Identity of Subjectivity and Objectivity

Knowledge is the object—the world—come to consciousness in the living organism, which in its organicism epitomizes the whole which it brings to consciousness. Knowledge, therefore, is from the first the self-consciousness of the object. It is the object aware of itself. Subject and object are thus *ab origine* identical; but they are also non-identical because the first is a higher phase in the dialectic through which the whole is realizing itself and has come to consciousness of itself. Hence, while it is itself of which it becomes aware, its awareness is a different and more adequate phase of itself than that of which it is aware, the immediately prior phase of its own dialectical development. In knowledge, the object (which is its own earlier phase) is sublated and transformed as self-consciousness. But this consciousness is not at first consciousness of self as object, but is consciousness of object as other than or nonidentical with self. In the first instance, then, it is inadequate to the completeness and coherence of the whole, which is dirempt in the opposition of object to subject.

As the nisus of the whole is constantly towards realization of itself as total and absolute, the persistent tendency of consciousness and knowledge is towards the unification of the duality in knowledge, which it effects by constant reflection upon itself. In coming to consciousness of itself, in the first instance, the world, or object, reflects *in* itself; and as awareness of itself, it reflects *upon* itself; and this reflection necessarily brings the subject to awareness of the relation between itself and its object and so makes it, with its object, object to itself, an awareness it expresses in referring to itself as "I." Henceforth, every endeavour to become more explicitly aware of the object takes the form of a further reflection upon the consciousness already achieved. It is a recurrent process of reflection upon reflection and a progressive advance in self-consciousness, in which at each stage the object is the previous stage reached. So the progress of knowledge is from perception, which is reflection upon sentience (itself the reflection of the organic internalization of the external world), to scientific reflection, and then from that to reflection upon science as knowledge of the world, and so to philosophy; and thence to reflection upon that as the theory of the relation between knowledge and its object, which is dialectical logic revealing the dialectical structure of the whole process. And as each phase is a more adequate realization of the whole than its predecessor, each phase is the norm and standard for, as well as the truth of, its predecessor. The final self-reflection, which brings the whole to awareness of itself as a dialectical scale culminating in that very self-awareness, is thus the self-awareness of the whole as ideal, as subject, as "I"; not merely as the finite ego confronting and reflecting upon an external object, but as the subject aware of itself as its object, and of its object as itself—the subject transcendent beyond the diremption of subject from object. It is thus a transcendental subject, though equally and at the same time a transcendent object since it is the object (the whole) aware of itself as subject. The truth of the conclusion and procedure of transcendental logic can thus be consistently reached only dialectically and only dialectically can transcendental logic be accomplished.

The transcendental subject is the indispensable condition of objective knowledge, for that is a coherent whole of interrelated elements which can be grasped as a whole and held together as a system only by a single unitary subject of awareness—the undeniable truth of Kant's transcendental deduction. This supplies the principle of unity and order which in the last resort is the criterion of factual and objective truth. And, as we have seen, it has been dialectically generated through the scale of physical and biological forms which constitute the factual world, to issue in self-conscious awareness and objective science, which is "the truth of" that world. Its culmination, however, cannot be realized in the mind of any one isolated finite organism, although it is necessarily immanent in every such mind. Because that culmination is the self-awareness of the whole which embraces all organisms, it must encompass their mutual relations, including that of persons, their intersubjective commerce and common awareness of their own self-transcendence. This, indeed, involves a necessary self-transcendence of the finite, which is inherent in all consciousness. The "problem" of other minds is, therefore, no real problem, because each mind is the world come to consciousness and that includes the mutual relation of minds. My awareness of other persons' organisms is an awareness of them, similar to my awareness of my own, as the media through which nature brings itself to awareness of itself. I am, thus, aware of them not just as bodies, but as living bodies, and not only so, but also as conscious and as self-conscious in referring each to him (or her-) self as "I," and as communicating with me in the I-thou relationship of persons. Their minds are thus brought to my consciousness, as mine is to theirs, in and through the dialectical coming to consciousness of the common world of which we are all members.

Moreover, this coming to consciousness of self-in-relation-to-other is possible only through the active intercourse of intelligent minds, so that all self-consciousness is *ab initio* at the same time a social consciousness. My knowledge of myself is also my knowledge of my relation to other persons, and only as a social activity can my knowledge of the world be properly brought to fruition in practical activity and in-science. This is one important reason why the consummation of knowledge in the philosophically reflective recognition of identity of subject and object cannot be achieved by any finite mind in isolation. It cannot be achieved except by way of a prior consciousness of community with others and through self-identification with others, both in contemporary community and in historical continuity. And no such identification is possible apart from practical interests and practical intercourse issuing sometimes in conflict but more generally in varying degrees of harmonious cooperation. Such practice is, of course, always informed, so that it involves concomitant community of knowledge and social development of theoretical competence.

The practical expression of this common experience issues in moral action and political order, and through and beyond these, reflection upon theory and practice gives art, religion, and philosophy. Thus are provided the ultimate standards of both truth and value, the objectivity of which has been dialectically established in a manner which overcomes and nullifies all relativism. The root cause of the contemporary predicament is thus extirpated, and we can proceed forthwith to consider the nature of value standards and how, in the light of the modern scientific world-view, they bear upon the solution of contemporary problems.

Notes

1. Cf. G. R. Mure, *Aristotle* (London, 1932), p. 173ff.; *Introduction to Hegel* (Oxford, 1940), pp. 44–49; Sir David Ross, *Aristotle* (London, 1937), p. 181; and my *Nature, Mind and Modern Science* (London, 1954), ch. V.

2. Cf. *Hypothesis and Perception*, chs. V, and VII; "Dialectic and Scientific Method," *Idealistic Studies* ch. III, p. 1 (1973).

3. Cf. Albert Einstein and Leopold Infeld, *The Evolution of Physics* (New York, 1954), chs. II and III.

4. Cf. H. Margenau, *The Nature of Physical Reality* (New York, 1950), pp. 437, and 445.

5. Cf. Sir Arthur Eddington, *The Expanding Universe* and *New Pathways in Science* (Cambridge, 1953); Edward Harrison, *Masks of the Universe*, p. 248; Paul Davies, *God and the New Physics* (Harmondsworth, 1985), p. 187.

6. Cf. E. A. Milne, *Relativity, Gravitation and World Structure* (Oxford, 1935); "Fundamental Concepts of Natural Philosophy," *Proceedings of the Royal Society of Edinburgh*, sec. A, vol. 62. 1943–44, pt. I; D. W. Sciama, *the Unity of the Universe*; David Bohm, *Wholeness and the Implicate Order*.

7. Cf. *Le Hazard et la Necessité* (Paris, 1970); Trans. A. Wainhouse (New York, 1970).

8. Cf. *ibid.*, and my discussion "Teleonomy and Mechanism," *Proceedings of the XVth. Internat. Congress of Philosophy*, 1973.

9. Cf. R. G. Collingwood, *An Essay on Metaphysics* (Oxford, 1940) and *The Idea of Nature* (Oxford, 1945).

10. Cf. Thomas Kuhn, *the Structure of Scientific Revolutions* (Chicago, 1962), ch. IX.

11. Cf. *The Foundations of Metaphysics in Science* (London, 1965); "Method and Explanation in Metaphysics," *The Future of Metaphysics* (Chicago, 1970); "Metaphysics and the New Physics", Forthcoming.

12. Good examples are: (i) the philosophy of Spinoza, who explicitly repudiates a superficial and inadequate version of teleological explanation, and appears at first sight to be advocating universal mechanism and determinism, but is throughout arguing for holism in reality and in knowledge in a system which is dialectically structured. (Cf. my *Salvation from Despair*, pp. 126–132). (ii) The philosophy of Husserl, who rejected the dialectical method, yet whose theory of phenomenology has, as observed above, been presented dialectically by de Muralt. (iii) The ideas of the later Wittgenstein, though presented in a sporadic and unsystematic fashion, reveal dialectical features; *e.g.*, the conception of "family resemblances" is a different notion of universals diverging from that of a class concept (abstract universality) in the direction of system (concrete universality). This tendency is more explicitly revealed in *On Certainty*, where Wittgenstein contends that assurance and conviction depend on the total system of experience, adumbrating a dialectical theory of perception and knowledge.

Chapter 14

Value

I

Dialectical Generation of Value

The most comprehensively coherent and articulate experience of the world is, then, the most truly objective. But it is inescapably an *experience* and therefore is also subjective. The best, most fully corroborated, and most widely accepted scientific theories are still products of the human intellect; but, as we can now see, they are not to be discredited on that account because the human intellect is the product and the fruition of the scale of nature, which is throughout teleonomic and so realizes the potentialities of its elementary forms by bringing them to consciousness in our minds. This knowledge, the systematically theorized concept of the natural world is what is objectively true; it is what the actual world objectively is, what is for us "the actual fact", as revealed to the self-conscious mind, a late stage in the dialectical development, the process of which *is* the actual world. The *objective* world of nature in its most highly developed form and the most completely explicated and systematically articulated *subjective* awareness therefore coalesce. As we said at the outset, knowledge is at once subjective and objective.

Once this essential correlation is recognized, a conception of value becomes available that is consonant with the holistic trend of contemporary scientific thinking. But the mind with its knowledge is never purely theoretical. Its awareness is objective also in a second sense, for it objectifies itself in practice, in activity which modifies the existing state of affairs and is "objective" to all observers and integral to their own consciousness in ways other than as merely theoretical revelation. Practical activitity is the outward expression in action of the mind's awareness of its world, of the condition in that world of its conscious self, and of its relation to other things and other selves. In that action the self is not isolated, but it is necessarily involved with the action of other persons whose awareness of it is as much practical as theoretical, for in large measure their practice may be identified with it, either as reaction to it or as cooperation with it.

The immanence in the individual mind of the principle of wholeness generates, from this consciousness of self and other, a conception of a more adequate and complete realization of that universal principle—in other words, of a better state of the self and of its world. The universal nisus towards wholeness is thus, in the self, the nisus toward self-fulfilment. It is desire, and what it aims at is "objective" for it in a third sense. It is its practical objective. This end, or aim, or object is in the last resort the ultimate object of the whole dialectical process. Hence, all three senses of objectivity converge. The word is not ambivalent although it is used in these three distinct ways, for they all coincide in the last, which transpires as the criterion at once of both value and truth.

II

Desire, Purpose and Objective Standards

Life and consciousness are successive phases in the dialectical scale. Each is the concrescence or focus in an individual organism of the entire world integrated as a system: in the organism through its coordinated reactions to its environment, and in consciousness through its active interrelating of its objects. Living activity (as merely physiological) is opposed to consciousness as unconscious, yet mentality is the developed outcome, the self-inwardizing and bringing to awareness of the organic whole. So each phase is a specific form, as well as a further degree of adequate actualization of the universal organizing principle.

The felt needs of the living organism, in its efforts to maintain its systematic wholeness, are experienced as appetites, as drives toward the satisfaction (or the fulfilment) of this whole. As feeling is organized in consciousness, these needs and their objects are brought to self-awareness. This occurs *pari passu* with the ordering of the sensed world, with the distinction from one another of external objects, and the identification, in that process, of the self as such. Needs are then felt as "mine," and their satisfaction becomes *my* satisfaction. Mere appetite is blind, but as it becomes conscious and aware of its object, it is transformed into desire. At the conscious level, desires are identified with the self, which is aware of their mutual relation. They are now grasped in context and seen in perspective. They have become the purposes of life and can be deliberately organized so as not to conflict and to be capable of harmonious realization. This harmonious realization of the self in a complete life is the purpose of living, what Aristotle defined as happiness or the good for man. The criterion of value thus turns out to be an ordered whole, in much the same way as did the criterion of factual truth.

The recognition of values is consequent upon purposive activity, which is characteristic of life and predominantly of human action. As human personality is the latest phase in the developing scale of natural forms, the subjectivity of values may be acknowledged without denying their equally objective significance. In fact, since objectivity has turned out to be systematically integrated wholeness, if that also proves to be the hallmark of value, its criteria will be just as objective and universal in their validity as are standards of truth.

Values are the goals of purposive action, and purposes derive from desire, which is the conscious phase of natural appetite and instinctive impulse. But these again are no more (nor less) than the expression of the urge intrinsic to all life to maintain itself as an organic system. Purposive action, therefore, is a late phase in the teleonomic development of natural forms. Though we think of it, not unnaturally, in terms of goals and end-states, strictly speaking all purpose is the endeavour to realize a design or structure of activity—the fulfilment of a whole. The principles of value for action, therefore, are the same principles of coherence and integration as prevail in the intellectual sphere. Let me try to explain this somewhat more in detail.

Desires arise from the material needs of life and from instinctive urges; but they are various and diverse, frequently coming into mutual conflict, not only with one another within the single individual, but also with the desires of other individuals. Such conflicts involve frustration and unrest. In a self-conscious, intelligent being, that unrest excites a new, secondary desire to remove the conflict. He can do so in himself

by adjusting his desires one to another, and in relation to other persons
by seeking cooperation in the achievement of ends sought in common.
The first recourse leads to internal regulation and self-organization, to
realize an integrated personality; the second leads to social organization and the regulation of social function. Both are the pursuit of order
and harmony and both are the activity of reason, as the principle of
organization. The satisfaction derived from the realization of them (for
they can only succeed in conjunction), the end at which they aim, is
the same: namely, a fully integrated personality in every individual.
The outcome in each case is a form of whole, the one personal and the
other communal, the grounds of both moral and social values.

The sources and origins of values are undoubtedly exceedingly
complex and diverse. It is hardly possible in a single chapter to give an
adequate account of them. It is commonly agreed that they are bound
up with our social tradition, but to say that is to say very little, for a
social tradition is itself a highly complex product of individual enterprises, cooperative endeavours, and a long history of conflicts and their
resolution in the effort to attain satisfaction. Were human beings
devoid of needs and desires, society would never come into being, and
it does come into existence because the needs and desires people do
have can be satisfied (if at all) only in cooperation. No person can survive, let alone attain satisfaction, in total isolation; accordingly, only in
community can needs be met and desires fulfilled. Human life is *essentially* social, if only because our survival depends on long parental care
in infancy, and thus requires familial association. But this is only the initial condition of sociality. Needs for sustenance, shelter, clothing, and
defence cannot be satisfied by persons in isolation; their supply with
any degree of efficiency calls for division of labour and the interlocking
of specialized skills and functions. Human society is thus from its
earliest beginnings an organized texture of activities requiring regulation, and demanding and providing a framework for institutions of
property and exchange, on which are built systems of law and administration. From this very fact results the complication and
sophistication of the simple needs of life, so that from them emerge the
further social needs for security, solidarity, and mutual dependability.
Out of these arise demands for personal and group loyalty, honesty,
and reliability in the transaction of business, and the concepts of
honour, fidelity, justice, and all the personal and social virtues. These
and kindred ideals are what people seek to realize in the course of the

long process of endeavour that constitutes a nation's history and develops a social tradition.

The obstacles to their realization are conflicts which inevitably arise between individuals and groups within the society, and equally and correlatively within individuals. Every individual experiences in his or her own personality frequent conflicts between desires and objectives. These may arise independently of relations to other persons, as for instance when gluttony interferes with health; but it is bound to occur whenever disputes arise between different persons because of clashes between their interests and aims. Such conflicts, whether within the single personality or between different individuals, are perpetual causes of frustration. Their removal is an objective common to all, and the attempt to effect it is known as the pursuit of happiness. It is the search for harmony and integrity, both personal and social, and neither without the other, covering every aspect of human life and including every individual. The ultimate aim of practice and the final criterion of practical value is a comprehensive conception of human welfare coincident with moral virtue.

Clearly, harmony and integrity imply a principle of organization (both in individual conduct and in social structure and administration) which is one of unity and conciliation. This then proves to be the ultimate principle of value, a principle of systematic integrate wholeness, as we anticipated, consonant with what we have already found to be the principle of objective truth. The objectivity of values is established by their universality, and, while personal ideals may be subjective to the individual, they can never be so exclusively because of the individual's unavoidable dependence for his welfare and his very survival on other people. Thus his ideals, if they are ever to be practically attainable, must also be the ideals of his society and must be shared in common with his fellow citizens. Accordingly, personal and social standards inevitably merge and are objective to all members of any particular community. Such values, however, remain relative to the society concerned in contrast to those of other societies. But when societies become interdependent and develop common interests, an essential relationship between their different value systems is bound to grow up in the course of time, and a new and wider system will evolve as the support for common values—a system objective to all societies. this unification can occur only through the exercise of the capacity common to all human beings to organize their lives and activities together—their rational capacity—so that a universal objective standard emerges.

An incipient recognition of such a standard is not entirely absent at the present day. There is general agreement, if at times and by many it is given only lip service, that there are universal human rights. Any nation that refuses to acknowledge them in principle (for example, South Africa) is widely condemned. Any nation that, while acknowledging the principle, violates them in practice, will not escape criticism. The recognition is not confined to the West, nor to any one ideology, and what is recognized is that human rights are universal. But, whether progress is being made toward such recognition of of universal standards of value, unless and until it is, our contemporary difficulties will not be surmounted.

In the final issue, the universal objective standard of value can only be the complete and comprehensive fulfilment of human personality, which is not, however, and cannot be, exclusively individual or subjective, because it can only be guaranteed through participation in a fully developed and comprehensive social structure. But the ultimate aim of that, again, must be the free and satisfactory development of individual capacities, without which the social order cannot be effectively maintained and dissension and conflict cannot be eliminated. It must be at once intellectual, emotional, and practical. It does not and cannot exclude the awareness of the comprehensive nature of the world—what is called a *Weltanschauung*—for that includes our view of ourselves and our place in the world and determines our conception of the worth and significance of the objectives we pursue. Once more, therefore, it becomes apparent that the criteri of factual truth and of ultimate value coincide.

Accordingly, complete personal fulfilment must be fully self-conscious and reflective, issuing not only in systematic scientific knowledge of the natural world, but also in art, religion, and philosophy, seeking, through them, to achieve that final atonement with the ultimate universal principle of the whole, that infinity, which in religion is identified with God. This final atonement is the supreme objective of all striving and all activity and is the ultimate standard at once of truth and of value. It is essentially an experience, and to that extent it is subjective; but it is also the fulfilment of the whole dialectical series that is, and is known as, the objective world. It is thus the final unification of subject and object, reconciling in itself the opposite poles of reality.

III

Dialectic and World Problems

Having thus reestablished objective standards both of theoretical truth and of value, by pursuing the course of the dialectic inherent in nature and in mind, in scientific thinking, in practical action, and in philosophical reflection, we are now in a position to consider the bearing that this dialectical approach has upon the practical problems of our age. These, however, are global: political, economic and ecological, cultural, moral and religious, and the sufficient treatment of any one of them would require at least a volume of its own. All that is possible here is to indicate briefly and schematically the sort of approach that has some prospect of success in finding solutions. The primary need is to reform our way of thinking to make room for dialectic and holism over and above mere formal analysis. What that requires has been the substance of the foregoing chapters.

The feasibility of solving any of our current major practical problems depends on the removal of the imminent threat of nuclear extinction, and to that end the resolution of the stubborn obstacle to peace presented by the persistent anarchy in international relations. For the major world problems are, as has been said, global, and they can be successfully tackled only by an agency with global capacity and power. Hitherto, no such agency has come into being, because the practical dialectic has so far brought us only to those forms of political order which have issued in the sovereign nation-state, and that, even as represented by modern superpowers, is not only inadequate and incompetent to act with global authority, but is the main cause preventing the pacific settlement of international disputes. What is needed, then, is to follow out the dialectic of what Hegel called "objective spirit" beyond the stage of the nation-state (as Hegel, in his day, could not have done), by developing the implications inherent in the concept of sovereignty in its modern context.

I have attempted to do this elsewhere.[1] The moments of the concept of sovereignty are legal supremacy and moral accountability, which may be identified respectively as its juristic and its ethical aspects. The ethical is based upon common interests, which today are worldwide and can neither be confined to separate nations nor served by national sovereignties. The juristic is the power and authority to enforce law and to maintain peace and order, which the sovereign independence of the several nations frustrates. The logic of common interests points to a world community and to the establishment of an international authority, representative of the world's peoples and constituted to give effect to their common (or "general") will. It would be equipped with legal institutions and invested with adequate power for enforcement of law in the international sphere and maintenance of world peace. Thus, it would be enabled to work through the appropriate agencies, providing them with the necessary resources to address the other problems outlined in the Introduction to this book.

There is a dialectic in ideological conflicts, the pursuit of which can bring about reconciliations. Democracy and socialism have ideals which often seem opposed, but they are both rooted in humanitarian ideas and in the conception of individual rights, both civil and economic. The equitable distribution and disposal of material resources would follow naturally upon the dialectical reconciliation of such oppositions as now inject themselves into international politics and are strident in the pronouncements of politicians. Despite these, the resolution of differences is rationally possible, and the solution of world problems becomes feasible. Environmental adjustments and measures for conservation follow upon the solution of the sociopolitical conflicts, but they require besides a new attitude towards nature. This derives from the revolution in scientific approach which has already been outlined, but perhaps it would not come amiss to dwell upon it somewhat more at length.

IV

Mankind and Nature

As was noticed above, nature for the Greeks was one vast living organism, sentient, self-moving, and conscious, in which human and other living beings were localized centres of the pervasive soul-substance. This soul-substance was, in the last resort, identical with, and the purest form of, that ultimate stuff (or nature) of which all things were made. The lesser souls, whether of gods, men, or animals, were differentiated by varying degrees of adulteration of the original stuff by its own less appropriate forms. The problem for the Greeks, therefore, both metaphysical and practical, was how the human soul could be purified and become wholly reidentified with the universal substance.

The birth of modern science in the sixteenth century A.D. produced an entirely different and opposite conception of nature, of which some account has already been given and the general effect of which has already been described. With the development of the notions of gravity and inertia, nature came to be viewed as an aggregation of bodies moved by forces calculable solely from their masses and positions. It was one great machine.

As stated earlier, this conception involved a cleavage between the machine—the total aggregate of material existence—and the conscious mind, whether of God (its putative creator) or of man (the subject of scientific knowledge). Various attitudes to nature arise from the dichotomy so created. Nature is first the object of human knowledge, set over against the knowing mind as an alien other to be observed from without. Next, as science succeeds in discovering natural laws, nature becomes an opponent to be conquered and controlled, a combination of forces to be subdued and domesticated, to serve the purposes of man. Subsequently, it becomes apparent that nature in the service of man has limitations, that resources of matter and energy can become exhausted, or so modified that man's purposes may be defeated by the very technology he employs to serve them.

Supervening upon these attitudes to nature, however, a third conception has arisen which complicates more radically the relation between nature and man. This new view emerged with the conception, in the mid-nineteenth century, of the idea of evolution. Henceforth, nature could not be regarded simply as a machine, but was conceived as a process of continuous development. Laws of mechanics are reciprocal and reversible, but an evolutionary process is unidirectional and progressive. Further, under this conception of nature, man is recognized as a product of evolution, and his knowledge the outcome of biological development. His relation to nature now comes to be envisaged in terms of that between organism and environment. The effect of this modification was not immediate or total, although its implications were revolutionary. Environment, at least in the first instance, was still regarded as external and set in opposition to the organism, which must adapt itself to alien conditions in order to survive. Man's adaptation follows upon that of lower species, which involves the development of sensibility, sense-organs for distance reception and cognitive apparatus. His capacity to know and to act intelligently, his conquest and control of nature, his social and technical advance, are thus seen as aspects of his adaptation to environment.

So conceived, social progress though very different in character and in principle from biological evolution, appears as an extension of the same process. Yet, as it proceeds, the development of human social organization, with its accompanying technical advances, reacts upon and bedevils biological adaptations. Species are decimated, energy sources are tapped and drained, the ambient life-giving envelopes of atmosphere and sea are polluted and the balance of nature is upset.

With the advance of biological science and the study of ecology, it has become apparent that the idea of adaptation of organism to environment was a misconception, for the environment is not static, nor is it a mere external setting for indwelling life. Evolutionary change involves the environment equally with the living thing. The two constitute a single organic whole, an open system in dynamic equilibrium. Modification of, or "control" over, the environment, therefore, becomes less a means than a menace to human survival, and the exploitation of nature more inimical than advantageous. Voices are then raised advocating conservation; but that involves a conflict between the demands of technical progress already made and those of environmental preservation. In some sense, the demand is for a reversal of the evolutionary process, which runs counter to the very conception of evolution itself. The use of technology to mitigate the ravages of technology is severely limited. The preservation of resources can be effected by new techniques only at the expense of other resources. Pollution of atmosphere and water can be limited by new devices but not eliminated. If population can be controlled, consumption may be limited, but the demand for progress and "development" will persist. The evolutionary process cannot be arrested, and if social progress could be reversed, it is not obvious that the results would be beneficial. The idea of nature hitherto engendered by science has, in its effects on practice, led men into an impasse—a labyrinth to escape from which we need a new guiding-thread, in the form of a new conception of nature and our own place in it.

The conception of nature as an evolutionary process, while remaining valid and fundamental, is, in certain respects, only provisional and transitional in modern science. Its adoption formed a bridge between mechanism and organism, providing for the emergence of the latter from the former; but it also served as a means of reducing the organic to the merely mechanistic. The dominant and characterizing feature of living things is their capacity for auturgic self-maintenance, a propensity which has never been wholly explicable, and was, in the last century, attributed by some thinkers to a mysterious vitalistic principle or entelechy. This perpetuated the cleavage between the animate and the inanimate and ran counter to the principle of evolution, for that requires the process of change from the inorganic to the organic and organismic to be conceived as continuous. The Darwinian version of evolution, most prevalent and best attested, alleges as the "mechanism" of the process nothing beyond chance mutation and natural selection, excluding any vitalistic principle, any teleological influence, or orthogenesis. Evolution, in consequence, comes to be regarded as a series of random changes in physico-chemical processes, leading by some form of natural selection, to more and more complex forms, from which have emerged the numerous diverse species of living things. The speculation that life has evolved from the non-living is, accordingly, accompanied by the conception of living processes as no more than highly complex chemico-physical activity. Reductionism became and remains the ideal of scientific explanation. And such reductionism is the counterpart of the technology that seeks to manipulate the process fundamental to life and ecology.

But what this approach overlooks, while it inevitably must and tacitly does always assume, is the integral, polyphasic coherence of the organism and the consequent forms of self-maintenance, through growth, regeneration, and reproduction. Without the dynamic coherence of living entities there could be no evolution and nothing to evolve. Adaptation is meaningless except on the presupposition of a systematically unified and self-maintaining organic whole, which maintains itself precisely by means of such adaptation. Without self-reproduction, mutation is equally meaningless; and, apart from organic integrity, selective advantage is an inapplicable concept.

Organismic wholeness is thus the indispensable presupposition of evolution and even the most radically physicalistic of biologists is constrained to admit that the fundamental distinguishing characteristic of life is "teleonomy"—quasipurposive determination to systematic wholeness. In essence, "teleonomy" is the dominance over constitutive parts, functions, and processes by the structure or the total organic system, the factor, whatever it is, that maintains or increases negative entropy in the ordered whole by mutual adjustment of its constituents, both among themselves and to environmental variations.

The mechanistic and the Darwinian conceptions of nature both involve some form of antithesis between the purely physical and the animate. In the former, it is a stark dichotomy between matter and mind; in the latter it is the persistent contrast of organism to environment. But the thoroughgoing organismic conception of the biosphere recognizes the unity and systematic interconnection of organism and its ambient world. Not only is the organism itself an open system, in constant commerce with its surroundings, exchanging matter and energy in continuous flow, but there is also a symbiosis among contiguous organisms forming a biocoenosis, limits to which can be set only relatively; so that in the final analysis the whole biosphere is a single organic whole. Nor can we stop here, for the description of the earth as a series of envelopes, lithosphere, hydrosphere, atmosphere, and so on, is valid only for limited purposes. These, along with the biosphere, are all intimately interdependent, and the whole earth must be taken as a single organic unity.

Lewis Thomas, giving expression to this idea, one which is perhaps the most recent development in the concept of nature, writes:

> I have been trying to think of the earth as a kind of organism, but it is no go. I cannot think of it in this way. It is too big, too complex, with too many working parts lacking visible connections . . . . If not like an organism, what is it like, what is it *most* like? then, satisfactorily for the moment, it came to me: it is *most* like a single cell.[2]

He repeatedly returns to this theme:

> Jorge Borges, in a recent bestiary of mythical creatures, notes that the idea of round beasts was imagined by many speculative minds, and Johannes Kepler once argued that the earth itself is such a being. In this immense organism, chemical signals might serve the function of global hormones, keeping balance and symmetry in the operation of various interrelated working parts, informing tissues in the vegetation of the Alps about the state of eels in the Saragossa Sea, by long, interminable relays of interconnected messages between all kinds of other creatures.[3]

As seen from the moon:

> Aloft, floating free beneath the moist, gleaming membrane of bright blue sky, is the rising earth. . . . It has the organized, self-contained look of a live creature, full of information, marvelously skilled in handling the sun.

The atmosphere is conceived as a membrane

> able to catch energy and hold it, storing precisely the needed amount
> and releasing it in measured shares.[4]

But not even the earth, taken as a self-contained unit, is separable from
what lies beyond its atmospheric skin. It is integrally dependent on the
stream of solar energy and inextricably involved with the whole solar
system. Then comes the cosmological physicist to assure us that no
terrestrial phenomenon is isolable from its interrelations with the rest
of the universe in both galactic and extragalactic space.

The outcome is a conception of nature as a single, individual totality, organismic throughout, in which distinctions are always relative,
and partial elements always determined in their individual form and detailed behaviour by the over-arching pattern of the totality.

It is not simply that the idea of nature in the advance of science has
come full circle and has returned to that entertained by the Greeks. In
some sense this has occurred, but the new conception is much more
elaborate and sophisticated than the original one, and is rather a combination and reconciliation of the two opposite notions of mechanism
and organism. The earlier mechanism rested in Newtonian physics,
which has today given place to relativity and quantum mechanics.
Physics has ceased to be mechanistic and has even adopted a conception of matter which is itself non-materialistic. Contemporary physics
is as teleonomic in principle as contemporary biology. It is the whole
structure of the physical world by which its details are determined.
The curvature of space-time dictates the laws of gravitation and elec-
trodynamics and fixes the fundamental physical constants. The enfold-
ment of space manifests itself as energy, wave systems suffuse the
whole of space, and the superposition of waves appears as material particles. The structure of energy fields determines the interlocking of
particles in the atom, and their mutual disposition the forms of the
molecule and its chemical valency. From these again arise the artistry
of crystalline forms, and no hiatus is found between them and those
aperiodic crystals which are the foundation of the chemical cycles of
living metabolism.

Each level provides the basis of that which succeeds, yet on every
level the characteristic properties of the appropriate entities depend
upon their total structure. They are "cooperative properties" impossible for less complex entities. Atoms have properties impossible for

free electrons, and molecules evince chemical affinities which are dependent solely upon the pattern of combination of their constituent atoms and are not characteristic of any atom in isolation. This is especially true of the macromolecules involved in the activities of living matter, which are not feasible at the inorganic level. It is the structure of each whole that determines its propensities, and structure is always whole, for it is not what it is unless structurally complete. We find, in consequence, that throughout the entire scale of natural forms, wholes predominate over and determine their parts. '*Totum in toto et totum in qualibet parte*' is true at every stage.

Consequently the cosmic organism, while it is one and indivisible, is at the same time a range of developing phases, which can be represented, and which display themselves, as a dialectical scale. The totality is constituted by the scale of its internal forms, and each level is in some sense self-contained and all-pervasive; yet each gives rise to the next above it by virtue of the potentiality within it infused by the immanent principle of the totality in which it is no more than a phase. This is an idea of nature, not merely as an all-embracing living animal, but as a dynamic organismic system, comprising a continuous range of wholes, on levels of progressively increasing complexity and integration. They are wholes mutually in dialectical relation, so that the entire system manifests itself as an evolutionary progression.

Let me once more recapitulate the dialectical relation in its full complexity. The wholes which it relates are each, in one aspect, self-contained and self-dependent, and, in another, mutually implicated and inseparably interrelated. Essentially the relation is serial, each successive whole being a fuller and more adequate realization of the systematic principle governing the entire series. So each is related to its predecessors as their fulfilment, requiring and incorporating the prior forms while actualizing potentialities of which they were incapable. For this reason, while the subsequent involves the antecedent, it also supersedes and, in some sense, negates its forebears. Each whole, then, is a grade, a developmental stage, within the total series, but also a distinct relatively self-subsistent phase standing in contrast and opposition to its neighbours. Yet because this opposition is resolved in the higher phase (which preserves the contrast while it supersedes it), the entire series remains continuous and coherent.

The relation of mankind to nature has now to be understood in the light of this dialectic conception. Human personality, developing within social structures peculiar to its appropriate level in the scale, is integral to the whole. On the other hand, as one level distinct from others, it confronts the prior phases as other and opposed. But this is only one aspect of its relation to them, for they are also its forebears and progenitors in which the potentiality of its emergence is instant. What humanity sees as nature is its own self in becoming; but more than this, nature is the very matrix from which its very being is contrived and the soil out of which it is nourished. It is not nature that man[5] has power to exploit, but man who is moulded and engendered by nature—not, however, as physical entities are determined by mechanical forces, but as expressing more explicitly the universal principle which through the natural processes has been bringing itself to fruition in human kind.

<h1 style="text-align:center">V</h1>

Residual Questions

Three major metaphysical questions arise out of this conception of mankind and nature. The first concerns the individuality and self-identity of man as a person, the degree of his self-sufficiency and freedom. How far is his identity submerged and overwhelmed in such a conception? If, *prima facie*, it may seem to be fatally subordinated to an all-absorbing totality, two considerations forbid any such conclusion. Apart from human thought and self-reflective consciousness there would be no idea of nature. It is his own self-determining and free thought that makes man aware of his world and his relation to it. So whatever idea of nature science generates, it is man's own science, his own construction, his own judgement of the world, and the interpretation, self-made, of his own experience. It cannot, therefore, be wholly subordinated to, and submerged within, the totality conceived as nature. Further, this reflection is not in conflict with that conception itself. For it is one form of a totality, self-generating in a scale of forms, each of which is more self-complete and self-maintaining than its predecessors. The human mind supervenes at a relatively highly developed stage and, accordingly, represents a high degree of self-sufficiency, integrity, and self-determination. It is the fruition of the natural process and cannot be reengulfed and submerged in its more primitive matrix.

The second major question is that of the ultimate character of the totality. Is it, as a whole, a consciousness, self-aware of its own identity? Or is it a mere schema correlating its diverse phases as we have conceived them? The latter is hardly plausible and is not consistent with the conception of a scale of concretely existing phases. First, so far from being a mere schema, the totality must be seen as a continuum of interwoven forms; and, secondly, among these forms human personality is one of the more highly developed, though in obvious ways incomplete and limited. Whatever transcends human consciousness can hardly be something more abstract, more diffuse, and less integrally whole. The implications which follow upon this reflection demand to be worked out in detail.

The third question follows naturally from these two. How does human life and purpose relate to the totality in which it is integral? What sort of self-determining conduct on the part of mankind is most appropriate to the conception of nature above outlined? The aspiration to conquer and control nature is now revealed as arrogant folly, liable to lead, as in our own day looks probable, to self-destruction. Man must somehow see himself as the instrument of nature's own purposes, which his science must divine and follow. Perhaps, in a new and more significant sense, we shall have to revive the ancient exhortation to live according to nature if we are to live successfully, satisfactorily and virtuously. But that does not mean that we must revert to what is primitive. Rather it implies that, when nature is adequately understood, the general direction of evolution will be more clearly seen, and human action and policy can then be properly alligned and assimilated to it.

These three questions are fundamentally metaphysical, even if also they have consequences for ethics, social theory, and technology. None of them is wholly new, but they all require reconsideration, and they must be reformulated in the light of a new conception of nature. Nor are they wholly separable, the answer to any one being implied in, and implying, the answer to each of the others. They are questions too large and difficult to receive the treatment they deserve in a single volume and I shall not attempt to do more than indicate an approach toward the answers.

(1) *The freedom and individuality of man*

If wholes are indivisible and teleonomic and in all cases determine the nature and behaviour of their parts; if the parts are thus reduced to integrants or moments within their wholes with no really independent existence, would men not be reduced to mere puppets whose strings are manipulated by alien hands? The whole to which they belong, nature, imposes its laws upon them. Does it make any difference whether they are mechanical, in the old classical sense of that word, or organismic, according to the new view of nature suggested in this chapter?

Indeed it does, for the totality is not just organic; it is dialectical and it issues in a whole on a level superior to organism. The organic is superseded and sublated in the psychical and epistemic. Consciousness and intelligence supervene upon organism and the higher phase, not the lower, is the dominant determining factor. Nature conceived as one vast organism is not a stupendous protozoon or an all-pervasive slime mould. The more advanced in the dialectical series the totality under consideration is, the more fully and distinctly is it articulated. Although its elements are inseparable, they are nevertheless distinct; and the more highly developed the whole, the more completely will be differentiated. Even at the organic level there is not just one vast organism but innumerable exquisitely variegated and diversified organisms organically interrelated. At any super-organic stage, therefore, there should be a totality differentiated into individuals each of which is more than merely organic.

It is precisely this that we do find. In the higher animals (at least) organism supports and burgeons into conscious mentality, and at the human level intelligence reaches the pitch at which social cooperation and theoretical reflection are possible. It is only here that the capacity develops to frame an idea of nature at all, itself testimony to a high degree of self-consciousness and all that that implies. In spite of what might be considered undesirable mystical associations, it would be not inappropriate to call this the spiritual level of the dialectical sequence.

If we review the course of that sequence throughout its length, we observe a continuous increase in the self-sufficiency and self-determination of the elements at each successive stage as the scale advances; and this applies equally to the differentiations and to the totality. At the spiritual level, therefore, the elements should be spiritual; that is, self-conscious, intelligent beings capable of a high degree of self-direction and self-determination. Their interrelations will be equally spiritual, or what we more ordinarily call social; and the totality of which they are members will be a community. But all this amounts to nothing less than the condition of individuality and freedom.

Freedom is not, despite frequent misconception, an indeterminate capacity to do all and sundry according to the unpredictable and unaccountable caprice of the agent. Unregulable caprice is not freedom; it is insanity. On the other hand, external determination equally precludes freedom. Intelligently directed action, however, is self-determined, because intelligent thinking is neither more nor less than the self-specification in conscious thought of a universal principle. Deliberate action, which depends on such self-determined consciousness, is the only sort of action which is entirely free, and only an intelligent being is capable of it.

Now such capability supervenes only at levels of development subsequent to organicism. It is the super-organic level which is both dependent on and regulative of the organic reactions that subserve it, where the capacity for thought and action emerges. Below this there can be no free individuality, and to call that independent because it is free would be a mistake. It is independent neither of its organic matrix nor of the social whole that it both generates and sustains, and which it nevertheless requires for its own efflorescence. The totality characteristic of this level, theefore, is a spiritual whole, approached through a social order and determined by rational self-awareness. It is thus a self-differentiating whole, which actualizes itself through and in self-conscious, rational individuals, just as analogously the organic totality specifies itself in and as determinate organisms. The analogy, moreover, is more than mere accidental similarity, for the self-conscious individuals are themselves organisms, and it is in them that organism realizes its potentialities.

Obviously, there is far more to be said about this matter. The essential nature, the process of development and the structure of an intelligent self-consciousness, as well as its social character, give ample scope for further development of the subject. Here I am concerned only to indicate the groundlessness of a possible objection to the idea of nature that has been adumbrated, to the effect that it would submerge and obliterate human personality.

That this is not the case becomes apparent when one reflects that free activity, understood as self-determined, is characteristic, in some degree, of all levels of natural process. It is only under the influence of the older, Newtonian physics that we tend to think of mechanical action as crassly determined. Contemporary physics is, as I have maintained, teleonomic, and whatever is a whole determining its own elements is self-determined and so to that extent free. Organic activity is a still higher degree of freedom. Metabolism is the self-regulating process of the organic system, and metabolism has been described by Hans Jonas as the first realization of freedom.[6] So we go up the scale: physiological processes are homeostatic, that is to say, self-regulating. They constitute the next degree of freedom. Instinctive behaviour is a grade higher, and then intelligent conduct. It is the new conception of nature that preserves the conditions of human freedom rather than destroys them. It is more compatible with human personality than any of the prior conceptions of nature.

(2) *The ultimate character of the universal whole*

Development of the last topic would naturally lead into reflection upon the second question raised for discussion. Is the universal totality merely a logical schema? Is it a spatiotemporal or a taxonomic structure? Or is it at once all these and more besides—a living, self-conscious, spiritual being? Of course the first two descriptions must be readily admitted, but they cannot be exhaustive. No dialectical system such as I have posited can be limited to a mere logical schema, or even to an evolutionary series extended in space and time. The dialectical relations require that the prior phases be retained sublated in their successors, even though they are superseded by them. Equally, the only complete, the only full reality which the prior phases enjoy is the realized actuality of their potentialities in the higher forms.

Without these the more primitive cannot even exist, because it is the immanence in them of the ultimate totality which brings them into being and makes them what they are. Our best, and perhaps in the last resort our only, clue to the nature of this ultimate reality is that of the highest stage with which we are acquainted. That, as has been seen, is the self-conscious, personal, and interpersonal. Can the existent universe as a whole be conceived as a being of this kind?

The answer, of course, is implicitly given in religion, which postulates a supreme being of the kind required. But that is not a complete or a distinct answer, because the question remains—how we are to conceive the Deity. Not only do different religions entertain different conceptions, but none of them is in itself clearly intelligible, for all of them are veiled in imagery or described in figurative language. No doubt that is unavoidable when finite minds seek to comprehend the infinite, but the metaphysician must strive to penetrate the obscurity, to interpret the metaphors, and to give the imagery meaning.

What we have so far maintained, is that the universe is one single, indivisible whole, self-specifying, self-differentiating, and proliferating as a continuous scale of interdependent forms dialectically related. Each form is itself a whole, self-differentiated in its own way and according to the principle operative at its own level. The later is superior to the earlier, inclusive of all that precedes and the fruition of prior potentialities. Each successively is more articulate, more fully integrated, and more self-determinately whole than its predecessors. Accordingly, the whole gamut is sublated and summed up in the final form, the extended series of its phases being not only compatible with, but necessary to, its all-encompassing unity.

If we have been right so far, it should follow that the highest from hitherto experienced, human mentality, is the closest analogy to the ultimate nature of the absolute whole. In that case, it must involve something like, yet somehow transcending, self-conscious personality. It must involve and yet transcend some form of organized community. It must be at once a physical, organic, intelligent, moral and spiritual whole, of which we (with all that is implicated in our nature) are integral members.

So regarded, nature cannot be limited to what we discover through the physical and biological sciences. We must add to these the social, psychological, and philosophical sciences, and must reflect upon the combined results of them all, if we are to arrive at an adequate metaphysical conception. Nature can no longer be thought of as the merely physical, devoid of all psychical and conscious elements, as the sort of abstraction by which it was represented in the nineteenth century. So far from excluding man and his mind, so far from standing over against and opposing humanity, as something to be subdued and exploited, nature and mind are to be seen as one—matter and mind fused into a single reality, as body and mind form one person.

Once again, the implications of all this demand further development than the scope of this chapter will permit.[7] But if we cannot now go further, what I have already said may give some indication of the answer that should be given to the third question: How does human life and purpose relate to the totality in which it is integral?

(3) *Man's relation to universal nature*

It would seem to follow from the position set out that the relation between mankind and nature must be sought at the upper end rather than in the lower or middle strata of the scale. The whole, in its ultimate character is of the nature of mind involved in and involving the interpersonal relations of a community. That again presupposes and sublates the biological and the physical. In relation to the whole, mankind must be seen as a single community, a kingdom of ends, the undivided interest of which is to maintain the integrity of the world that it inhabits. That maintenance is a responsibility upon man, so that his relation to nature is ethical, rather than simply biological or technical. The conception we need to deploy is that of a spiritual community of persons, mutually responsible for the welfare of all and for the material basis on which that depends. Nature must be pictured as man's Garden of Eden in which he is its latest product—the latest species generated in the process of its self-evolution. As its intelligent progeny, he has the responsibility of keeping it fertile, healthy, and beautiful. He must be its cultivator, not its exploiter. His is a moral responsibility, at once to nature and to his fellows; that is, a responsibility to the ultimate totality. It can, therefore, be fulfilled only in a spirit of unreserved self-giving, if it is to be fulfilled adequately. It must not be simply a duty imposed, but, in a consciousness of identity with the whole, a service freely rendered. In short, it must be, in the final outcome, the tendance of a spiritual *Heimat* in which the human spirit finds itself, because man and nature are one, and what is done to nature is *ipso facto* done to mankind.

Notes

1. In *The Survival of Political Man* (Johannesburg, 1950) and *Annihilation and Utopia* (London, 1966). Hegel, who argued dialectically, rejected Kant's recommendation for perpetual peace, and rightly, because Kant failed to see its incompatibility with national sovereignty, which he sought to retain in a world federation. Hegel's political vision was necessarily limited to his own historical period and so terminated with the state. He could not have envisaged the sort of dilemma we face today in the nuclear age, or have anticipated the conditions of world-wide common interest. His principles are sound, however, and need only be applied to international relations in our present situation. See my "Hegel's Theory of Sovereignty, International Relations and War," in *Hegel's Social and Political Thought*, ed. D. P. Verene (New Jersey, 1980).

2. *The Lives of a Cell*, p. 5.

3. *Op. cit.*, p. 41.

4. *Op. cit.*, p. 145.

5. "Man" is used here and throughout as a generic term including both sexes and without gender.

6. *The Phenomenon of Life* (New York, 1966), pp. 81–84.

7. Cf., however, my *Atheism and Theism* (New Orleans: Tulane University Press, 1977), ch. V.

Selected Bibliography

Allport, Floyd. H., *Theories of Perception and the Concept of Structure*, Wiley, New York, 1955.

Aristotle, *Physics*, Trans. Edward Hassey, Oxford at the Clarendon Press; Oxford University Press, New York, 1983.

Austin, J., *Sense and Sensibilia*, Oxford at the Clarendon Press, (England), 1962.

Ayer, A.J., *Metaphysics and Common Sense*, San Francisco, 1970.

Bachelard, Gaston, *Le nouvel ésprit scientifique*, Presses Universitaire de France, Paris, 1968.

Bartlett, Sir Frederick, *Remembering*, Cambridge University Press, Cambridge (England), 1961.

Bates, M., *The Forest and the Sea*, New York, 1964.

Bertholet. M.P.E., *La revolution chimique: Lavoisier*, Paris, 1964.

Blanshard, B., *The Nature of Thought*, George Allen and Unwin, London, 1939

———, *Reason and Analysis*, Open Court, La Salle, Illinois, 1969.

Bosanquet, B., *Knowledge and Reality*, London, 1885, 1892, 1968.

———, *Logic, The Morphology of Knowledge*, Oxford at the Clarendon Press (England), 1911.

———, *The Principle of Individuality and Value*, Macmillan, London, 1912.

———, *Implication and Linear Inference*, Macmillan, London, 1920.

Bohm, David, *Fragmentation and Wholeness*, van Leer Foundation Series, Jersualem, 1976.

————, *Wholeness and the Implicate Order*, Routledge and Kegan Paul, London; Boston, 1980, 1983.

Bradley, F.H., *The Principles of Logic*, Oxford at the Clarendon Press (England), 1922.

————, *Appearance and Reality*, Oxford at the Clarendon Press (England), 1897, 1930.

————, *Ethical Studies*, Oxford at the Clarendon Press (England), 1927.

Brain, Sir W. Russell, *Mind, Perception and Science*, Blackwell, Oxford (England), and Springfield, Illinois, 1951.

Braithwaite, R.B., *Scientific Explanation*, Cambridge University Press, Cambridge (England), 1953.

Brouwer, L.E.J., *Collected Works*, Amsterdam, New York, 1975–1976. *Brouwer's Cambridge Lectures on Intuitionism*, D. van Dalen, Ed., Cambridge University Press, Cambridge (England), 1981.

Cabrera, C., *Paramagnetisme et structure des atomes combines, Activation et structures des molecules*, Paris, 1982.

Capra, Fritjof, *The Tao of Physics*, London, 1975, 1983.

————, 'The Role of Physics in the Current Change of Paradigm,' Symposium on *The World View of Contemporary Physics*, Richard Kitchener, Ed., Forthcoming.

Cohen, R., and Wartoffsky, M., eds., *Hegel and the Sciences*, Boston Studies in the Philosophy of Science, Reidel, Dordrecht, Boston and London, 1984.

Collingwood, R.G., *an Essay on Metaphysics*. Oxford University Press, Oxford (England), 1940.

————, *An Essay on Philosophical Method*, Oxford University Press, Oxford (England), 1934, 1965.

————, *The New Leviathan*, Oxford University Press, Oxford (England), 1942.

————, *The Idea of Nature*, Oxford University Press, Oxford (England), 1945.

Copernicus, *De Revolutionibus Orbium Coelestium*, Culture et Civilization, Bruxelles, 1966.

Cornford, F., *From Religion to Philosophy, A Study in the Origins of Western speculation*, London, 1912.

d'Abro, A., *The Rise of the New Physics*, 2 vols., Dover, New York, 1951.

Davies, Paul, *God and the New Physics*, London, 1983, Penguin Books, Harmondsworth, 1986.

de Muralt, A., *l'Idée de la phénomenologie: l'Exemplarisme Husserlien*, Presses Universitaires de France, Paris, 1958.

Eddington, Sir Arthur, *New Pathways in Science*, Cambridge University Press, Cambridge (England), 1935.

———, *The Nature of the Physical World*, Cambridge University Press, Cambridge (England), 1928.

———, *The Expanding Universe*, Cambridge University Press, Cambridge (England), 1933.

———, *The Philosophy of Physical Science*. Cambridge University Press, Cambridge (England), 1939.

———, *Space, Time and Gravitation*, Cambridge University Press, Cambridge (England), 1950.

Einstein, A., *Relativity, the Special and General Theories*, London, 1954.

———, *The Meaning of Relativity*, London, 1956.

Einstein, A., and Infeld, L., *The Evolution of Physics*, New York, 1954.

Fichte, J.G., *Grundlage der Gesamten Wissenschaftslehre*, in *Sammtliche Werke*, Mayer und Muller, Leipzig, 1845–46.

———, *Science of Knowledge*, Peter Heath and John Lachs, Trans., Cambridge University Press, New York, 1982.

Frege, Gottlob, *Die Begriffschrift*, G. Olms. Hildersheim, 1964.

———, *Die Grundlagen der Arithmetik*, G. Olms, Hildersheim, 1961.

———, *Grundgezetze der Arithmetik*, G. Olms, Hildersheim, 1962.

———, *Translations from the Writings of Gottlob Frege*, P. Geach and M. Black, Blackwell, Oxford (England), 1952, 1980.

———, *Foundations of Arithmetic; a Logico-mathematical Enquiry*, J.L. Austin, Trans., Philosophical Library, New York, 1950.

Galilei, Galileo, *Dialogue Concerning the Two Chief World Systems*, Stillman Drake, Trans., University of California Press, Berkeley, California, 1962.

Gibson, J.J., *Perception and the Visual World*, Boston, 1950.

Gödel, Kurt, *Collected Works*, Solomon Feferman et al. Eds., Oxford University Press, New York, Oxford at the Clarendon Press, Oxford (England), 1986.

————, "Über formalunentscheidbare Sätze der Principia Mathematica und verwandter Systeme," *Monatshefte für mathematik und Physik*, Band XXXVII, 1931.

Hanson, N.R., *Patterns of Discovery*, Cambridge University Press, Cambridge (England), 1958.

Harris, E.E., *An Interpretation of the Logic of Hegel*, University Press of America, Lanham, Maryland, 1983.

————, *Atheism and Theism*, Tulane University Press, Martinus Nijhoff, The Hague, 1977.

————, *Annihilation and Utopia*, George Allen and Unwin, London, 1966.

————, *Hypothesis and Perception, The Roots of Scientific Method*, George Allen and Unwin, London 1970.

————, "Epicyclic Popperism," *The British Journal for the Philosophy of Science*, vol. 23, 1972.

————, *The Foundations of Metaphysics in Science*, George Allen and Unwin. London, 1965. Reprinted by The University Press of America, Lanham, Maryland, 1983.

————, *Nature, Mind and Modern Science*, George Allen and Unwin, London, 1954.

————, *Perceptual Assurance and the Reality of the World*, Clark University Press, New York, 1974.

————, *Salvation from Despair, A Reappraisal of Spinoza's Philosophy*, Martinus Nijhoff, The Hague, 1973. *The Survival of Political Man*, Witwatersrand University Press, Johannesburg, 1950.

————, "Dialectic and Scientific Method," *Idealistic Studies*, vol. III, no. 1, 1973.

————, "Teleonomy and Mechanism," *Proceedings of the XVth. International Congress of Philosophy*, 1973.

Harrison, Edward, *Masks of the Universe*, New York and London, 1985.

Harvey, William, *De Motu Cordis*, Chauncy, D. Leake, Ed. and Trans., Springfield, Illinois, 1941.

Heb, D.O. *The Organization of Behaviour*, London, 1949.

Hegel, G.W.F., *Gesammelte Werke*, F. Hogemann and W. Jaeschke, Eds., Felix Meiner Verlag, Hamburg, 1981–.

———, *The Science of Logic*, A.V. Miller, Trans., George Allen and Unwin, London, 1959.

———, *Encyclopaedia of the Philosophical Sciences: Logic*, W. Wallace, Trans., Oxford at the Clarendon Press, 1892. Revised by A.V. Miller, with a foreword by J.N. Findlay, Oxford University Press, Oxford (England), 1975.

Heidegger, Martin *Holzwege*, Frankfurt-am-Main, 1952.

Heisenberg, W., *Philosophical Problems of Nuclear Science*, London, 1952.

———, *Physics and Philosophy*, New York, 1962.

Heyting, A., *Intuitionism; and Introduction*, North Holland Publishing Co., Amsterdam, 1956.

———, *Logic and foundations of mathematics, Essays dedicated to A Heyting*, Wolters-Noordhoff, Groningen, 1968–69.

Hilbert, David, in *Verhandlungen der dritten Internationalen Mathematiker-Kongresses*, 1904.

Hilbert, D., and Ackermann, W., *Gründzuge der theoretischen Logik* Springer, Berlin, 1959.

Hofstadter, D.R., *Godel, Escher, Bach*, Vintage Books, New York, 1980.

Hume, David, *Treatise of Human Nature*, Selby-Bigge, Ed., Oxford at the Clarendon Press; Oxford University Press, New York, 1978; Dutton, London, 1911.

Husserl, E., *Die Krisis der europäischen Wissenschaften und die transcendentale Philosophie*, herausgegeben von E. Stroker, Felix Meiner Verlag, Hamburg, 1977.

———, *Erfahrung und urteil*, Felix Meiner Verlag, Hamburg, 1972. *Husserliana. Gesammelte Werke*, Martinus Nijhoff, The Hague, 1950–.

———, *Formule und Transcendentale Logik, Husserliana*, Band, XVIII.

———, *Ideen zu einer Phänomenologie und phanomenoligische Philosophie*, Martinus Nijhoff, The Hague, 1982.

———, *Logische Untersuchungen*, M. Niemeyer, Tübingen, 1968.

————, *Experience and Judgment*, J.S. Churchill and K. Ameriks, Trans., Northwestern University Press, Evanston, Illinois, 1973.

————, *Formal and Transcendental Logic*, Dorian Cairns, Trans., Martin Nijhoff, The Hague, 1969.

————, *Ideas*, W. Boyce Gibson, Trans., George Allen and Unwin, London, 1931, 1956.

————, *Logical Investigations*, John Findlay, Trans., Routledge and Kegan Paul, London, 1970.

————, *The Crisis of the European Sciences*, David Carr, Trans., Northwestern University Press, Evanston, Illinois, 1970.

Ittleson, H.W., "Size as a Cue to Distance: Static Localization," *American Journal of Psychology*, vol. 64, 1951.

Ittleson, H.W., and Cantril, H., *Perception, a Transactional Approach*, Doubleday, Garden City, 1954.

Ittleson, H.W. and Kilpatrick, F.P., "Experiments in Perception," *Scientific American*, 185, no. 2, 1951.

Jasper, H.H., (Ed.), *The Reticular Formation of the Brain*, Henry Ford Hospital International Symposium, 1958.

Jeans, Sir James, *Physics and Philosophy*, Cambridge University Press, Cambridge (England), 1942.

Jonas, H., *The Phenomenon of Life*, New York, 1966.

————, *Philosophical Essays*, Englewood Cliffs, NJ, 1974.

Jordan, Z.A., *Philosophy and Ideology*, Dordrecht, 1963.

Joseph, H.W.B., "A Plea for Free-thinking in Logistic." *Mind*, vols. XLI, XLIII, N.S. 1932–1934.

————, *Introduction to Logic*, Oxford at the Clarendon Press, (England), 1916.

Kant, Immanuel, *Kritik der Reinen Verunft*, herausgegeben von G. Hartenstein, Leopold Voss, Leipzig, 1853; Raymond Schmidt, hrs., Felix Meiner Verlag, Leipzig, 1926, 1930.

————, *Critique of Pure Reason*, Kemp Smith, Trans., Macmillan, London, 1929.

Kepler, J., *Astronomia Nova*, Prague, 1609. *Werke*, Munich, 1937.

Kneale, Martha and William, *The Development of Logic*, Oxford University Press, Oxford (England), 1962.

Koffka, K., *Principles of Gestalt Psychology*, Routledge and Kegan Paul, London; Harcourt Brace, New York, 1935.

Kuhn, T., *The Structure of Scientific Revolutions*, Chicago University Press, Chicago, 1962, 1970.

Lakatos. I, and Musgrave, A., *Criticism and the Growth of Knowledge*, Cambridge University Press, Cambridge (England), 1970.

Langer, S., *Mind: An Essay on Human Feeling*, John Hopkins Press, Baltimore, 1967–1983.

————, *Philosophical Sketches*, John Hopkins Press, Baltimore, 1962.

Lashley, K.S., *Brain Mechanisms and Intelligence*, Chicago, 1929.

Laviosier, A.L., *Traité elementaire de Chimie*, Paris, 1789; Brussels, 1965.

Lukasiewicz, J., "On the Intuitionistic Theory of Deduction," *Nederlands Akademie voor Wetenskap, Proc.*, Ser. A., 55, 1952.

MacIntyre, A., Ed., *Hegel*, University of Notre Dame Press, Notre Dame, London, New York, 1972.

Margenau, H., *The Nature of Physical Reality*, New York, 1950.

Merleau-Ponty, M., *The Phenomenology of Perception*, C. Smith, Trans., Routledge and Kegan Paul, London, 1962.

————, *The Structure of Behaviour*, A.L. Fisher, Trans., Boston, 1963.

Milne, E.A., "Fundamental Concepts of Natural Philosophy," *Proceedings of the Royal Society of Edinburgh*, Sec. A, vol. 62, 1943–44, Part I.

————, *Relativity, Gravitation and World Structure*, Oxford University Press, Oxford (England), 1935.

Monod, J., *Le hazard et la necessité*, Paris, 1970. *Chance and Necessity*, A. Wainhouse, Trans., New York, 1970.

Mure, G.R., *Aristotle*, London, 1932.

————, *Introduction to Hegel*, Oxford University Press, Oxford, (England), 1940.

————, *A Study of Hegel's Logic*, Oxford University Press, Oxford, (England), 1950.

Natanson, M.A., *Edmund Husserl, Philosopher of Infinite Tasks*, North-western University Press, Evanston, Illinois, 1973.

Newton, Sir Isaac, *Philosophiae Naturalis Principia Mathematica*, 3rd. edn., Alexander Koyre and Bernard Cohen, Eds., Cambridge University Press, Cambridge (England), 1972.

————, *Mathematical Principles of Natural Philosophy*, F. Cajori Ed., Motte, Trans., University of California Press, Los Angeles, California, 1966.

————, *Opticks*, Dover Publications, New York, 1952.

Piaget, J., *The Psychology of Intelligence*, London, 1950.

Planck, M., *The Philosophy of Physics.* London, 1936.

————, *The Universe in the Light of Modern Physics*, London, 1937.

Plato, *Dialogues of Plato*, Benjamin Jowett, Trans., Oxford at the Clarendon Press, (England), 1953.

————, *The Works of Plato*, Edith Hamilton and Huntington Cairns, Eds., Princeton, New Jersey, 1963.

————, *Plato's Theory of Knowledge; Theatetus and Sophist*, F. Cornford, Trans., Routledge and Kegan Paul, London, 1935.

Poincare, H., *Science and Hypothesis*, Dover Publications, New York, 1952.

Popper, Sir Karl, *Conjectures and Refutations*, Basic Books, New York; London, 1962, 1963.

————, *Objective Knowledge; An Evolutionary Approach*, Oxford, at the Clarendon Press, Oxford (England), 1979.

————, *The Logic of Scientific Discovery*, London, 1959.

————, *The Open Society and its Enemies*, Princeton University Press, Princeton, New Jersey; London, 1950, 1966.

Price, H.H., "Appearing and Appearances," *American Philosophical Quarterly*, Vol. I, 1964.

————, *Perception*, Methuen, London, 1950.

Prior, A.N., *Formal Logic*, Oxford University Press, Oxford, (England), 1962.

Reichenbach, H., *Experience and Prediction*, Chicago, 1938.

————, "On the Justification of Induction," *The Journal of Philosophy*, 37, 1940.

Rescher, N., *The Coherence Theory of Truth*, Oxford University Press, New York, 1937.

Richter, D., (Ed.), *Perspectives in Neurophysiology*, London, 1950.

Ross, Sir David, *Aristotle*, London, 1937.

Russell, Bertrand, *Human Knowledge, its Scope and Limits*, George Allen and Unwin, London, 1948.

———, "Logical Atomism," *Contemporary British Philosophy*, Series I, George Allen and Unwin, London, 1924.

———, *Our Knowledge of the External World*, Norton, New York, 1929.

———, *The Philosophy of Logical Atomism*, University of Minnesota Press, Minneapolis, Minnesota, 1959.

Russell, B. and Whitehead, A.N., *Principia Mathematica*, Cambridge University Press, Cambridge (England), 1927. Reprinted 1973.

Schelling, F.W.J., *System des Transcendentalen Idialismus*, Klett Cotta, Tübingen, 1800; Felix Meiner Verlag, Leipzig, 1957.

———, *System of Transcendental Idealism*, Peter Heath, Trans., University of Virginia Press, Charlottesville, Virginia, 1978.

Scher, J., (Ed.) *Theories of the Mind*, New York, 1962.

Schlipp, P.A., Ed., *the Philosophy of A.N. Whitehead*, Northwestern University Press, Evanston Ilinois, 1941.

———, *Albert Einstein, Philosopher, Scientist*, Northwestern University Press, Evanston, Illinois, 1949.

Schroedinger, E., *Space-Time Structure*, Cambridge University Press, Cambridge (England), 1950.

———, *Science and Humanism*, Cambridge University Press, Cambridge (England), 1952.

Sciama, D.W., *The Unity of the Universe*, New York, 1961.

Snell, B., *The Discovery of the Mind, The Greek Origins of European Thought*, Blackwell, Oxford, 1953.

Spinoza, B., *Collected Works*, E. Curley, Trans. and Ed., Princeton University Press, Princeton, New Jersey, 1985–.

———, *Ethics*, A. Boyle, Trans., M. Dent, London, 1910.

———, *Ethics, and Selected Letters*, S. Shirley, Trans., Hackett, Indianapolis, Indiana, 1982.

————, *Opera quotquot reperta sunt*, van Vloten en Land, Eds., Martinus Nijhoff, The Hague, 1913–1914.

Stonier, T., *Nuclear Disaster*, Penguin Books, Harmondsworth, 1963.

Teilhard de Chardin, P., *Le phénomene humain*, Editions du seuil, Paris, 1955.

————, *The Phenomenon of Man*, B. Wall, Trans., Introduction by Julian Huxley, Collins, London, Harper and Rowe, New York, 1959.

Thirring, W., *"Urbausteine der Materie,"* Almanach der Osterreichischen Akademie der Wissenschaften, Band, 118, 1968 (Imp. 1969).

Thomas, L., *The Lives of a Cell*, New York, 1974.

Thorpe, H., *Learning and Instinct in Animals*, London, 1963.

Tinbergen, N., *A Study of Instinct*, Oxford University Press, Oxford (England), 1952.

United States Atomic Energy Commission, *The Effects of Nuclear Weapons*, Washington, D.C., 1964.

United States Congress, The Holifield Committee Hearings on Radiation, 1959.

Verene, D.P., (Ed.) *Hegel's Social and Political Thought*, Humanities Press, Atlantic Highlands, New Jersey, 1980.

Vernon, M.D., *Experiments in Visual Perception*, Penguin Books, Harmondsworth, 1966.

————, *The Psychology of Perception*, Penguin Books, Harmondsworth, 1969.

von Wright, G.H., *The Logical Problem of Induction*, Blackwell, Oxford (England), 1957.

Whitehead, A.N., *Adventures of Ideas*, Cambridge University Press, Cambridge (England); Macmillan, New York, 1933.

————, *An Enquiry into the Principles of Natural Knowledge*, Cambridge University Press, Cambridge (England), 1919, 1925; Dover, New York, 1982.

————, *Process and Reality*, Cambridge University Press, Cambridge, (England), 1929. D.R. Griffin and D.W. Sherburn, Eds., Free Press, New York, 1978.

————, *Science and the Modern World*, Cambridge University Press, Cambridge (England), 1926. Macmillan, New York, 1925, 1948; New American Library, New York, 1953.

————, *The Concept of Nature*, Cambridge University Press, Cambridge (England), 1920, 1971.

Whitehead, A.N., and Russell B., *Principia Mathematica*, Cambridge University Press, Cambridge (England), 1927 (Reprinted 1973). England, 1920, 1930, 1964, 1978.

Whitrow, J.G., "On Synthetic Aspects of Mathematics," *Philosophy*, vol. XXV, no. 95, 1950.

Whittaker, Sir Edmund, *From Euclid to Eddington*, Cambridge University Press, Cambridge (England), 1949.

Williams, D., *The Ground of Induction*, Harvard University Press, Cambridge, Massachusetts, 1947.

Wilson, J. Cook, *Statement and Inference*, Oxford at the Clarendon Press (England), 1926.

Wittgenstein, L., *On Certainty*, Blackwell, Oxford (England), 1969. *Philosophical Investigations*, Routledge and Kegan Paul, London, 1967.

————, *Tractatus Logico-Philosophicus*, Routledge and Kegan Paul, London, 1960.

Zeman, J.J., "Quantum Logic with Implication," *Notre Dame Journal of Formal Logic*, 29, 1979.

Index

Absolute, 111, 117, 184; irregularity, 138; provisional definition of, 184
Abgehobenheiten, 96, 100, 181
Abschattungen, 95
Abstraction, 43, 132, 144, 183, 192; extensive, 43
Action, 153, 203, 245; discriminatory, 203; reciprocal, 192
Actual entity, 196
Actuality, 193, 195f; concrete, 196; sub-categories of, 196
Adequation, 150
Aether, 224; incoherencies of, 224
Aggregate, 90, 125, 131f, 140, 147, 161, 191f; of unit elements, 183; open-ended, 140
Alphabet, 159
Anaxagoras, 229
Anaximander, 230
Anaximenes, 229
Ancient Greece, 190
Anderson, C.D., 63, 214
Anschauung, 77
Anstoss, 83, 117
Anthropology, 10
Antithesis, 85, 116
Apophantics, 89, 107; formal, 89, 91, 107
Appearances, 82
Apperception, 86n2, 110
Appresentation, 114
Archimedes, 207; screw, 237

Aristarchus of Samos, 223, 225n10
Aristotle, 45, 64, 89, 128, 177, 187n15, 191, 209ff, 229f, 245
Arithmetic, 25, 30, 32, 207
Arms race, 5
Association, 82f
Atom, 132f, 137, 143, 148, 151, 179, 193, 196; Bohr's, 223; chemical affinities of, 133; hydrogen, 176, 194; structure of, 222f
Atomic. *See* Fact, Proposition
Atomism, 190, 192f; Logical, 30f, 40, 42f
Attention, 100, 177f, 180; cognitive, 181
Aufheben, 154. *See* also Sublation
Austin, John, 67, 70n35
Auturgy, 142
Axiology. *See* Value
Axiom, 209, 211ff
Ayer, A.J., 70n36

Bachelard, G., 194, 207
Background, 96; systematic, 191. *See also* Horizon
Bartlett, Sir F., 70n35, 156n15, 219f
Bates, M., 69n19
Becoming, 173–181, 186
Being, 182, 186, 192; and becoming, 173–181; Doctrine of, 110; spiritual, 261; supreme, 261; thinking, 153
Berkeley, G., 118

Biochemistry, 9f, 232
Biocoenosis, 61, 195
Biology, 9, 58, 61, 186, 255; continuity with physics, 227
Biosphere, 61, 195; organismic conception of, 254
Black, M., 55
Blanshard B, xi, 34, 46n31, 69n21
Bohm, D., 60, 69n16, 187n8, 231
Bohr, N., 223
Bosanquet, B., 46n23, 69n21, 93
Bradley, F.H., 46n23, 93, 133f, 155n4
Brahe, Tycho, 64, 208, 220f
Brain, Sir W. Russell, 70n34
Braithwaite, R.B., 56
Broad, C.D., 70n36
Brouwer, L.E.J., 43f
Buffon, 223

Cabrera, C., 194
Calculation, 31f, 207, 215
Calculus, 56, 154, 207f, 215; formal, 208f; propositional, 184
Cantor, 28f
Capra, F., 69n16, 175
Catalyst, 137
Categories, 75, 78f, 85, 99f, 102, 117, 122, 167, 172, 178, 182; are concepts, 200; dynamic, 191; Hegelian, 179; of actuality, 193ff; of contemporary science, 193–197; of Perception, Ch. 10, 171–186; of Reflection, Ch. 11, 189–197; of systematic thinking, Ch. 12, 199–224; provisional definitions of the Absolute, 184; scientific, 197
Causation, 145, 192; final, 8, 229
Cause, 51, 126, 190f; and effect, 126; efficient, 229; final, 229
Cell, 61, 142, 147, 194, 245
Chance, 51
Charge, 174
Chemical, bonds, 152; cycles, 61, 137, 141f 152; elements, 137, 186, 192
Chemistry, 10, 194; contemporry, 231; continuity with physics and biology, 227

Chomsky, N., 68
Circle, 142, 212
Circular argument, 212
Civilization, 3; European, 3; modern, ix, 4
Clark, Le Gros, 71n40
Class, 27ff, 32, 49, 183; concept, 152
Classification, 209
Cogito, 79, 94, 108ff, 116, 173
Cognition, 81, 173f, 177; immediate, 190; object of, 200
Coherence, 77, 81f, 102, 110, 118, 121, 163, 166, 201, 204, 208, 211, 228, 238; logic of, 98; of conceptual scheme, 222; polyphasic, 253; systematic, 235. See also Truth
Collingwood, R.G., 14, 80, 234
Colombo, 207, 217
Colour, 127, 137, 185
Combustion, 63, 217f
Common sense, 189f; and Newtonian science, 190–193
Community, 236f, 240, 246f, 259, 262; organized, 262
Commutation, 32f
Comparison, 135, 178
Complement, 157
Complementarity, 148, 167, 196f
Complementary, 158, 170n2
Complementation, 146
Complexification, 196, 232
Concatenation, 123f, 191
Concept, 24, 31, 43, 75ff, 80, 84, 90, 93, 96, 102, 154, 178f, 181, 182f, 199f, 227; abstract, 43, 49, 92, 199; and function, 26; a priori, 101; class, 27f; Doctrine of, 110, 193; dynamic, 174; extension of, 27f; Hegelian, 197; is theory of theory, 199; objective, 199; specification of, 199; theoretical, 199; theory of, 76, 81, 131, 172, 199; transcendental, 120; universal, 85, 174
Conception, 81
Conceptual scheme, 201ff, 210f, 219, 222, 224, 234
Concrescence, 196f

Conditional, 206; Philonian, 33f, 45
Conduct, 199; intelligent, 260
Configuration, 135, 148, 158, 194
Consanquinity, 137
Consciousness, 8, 111, 114, 116, 153, 238, 259; absolute, 94, 128; human, 257; primordial dator, 95, 115; religious, 237; self-reflective, 153; social, 239; transcendental, 97, 115; world come to, 237
Consistency, 163f, 208; self-, 164
Constant conjunction, 50, 52, 215f
Constants, physical, 59, 127, 231
Constitution, 93, 97, 105, 108f, 115, 128. *See* also Self
Construction, 63, 219
Content, and form, 24, 154
Context, 162, 210, 212
Continuum, *135-140*, 158, 160; heterogeneous 138f; homogeneous, 137f, 162; of graded forms, 230
Contradiction, 84, 93, 146, 150, 164, 201, 208, 217, 219, 225n9, 230; Law of, 163–169
Contradictories, 158, 167
Contraries, 158, 167, 169n2
Contrast, 174, 177, 182
Cook, Wilson, 155n4
Copernicus, 64, 133, 223, 225n10, 230
Copula, 27
Correlatives, 192
Corroboration, 56, 63, 65, 204, 217f
Cosmology, 64, 223; heliocenteric, 224
Creativity, 196
Crystal, 61, 137, 176, 181, 196; aperiodic, 61, 196, 255; periodic, 196

Darwin, C., 63, 65, 223
Data, 56, 117f; hard, 56; hyletic, 102; sense, 67
Davies, Paul, 60
Deckung, 96
Deduction, 49f, 62f, 65, 76, 206, *209-215*; analytic, 210; from phenomena, 63, 211; transcendental, 77, 239
Definition, 209, 212f; *per genus et differ-*

entiam, 210; real, 210; stipulative, 210
Degree, 136; of truth, 224; scale of, 152, 158, 160. *See also* Scale
Deity, 261
Descartes, R., 66, 79, 94, 207
Desire, 119, 244–248
Detachment, rule of, 33f
Determinacy, 174f, 180, 186; quantitative, 182
Deterrence, 5
Development, dialectical, 149, 218; teleonomic, 245
Dialectic, 81, 82–86, 89, 105*e.s.*, 119f, *Pt. III*, 149, 166, 169, 173, 215, 230, 234, 237; and the Law of Contradiction, 163–169; and world problems, 249f; of knowledge, 184; Plato's, 7, 107
Dialectical, 258; concretion, 184; logic, 163, 167. *See also* Logic; movement, 209; order, 179; process, 165; relation, 256; scale, 154, 158, 165, 172; sequence, 259; series, 171; stirrings, 161
Difference, 157–163, 164, 166, 191f; qualitative, 182; relevant, 219
Differentiation, 144, 177. *See also* Principle of
Diogenes of Apollonia, 229
Dirac, P.A.M., 214f, 231
Discursus, 144f, 165, 178f, 181; inductive-deductive, 208; logical, 174; logico-epistemic, 175
Distincta (Distincts), 136, 158, 162; qualitative, 177
Distribution, 32f
Double helix (DNA), 141
Duration, 144

Earth, 161, 195, 254f
Eddington, Sir Arthur, 29, 127, 138, 176, 224, 231, 235
Ecology, 252f
Effect, 126. *See also* Cause
Ego, 78f, 83f, 94, 96, 109ff, 115ff, 119, 153, 238; Transcendental, 83f,

94, 97, 108ff, 115ff, 119f. *See also* I

Eide (εξόη), 229

Eidos, 102, 105

Eighteenth century, 58

Einstein, A., 59, 192, 224, 235

Electro-magnetism, 230

Electron, 63, 132, 137, 148, 214,, 222f, 231; orbiting, 222f, 231

Empedocles of Acragas, 230

Empiricism, 9, 14, 49*e.s.*, 57f, 63, 118f; contemporary, 192; Logical, 235

End, 151

Energism, 193

Energy, 135, 138, 143, 148, 151, 175, 196; atomic, 4; radiant, 151; systems, 186, 231

Engels, F., 167

Entailment, 24

Environment, 61, 195, 251; organic, 195

Epistemology, 76, 79, 81, 118, 173, 231, 234

Epochē, 95, 98, 108, 180

Erdmann, 90

Error, 201

Escher, M.C., 140f

Essence, 96, 108, 123, 171; and existence, 193; categories of, 192f, 197; Doctrine of, 110, 191f; generic, 158, 160

Ethics, 10, 12, 79, 258

Evaluation, quantitative, 189. *See also* Value

Evening star. *See* Venus

Evidence, 65, 93ff, 97f, 102, 109, 202, 216; coherence of, 222; empirical, 14; system of, 218; falsifying, 14; physiological, 178; primordial, 96; psychological, 178

Evolution, 63, 173, 230, 251ff; direction of, 258

Excluded Middle, 94. *See also* Law of Exclusion. *See* Principle of

Existence, 122, 193

Existentialism, 13

Experience, 78, 80, 98, 208; primordial, 113

Experiment, 201f, 213; Harvey's, 207; Lavoisier's, 217

Expertise, 204

Explanation, 190; teleological, 241n12

Extension, 26ff, 91, 145; of concept, 27f, 30, indifferent to quality, 183

Extent, 182; continuous, 186

Fabricius, 207

Fact, 30, 106, 153, 204, 206, 208, 230; actual, 243; atomic, 42, 49, 60, 65, 192; coherent organization of, 221; form of, 42, 154, 171ff, 180; organized body of, 211

Falsification, 14, 63

Feeling, 119, 197

Feyerabend, P., 15

Fichte, J.G., 82–86, 89, 98, 103n2, 105, 107, 111, 116f, 119f

Field, 135, 143, 175, 196, 231; continuous, 135; metrical, 193, 231; psychical, 115, 200; sensuous, 178f; unified, 59; universal, 175

Figure, and ground, 77, 158, 177ff, 202; geometrical, 141f, 147f, 185

Finite, 239; organism, 239; self-transcendence of, 239

Folklore, 190

Force, and expression, 191ff; Coulomb, 143; gravitational, 231; inner, 191f; saturation, 143, 193

Form, 152ff, 172, 191f; and content, 24, 154, 191; intelligible, 229; specific, 159; of the facts. *See* Fact; *Platonic*, 229

Formal Logic. See Logic

Formalism, 89–92

Formalization, 153

Formula, 209; for ellipse, 221

Foundation, 100, 122ff, 127

Frege, G., 17, 25–31, 32, 40, 42, 44, 46n15, 67, 90, 183, 209

Freedom, 257, 258ff

Function, and concept, 26; argument of, 26f; mathematical, 26

Fürsichsein, 181

Galaxy, 181
Galen, 64, 204, 207
Galileo, 63f, 230
Gametes, 137
Gedankenexperiment, 64
Gegenstandslehre, 107
Gene, 137
Genetic code, 11
Genus, 158
Geodesic, 193
Geometry, 132, 147, 185; Euclidean, 190f
Germplasm, 137
Gestalt, 77, 135
Gibson, J.J., 70n35
Gleichzahlig, 28f
God, 117, 248, 251; consequent nature of, 196; did not make man merely two-legged, 209; immanent and transcendent, 230; unmoved mover, 230
Gödel, K., 44, 47n30
Gradation, 123, 136, 138, 148, 150; specificity of, 160
Gravity, 151, 251; law of, 142
Greeks, 225n10, 228f, 250, 255
Green, T.H., 69n21
Ground, 159

Hanson, N.R., 14, 63, 68
Harmonics, 185
Harrison, E., 175
Harvey, W., 63f, 204, 207, 217, 223
Hegel, F.W.G., x, 69n21, 81, 89, 93, 103n11, 105, 110f, 119f, 152, 154, 166ff, 174, 178f, 181, 184f, 191f, 196f
Hegel's Logic, x, 81, 110f, 154, 161, 192f, 196f, 197n2, 249, 263n1
Heidegger, M., 13
Heisenberg, W., 59, 176, 235
Helium, 194
Heterogeneity, 139. *See also* Continuum
Heyting, A., 43f
Hilbert, D., 47n30
History, 228, 247; of science, 227, 234

Hofstadter, D.R., 46n17
Holism, 60, 100, 133*e.s.*, 181, 195, 231f, 241n12, 249
Hologram, 60
Holomovement, 60, 187n8
Homogeneity, 137ff. *See also* Continuum
Horizon, 94ff, 100, 102, 109, 190f
Hume, D., 51ff, 76, 118, 125
Husserl, E., 13, 18n5, 18n6, 87n3, 89–128, 180f, 235, 241n12
Hutton, E.L., 71n40
Hylē, 109, 111, 115, 126
Hylozoism, 228, 230
Hypotheses, 62, 204f, 211, 219; consilience of, 233; Copernican, 221, 223, 225n10; higher level, 209; lower level, 209; primitive explanatory (myths), 190; scientific, 14, 208; not mere conjectures, 208; working, 201
Hypothetico-deductive. *See* Method

I, 83f, 97, 109, 113, 115, 238f; –thou relationship, 239. *See also* Ego
Idea, 111, 118, 120, 193; absolute, 111; agreement between, 222; legal and moral, 137; of Good, 229; of number, 183; Platonic, 196
Idealism, 86; British, 14; transcendental, Ch. 6, 113–120
Ideals, 246f
Identity, 84f, 157–163; and difference, 166, 169, 191f, interdependence of, 159; bare, 160, 162; in difference, 99, 136, 203; of differences, 159; of opposites, 173; Law of, 158; philosophy of, 168; through difference, 160, 219; uniform, 183; within system, 164. *See also* Law
Ideology, 248; conflict of, 250
Imagination, 85, 87n8, 98
Immanence, 144, 146, 261
Immediacy, categories of, 184; perceptual, 173
Implicate order, 60
Implication, 24, 33–42, 218; formal,

37f, 41; material, 34–37, 41, 167; strict, 34, 41
Individual, 200, 227
Individuality, 257–260
Induction, 49–58, 63, 65, 76, 206, 215–221; enumerative, 216; justification of, 52; mathematical, 225n17; principle of, 51, 53
Inertia, 230, 251
Inference, 24, 34, 85, 89, 93, 118, 208, 219, 227; based on system, 218; deductive, 49, 52; extension of judgement, 208; linear, 209; principles of valid, 24, 80; scientific, 206–221; synthetic *a priori*, 214
Infinite regress, 133f
Infinity, reiterative, 93
Insight, 207
Integration, 196; organic, 253
Intensity, 182
Intention, 98, 105, 109, 116
Intentional performance, 94, 109, 115. *See* Object
Intentionality, 108
Interests, 247; common, 249f, 263n1
International, Law. *See* Law; relations, 249
Interrelation, 177
Interval, 138; musical, 186
Intuition, 50, 95f, 178; blind, 178; direct, 218; pure, 122, 125f; sensuous, 180
Ittleson, H.W., 70n35

Jeans, Sir James, 176, 180
Joachim, H.H., 69n21
Jonas, H., 12, 260
Jordan, A.A., 170n3
Joseph, H.W.B., 34, 46n21
Judgement, 78, 85, 93, 96, 219, 227; affirmative, 203; *a priori* synthetic, 75, 82, 86n2; categorical, 204f, 224n4; classification of, 205; disjunctive, 205; hypothetical, 205; incipient, 169n1, 177; negative, 203; particular, 206; perceptual, 202f; scientific, 202–206; traditional forms of, 204f; universal, 206

Kant, I., 47n34, 55, 67, 69n21, 75–86, 89, 92, 97, 99, 102, 107, 117f, 120, 127, 145, 166ff, 178, 191, 201, 225n8, 235, 239, 263n1
Kepler, J., 63f 208f, 220f, 222, 254
Key pattern, 141
Klever, W., xii
Kneale, Martha and William, 26, 29f, 44, 45n3, 45n6, 46n19, 46n24
Knowledge, 153, 171f, 199, 237; background of, 211; not representation, 171; not static, 222; objective, 78, 80, 199, 237; organized, 212; outcome of natural processes, 171; scientific, 201; systematically ordered, 227
Kosok, M., 154
Krebs cycle, 141
Kuhn, T., 14f, 63, 68, 234

Lakatos, I., 14
Language, 203
Laplace, P.S., 59
Lashley, J.D., 71n40
Lavoisier, A.L., 63f, 217ff, 224
Law, 246; algebraical 32, 153; empirical, 90; fundamental, 201; general, 216; International, 4; Logical, 90; of association, of commutation, of distribution, 32, 153, 189n6; of Excluded Middle, 94, 158, 160; of identity, 158, 160, 163, 166; of motion, 151, 211, 224; of Nature, 11; of Noncontradiction, 94, 158, 160, 162f, 166ff; of thought, 157–169; physicochemical, 142; psychological, 90; universal, 229
Leptocosm, 176
Lebenswelt, 96, 108, 110f, 180f, 190. *See also* Life-world
Leeper, F., 71n40
Leibniz, G.W., 149
Leistung, 109
Lenin, I., 165
Lewin, K., 71n40
Life, 180, 244; human, 258
Life-world, 13. *See also Lebenswelt*
Locke, John, 52, 101, 209, 222

Logic, ixf, 1f, 80f, 118, 154, 172, 179; apophantic, 87n3, 100f, 120; dialectical, x, Pt. III, 131–154, 166, 171, 184, 238; genealogy of, 100; first order, 43; formal, 9, 17, Pt. I, 23–45, 31, 49–68, 58, 62, 76, 78, 85, 89, 91f, 131, 133f, 152, 157, 166f, 169, 171, 182–186, 184, 195, 199, 207, 213; anathema to, 160, and scientific method, Ch. II, 49–68; inadequacy of, 91ff, 108, presuppositions of, *see* Presuppositions; mathematical, 25f, 29; objective, 89; of being, 108; of confirmation, 207; of discovery, 207; of knowledge, 154; of logic, 107; of movement and life, 166; of quanta, 184; relevance of, 1f; subject matter of, 179; subjective, 89; symbolic, xi, 9, 31f, 153f, 184; traditional, 9, 78, 108. *See also* formal; transcendental, x, Pt. II, 75–128, 131, 239

Logical Atomism. *See* Atomism

Lukaseiwicz, J., 47n33

Machine, 142, 251

Macrocosm, 231

Magnitude, 182; concept of, 184

Manifold, 30, 81, 109, 160; of sense, 79, 167, 178; theory of, 91

Many, 182

Margenau, H., 231

Mars, orbit of, 63f, 208f, 220ff

Marx, Karl, 166ff

Mass, 58ff; points, 231

Materialism, 192f, 229

Mathematics, 7, 43, 75, 91, 154n1, 183, 195, 215; language of, 30f

Matrix, 135f, 143, 151, 256; dynamic, 187n8; energy, 180; indeterminate, 182; physical, 179f; universal, 135, 196

Matter, 135, 138, 175, 192f, 196, 214; and form, 191f, 230; anti–, 214; equation of motion for, 176; living, 229; proximate, 177

Meaning, 97, 108

Measurement, 189f

Mechanism, 11, 192f, 230, 251ff

Mediaevals, 193, 228, 230

Meiosis, 137

Memory, 98

Menge, 27ff, 182f

Mentality, 176f, 244, 259; human, 262; primitive phase of, 176

Merleau-Ponty, M., 68, 71n39, 235

Metabolism, 61, 137, 141, 176; first realization of freedom, 260

Metaphysics, 23fd, 31, 75, 79ff, 118, 171, 234f, 258, 262; inseparable from science, 234

Method, 54f; hypothetico-deductive, 62, 216; scientific, 47–68, 62–65, 196

Microcosm, 144, 147ff, 151

Middle Ages, 190

Mill, J.S., 90

Milne, E.A., 231

Mind, 8, 154, 197, 230, 262; human, 153, 257; knowing, 199

Modus ponens, 94

Modus tollens, 94

Molecule, 61, 137, 142, 179, 181, 196; macro– 61, 152, 194, 232, 255

Moment, 123f, 144, 151, 158, 183, 227; conceptual, 200ff; negative, 160; particular, 204; of concept, 200; of sovereignty, 249; universal, 204

Monod, J., 231

Moore, G.E., 70n36

Morning star. *See* Venus

Morveau, G. de, 64, 217

Multiplicity, 144, 182

Mundanization, 115

Muralt, A. de, 103n11, 105–111, 119, 241n12

Mure, G.R., 168

Mythology, 190

Nation-state, 4, 249

Natural attitude, 91f, 122 190

Nature, 154, 171, 233, 250–257, 259, 262; and mind, 262; control over, 252; exploitation of, 252; idea of, 228,

256f, 259; of things, 228, 231; philosophy of, 235. *See also* Law of

Negation, 84, Ch. 9. 157–169, 174f, 180f, 191; bare, 157; of negation, 181; significant, 157f, 167; the instrument of specification, 158

Negative, 203f; identity with self, 162; moment, 160; relation to self, 160

Neurophysiology, 10

Neutron, 214f

Newton, Sir Isaac, 63, 141, 211ff, 219, 224; *Opticks*, 212ff, 219; *Principia*, 213, 219

Nineteenth century, 58

Nisus, 146

Noema, 108, 110

Noesis, 108f

Non-being, 175, 182, 186. *See also* Not-being

Noncontradiction. *See* Law of

Non-ego, 116

Not-being, 157, 192. *See also* Non-being

Nothing, 173f, 178, 182, 185

Not-I, 84. *See* also Non-ego

Noumenon, 79

Nous, 229

Nucleon, 132

Nucleus, 222

Number, 25f, 28ff, 182–186; atomic, 137, 194; definition of, 25; imaginary, 32; irrational, 32; negative, 32; Pythagorean, 229

Object, 25ff, 29f, 40, 80, 83, 86, 96, 106ff, 115f, 121; and subject, 110, 197; concept of, 199; definite, 179, 181; empirical, 109; eternal, 196; experience of, 81; external, 245; factical, 105; form of, 172; independent, 121–128; intentional, 87, 102, 122; material, 95f; non-independent, 121–128; primordial, 95; qualified, 182; substrate, 100f; transcendent, 239; universal, 174

Objectivity, 6ff, 12, 16, 57, 94, 118, Ch. 13, 227–240; identity with subjectivity, 237–240

Observation, 8, 56, 76, 201, 216; scientific, 204; theory-laden, 63, 210, 216

One, 27, 182, 185; among many, 182; of many, 182

Ontology, 89, 231; formal, 89, 107

Opposite, 158, 178, 181

Opposition, 83, 147, 150, 221, 224; square of, 169n2

Order, 135, 138, 200, 221; prior to disorder, 139; rule of, 140; social, 248. *See also* Principle of

Organism, 61, 147, 172, 179, 194f, 229, 251f; finite, 239; individual, 244; living, 156n13, 244; multicellular, 194, 196

Organization, 135, 138, 140–144, 200; activity of, 181; principle of, 75, 81. *See also* Principle

Other, 157, 160, 174, 177f; something and, 191

Overlap, 158, 165, 169. *See also* Terms, overlap of

Own, my primordial, 114f

Pairing, 115

Palaeontology, 143

Paradigm, 14f, 63, 234

Parmenides, 157, 173; Plato's *Parmenides*,

Part, 107, 121–124, 143, 145, 191

Particles, 175, 193, 231, 255; elementary, 11, 59f, 143, 151, 176, 180f, 195, 214; virtual, 175

Particulars, 90, 160, 182, 194, 200f, 227; atomic, 153, 161; bare, 33, 49, 92, 183, 209f, 218; in external relation, 183

Pauli, W., 143, 153, 195, 231

Percept, 175

Perception, 63, 65–68, 77, 81, 98f, 102, 109, 145, 172, 177, 189, 200f; categories of, Ch. 10, 171–186; immediate, 162; judgement of, 203; minimal object of, 158; theory of, 102, 118

Perihelion, 205

Peripatetics, 221
Personality, 246, 248; human, 256, 260; self-conscious, 262
Person, 233, 239f; other, 245ff
Pfander, A. 103n11
Phaedo, 190
Phenomena, 81; cooperative, 231; explanation of, 231
Phenomenology, 91, 100, 108, 181
Philo of Megara, 46n18
Philonian, 34, 38, 40, 45. *See also* Conditional
Philosophers, 2; Greek, 228ff; Ionian, 228
Philosophy, 1f, 6, 17, 154, 234f; contemporary, 16f; identified with logic, 2, 17; of common sense, 192
Phlogiston, 64, 217; inconsistencies of the theory, 224
Photon, 148
Physical world, 151; matrix of, 179
Physicialism, 10
Physics, 9f, 58–62, 75, 127, 186; continuity with biology, 227; contemporary, 174ff, 178, 193, 196, 232, 255, 260; Newtonian, 255; particle, 175
Physiology, 9, 66f, 118, 173, 178, 186, 260
Piaget, J., 145, 156n14
Pi-meson, 175
Planck, M., 59, 192, 223, 235
Plato, 7, 45, 103n11, 106f, 118, 157, 196, 200, 229, 234
Poincaré, H., 195, 207f, 215, 225n17
Point, 138, 144; definition of, 137, 155n9
Pollution, 3
Polygon, 132, 141f
Popper, Sir Karl, 14, 55ff, 62, 68, 69n21, 69n25, 166ff, 208
Positron, 63, 214
Power, balance of, 5; politics, 4ff
Practice, 119, 199, 244, 246; and theory, 236f
Predicate, 27, 125
Preestablished harmony, 117

Prehension, 196
Presocratics, 229
Presuppositions, 90, 92, 101, 108; absolute, 14, 234; metaphysical, 44, 50, 57, 101; of formal logic, Ch. 1, 23–47, 49, 61, 65, 90f, 134, 154n1, 166, 195; of science, 58, 62, 80, 228
Price, H.H., 70n36
Principia Mathematica, 34, 37, 42–44, 46n20, 46n22, 47n28
Principle, 24; abstract, 200; explanatory, 232; generic 150, 152; immanent, 256; logical, 142, 208; of differentiation, 143; of Exclusion, 143, 151, 153, 193, 195, 231; of order, 147, 159, 203, 206, 218, 221; of organization (organizing), 75, 81, 132, 135, 143, 151f, 164, 193, 195, 200, 211, 213, 219, implied by harmony, 247; of structure, 135, 139f, 143–146, 149, 154, 172, 219; of system, 208; of valid inference, 24, 80; of value, 247; of wholeness, 146, 150, 244; of unity, 239; universal, 143, 149, 153f, 172, 200, 208, 219
Prior, A.N., 44, 47n32
Probability, 51, 53, 216
Process, 151; dialectical, 153, 165; dynamic, 177f; evolutionary, 173
Prominences, 181. *See also Abgehobenheiten*
Proportion, 185
Proposition, 26; atomic, 30, 49f, 167, 183, 192
Protention, 109
Proton, 175, 214, 231
Protoplasm, 180
Psyche, 94, 113
Psychical field. *See* Field
Psychologism, 89f
Psychology, 9, 58, 61, 66, 76, 90f, 118, 235
Purpose, 199, 231f, 244–248; human, 258

Quality, 127, 173f, 180f, 185; measured,

185; Primary, 8; pure, 180; secondary, 8, 9; sensible, 50, 173; whole of, 185

Quantity, 182–186; concept of, 184; conjugate, 193; continuous, 185; determinate. *See* Quantum; discrete, 185; extensive, 185; intensive, 185; dialectical opposite of quality, 184

Quantum, 185f; determinate, 186; discrete, 186; –field theory, 60; laws, 151; mechanics, 198n6; number, 132; Planck's 223; physics, 142; relations, 195; theory, 231

Quark, 60

Quine, W.V.O., 17, 39, 67; *Word and Object*, 17, 67

Quinton, A., 17, 67

Random, 137, 139

Ratio, 185

Realism, naïve, 95

Reality, 114

Reason, 117, 119, 168, 221; dialectic of, 227; ideal of, 119; ideas of, 79, 83, 167; phenomenology of, 98f, 102; practical, 119

Reasoning, 93; circular, 212; constructive, 208; deductive, 8, 206f; inductive, 8, 14, 206f, 211; mathematical, 31; precise, 232; synthetic *a priori*, 215, 226n17

Reciprocity, 192, 196, 200; category of, 195

Reduction, 114. *See also* Transcendental

Reductionism, 232, 253

Reference-frame, 127

Reflection, 108, 190; categories of, Ch. 11, 189–197; philosophical, 234; self–, 153

Reichenbach, H., 53, 58n5

Relation, 128, 131–134; asymmetrical, 122; external, 33, 67, 85, 101, 121, 131–134, 184; internal, 33, 61, 67, 75f, 82, 85, 100, 120, 121, 124, 131–134, 195; logic of, 101; measured, 186; one-one, 28f; symmetrical, 122

Relativism, 10, 12f, 15f, 80, 240

Relativity, 145, 151, 155n7, 175, 193, 224, 231

Religion, 190, 237

Renaissance, ix

Representation, 85f, 171f

Reproduction, 194

Rescher, N., xi

Retention, 108

Revolution, scientific. *See* Scientific

Rule, 221; for insight, 207, 225n8; of procedure, 209; social, 137; transformation, 209

Russell, Bertrand, ix, 17, 25, 30, 37, 40, 44, 51, 53, 56, 67, 134, 154

Rutherford, Lord, 222

S-matrix theory, 60

Sainte-Hilaire, Geoffroy, 223

Sartre, Jean-Paul, 13

Scala naturae, 235

Scale, 136, 154; dialectical, 154, 158, 165, 208, 222, 244; of degrees, 150, 152, 160; of forms, 107, 148, 151, 154, 200f, 229, 235, 245, 256f, 261; of nature, 243

Schelling, F.W.J., 79f, 84ff, 98, 105, 116f, 119f, 168

Schema, 167; logical, 261

Schroedinger, E., 59, 61, 148

Sciama, D.W., 60, 127, 231

Science, x, 3, 6 *e.s.*, 55f, 75f, 106, 137, 153f, 171; advance of, 201, 208, 221–224; as objective knowledge, 6–11; categories of, 196; contemporary, 133, 192, 193–197, 231ff; eidetic, 90; empirical, 197, 209ff; exact, 210; experimental, 179; Greek, 235; mechanistic, 192; modern, 251f; Newtonian, 58, 190ff, 228; objective, 6ff, 11f, 239; of science, 89, 107; presuppositions of. *See* Presuppositions; seventeenth century, 191; theoretical and practical, 236f; social, 2, 9f, 227; system of, 222; value-free, 8, 58

Sciences, 172, 227; biological, 262; natural, 23, 32; philosophical, 234, 262; physical, 262; positive, 91; social, 2, 9f, 227; special, 92, 184; system of, 222

Scientific, community 236f; investigation, 190; method. *See* Method; outlook, ixf, 3, 11ff, bankruptcy of, 11ff; revolution, 14f, 225, 227; theory, 141f, 153f

Selection, 177

Self, 83, 114, 245; empirical, 114f, 118

Self-consciousness, 83, 117, 237ff, 259

Self-constitution, 112–117

Self-deployment, 146

Self-development, 146

Self-differentiation, 132, 144–149, 150

Self-enfoldment, 196f

Self-maintenance, 194

Self-specification, 150, 179, 196, 200, 259

Sensation, 8, 85

Sense, 97, 108f; data, 67; manifold of, 79; perception, 50, 63, 95, 173; as criterion of scientific validity, 14, 63

Senses, 8

Sentience, 99, 111, 115, 153, 173, 176f, 180, 197; non-cognitive, 178; primitive, 178, 182; unity of, 181

Sentiment, 119

Series, 159; compact, 185; dialectical, 150; evolutionary, 261; ordered, 146

Set, 27ff, 30ff, 91f, 182ff; abstractive, 137

Seventeenth century, 7, 11, 58, 191, 233

Sigwart, 90

Sinngebung, 98

Skinner, B.F., 68

Society, 137, 237, 246

Sociology, 10

Socrates, 190

Solar system, 133, 141, 161, 181

Solipsism, 89, 98, 114

Sophists, 157, 234

Sophist, 157, 200

Soul, 229, 250; akin to the forms, 229

Sound, 127

Sovereignty, 249f, 263n1

Space, 58, 126, 145, 185; and time, 79, 126; empty, 138

Space-time, 59, 61, 127, 135, 138; continuum, 151; curvature, 152, 230, 255; structure, 231

Species, 150

Specification, 143, 147, 149, 158; self-, 150

Spectroscopy, 194

Spencer, Herbert, 90

Spin, 174

Spinoza, Benedict de, 80, 97, 241n12

Standard, 248f; objective, 10, 12, 16, 80, 244–248; personal, 247; social, 247

State, 4, 249; sovereign, 4, 249. *See also* Nation

States, of physical entities, 174

Stimulus, 68

Stonier, T., 18n1

Structure, 135, 177, 200, 245, 255; elements of, 143, 216, 219f; holistic, 153; logical, 180; molecular, 141; social, 248; systematic, 152, 163, 181, 208. *See also* Principle of

Subject, 77, 81, 83, 85, 118, 238; and object in one, 110, 197; of consciousness, 153; transcendental, 102, 128, 239

Subjectivism, 15, 89, 114, 117f

Subjectivity, 7, 75, 82, 118, 228, 233–236; transcendental, 75–82, 98f, 108, 111; union with objectivity, 237–240

Sublation, 146, 172f, 180, 215. *See also* Aufheben

Substance, 50, 190, 193, 195; and attribute, 192

Succession, 145

Sum, 183, 185f

Sun, 161

Supplementation, 146

Symbiosis, 195

Symbol, 33

Synthesis, 75–81, 83, 85f, 96, 98f, 109, 116

System, 78, 85, 98, 128, Ch. 8, 131–154, 134, 140–154, 181, 221, 227, 232; a structure of relations, 140; chemical, 153; closed, 141; concept as, 199; coherence of, 194, 223; deductive, 91, 209; development of, 222; dialectical, 234; eco–, 61, 195; elements of, 158; general nature of, 140; identity within, 164; inter-relation in, 160; living, 153, 181; logical, 142f; Logic of 131–154; mechanical, 57; Newtonian, 204n4; of classification, 209; of evidence, 202; of laws, 201; of science, 222; of systems, 222; of theoretical systems, 201, 222; open, 155n13; open-ended, 140, 155n13; organic, 194, 256; physical, 153; relational, 159; self-differentiation of, 144–149; structure of, 181. *See also* Logic, and Principle

Tarski, 44

Tautology, 40ff, 161, 169, 211, 231

Technology, 2, 10f, 57, 237, 251, 258

Teilhard de Chardin, P., 198n8

Teleology, 106, 109, 171, 228, 230, 241n12, 153

Teleonomy, 142, 231f, 253

Temperature, 185

Terms, 135*e.s.*; empirical, 210; in relation, 146; overlap of, 135–140, 152f; physico-chemical, 232; primitive, 209

Tetraktys, 141, 147f

Thales, 228

Theaetetus, 157

Theory, and practice, 236f; social, 258. *See also* Scientific

Thesis, 85

Things in themselves, 81f, 117f

Thing, 180; and its properties, 191; material, 191f

Thirring, W., 175

Thomas, Lewis, 61, 254

Thompson, J.J., 222

Thorpe, W.H., 71n40

Thought, activity of, 174

Time, 79, 126, 145; and change, 166; and space, 126; whirligig of, 13f

Tinbergen, N., 71n40

Togetherness, 140

Totality, 106, 144, 256ff; deployment of, 144; immanent, 146; ultimate, 261; universal, 149

Transcendental, Analytic, 79; Idealism. *See* Idealism; reduction, 95, 108, 111

Transcendentalism, 153

Treaties, 4

Truth, 16, 76, 94, 118, 153, 171, 199, 227f; absolute, 228; coherence theory of, xi, xiin, 77, 96, 102, 109; criterion of, 16, 82, 244f; degree of, 224; objective, 13, 228, 247; standard of, 119, 239; –value, 183

Understanding, 100, 168, 189; Principles of, 79, 99

Unit, 144, 182f, 186

United Nations, 4

Unity, 77, 79, 124, 143; all-encompassing, 262; blank, 144; in difference, 78f, 81, 84f, 101, 143, 193, 202; of differences, 200; of subject and object, 237–240, 248; polyphasic, 193, 197

Universal, 100f, 151f, 158f, 160, 183, 194, 201f; abstract, 101, 148, 152, 182, 184; concrete, 152, 165, 179; immanent, 171f, 236; matrix, 135; self-specifying, 154; specification of, 172, 201, 210, 221f; structure, 150; theoretical element in science, 201

Universality, 135, 227

Universe, 60, 231; as a single whole, 193, 261; as evolutionary process, 234; conceptions of, 228ff; mechanical, 230; objective, 228, 230; physical, 127

Urmson J.O., 45n1

Valency, 194

Value, 8, 10, 15f, 57, 80, 118, 230, 237, Ch. 14, 243–263; and truth, 244; criterion of, 244f; dialectical generation of, 243f; objective, 12f, 247; practical, 247; standard of, 16, 119, 240; truth–, 183
Variable, 37, 62, 151, 210
Venus, 161
Vernon, M.D., 70n35
Virtue, 246f
Void, 175
von Wright, G.H., 54f

Waismann F., 23
War, 5f
Warnock, G.J., 45n1
Waves, 176; standing, 193, 231; superposed, 176, 193, 196, 231, 255; –packets, 179f, 193
Wechselbestimmung, 85, 121, 165
Weltanschauung, 228, 248
Wesenserschauung, 96f
Wayl, H., 59
Whitehead, A.N., ix, 25, 137, 149, 196f
Whole, 33, 78, 82, 101, 107, 121–124; 132 *e.s.*, 140, 142ff, 172, 177, 193, 200, 237f; absolute, 262; and part, 191, 194; both one and many,

144; coherent, 239; conceptual, 237; identity of, 159; immanent, 179; individual, 182; integral, 231; not a mere aggregate, 184, 193; organic, 127, 195, 244; priority of, 194, 231; provisional, 149; self-inwardizing of, 244; self-specification of, 150; social, 260; structured, 177, 231; universal, 261f
Wholeness, 77, 125, 156n13; organismic, 253
Williams, D., 53
Wissenschaftslehre, 79, 83, 103n2, 107, 111, 116, 131
Wittgenstein, L., 23, 30, 40, 42, 45n1, 67, 154, 156n20, 195, 241n12; *Tractatus Logico-Philosophicus*, 67
World, 151; as living organism, 61, 229; come to consciousness, 237; conception of, 222; perceived, 189; physical, 151, 228
World-view, 222, 228ff, 234; Renaissance, ix; scientific, 222; seventeenth century, 232

Zeman, J.J., 47n27
Zeno, 166
Zerstückbar, 125f
Zerstückung, 122f, 191